I0763149

GO-BETWEEN GIRL

PRAISE FOR *GO-BETWEEN GIRL*

"Precise, sardonic, and thoroughly compelling, Gunraj's writing is a marvel. She scales hard terrain—multi-hyphenate identity, the push and pull of family history, and the centuries of offhand cruelty that have shaped modern Canadian society—with remarkable lightness and humour, and in so doing has created a collection that is both indispensable and totally engrossing."

—Dan Werb, social scientist and award-winning writer of *The Invisible Siege*

"An accomplished novelist, Andrea Gunraj writes with humour and language that sparkles of what it means to have been born and raised in the salad bowl of present-day Canada. In emotionally and intellectually engaging chapters, part personal memoir and part social analysis, she teases and probes the hazy borderlines separating whiteness from otherness, servitude from sovereignty, illuminating the in-betweenness that shaped our world and points us to our interlinked future and shared identity as Canadians."

—Karim Alrawi, author of *Book of Sands*, former media and civil society advisor to the United Nations Development Programme

"A sharp, generous, and revelatory book. Gunraj's powerful and tender insights will stay with you long after reading."

—Allison LaSorda, Contributing Editor, *Brick, A Literary Journal*

"In *Go-Between Girl*, Gunraj self-excavates to tenderly eviscerate our understandings of power and belonging. With instinctual precision, Gunraj turns her eye inward to inspect the looping threads of her personal history, the muddied pathways of indentured servitude echoing in shadows across generations of women who grasp for meaning and survival. Gunraj's voice resounds with deep honesty; she invites us into her consciousness with such warmth and intimacy, then guides us with rooted expertise through difficult revelations about the things that matter to us so urgently today—questions about what it means to linger in the in-between when confronting race and responsibility, personal betrayals of justice, the hauntings of poverty and family, and all the stifling, heart-rending pains of finding our place in the world. Gunraj treads the in-between with deep empathy and sharp-eyed observation; this is an urgent and essential work of self-shattering recognition."

—Shoilee Khan, writer and editor

"A brilliant exploration of the ghost in the machine of global capitalism, linking colonization and indentured servitude with the gig work of today. Driven by the author's own personal journey, this is essential reading for anyone interested in labour, history, race, class, migration, and the buried history of the money that makes the world go round. Grateful for this addition to our cultural conversation."

—Hannah Sung, culture commentator

"Andrea Gunraj's *Go-Between Girl* is a triumph of curiosity, insight, and heart. In a series of stylistically exquisite essays, Gunraj explores the insidious aftermath of indentured servitude, the hollow benevolence of white feminism, and the quest for authentic representation. Gunraj shows a breathtaking willingness to challenge herself in these essays. She brings us close, examining her own contradictions and complacencies, all the while offering an incisive study of broader failures within our systems and communities. *Go-Between Girl* is electric. Gunraj's words serve as a rich and vital reminder that scrutiny is not an antithesis to hope: it's a precursor. A reminder that we don't need to hold our tongues to hold space for each other."

—Hollay Ghadery, award-winning author of *Fuse*

ALSO BY ANDREA GUNRAJ

The Lost Sister

The Sudden Disappearance of Seetha

GO-BETWEEN GIRL

MY INDENTURED ROOTS
AS RECLAIMED PRESENT

ANDREA GUNRAJ

McCLELLAND & STEWART

Hardcover edition published 2026

The authorized representative in the EU for product safety and compliance is Penguin Random House Ireland, Morrison Chambers, 32 Nassau Street, Dublin D02 YH68, Ireland, https://eu-contact.penguin.ie

Library and Archives Canada Cataloguing in Publication
Title: Go-between girl : my indentured roots as reclaimed present / Andrea Gunraj.
Names: Gunraj, Andrea, 1978- author
Identifiers: Canadiana (print) 20250320029 | Canadiana (ebook) 20250320061 | ISBN 9780771020346 (hardcover) | ISBN 9780771020353 (EPUB)
Subjects: LCSH: Gunraj, Andrea, 1978- | LCSH: Women authors, Canadian—21st century—Biography. | LCSH: Authors, Canadian—21st century—Biography. | LCGFT: Autobiographies.
Classification: LCC PS8613.U58 Z46 2026 | DDC C813/.6—dc23

Certain identifying details have been changed to protect individuals' privacy.

Cover design by Talia Abramson
Cover art: (figure) Eugen Klein / Rijksmuseum; (buildings) tashechka / Getty
Typeset in Portrait Text by Erin Cooper and Six Red Marbles
Printed in Canada

McClelland & Stewart
A division of Penguin Random House Canada
320 Front Street West, Suite 1400
Toronto, Ontario, M5V 3B6, Canada
penguinrandomhouse.ca

1 2 3 4 5 30 29 28 27 26

For David

CONTENTS

PROLOGUE: ON RECLAMATION

Mountains extended into the distance, washed by brown and blue, pinched ridges melting into mist. I used my fingertip to trace rivers that rambled through the evergreens of the horizon below. The water was as luminous as gemstone, a perfect aquamarine. Waterfalls spilled like capillaries over rock, foamy white, too numerous to count. Above my head, clouds skidded across the sky, casting swaths of shadow.

When the gondola had hoisted me along the incline of Mînî Rhuwîn, Sulphur Mountain, in Alberta, I hadn't expected all of this. Bumping over the crest, I understood the true extravagance of the unfurled landscape. The town of Banff, where I'd been staying for weeks, had seemed so significant an hour ago. At this vantage point, it was a smatter of debris at the base of a fertile mound, encircled by stone giants.

The legacy of indentured and coerced labour was here. Chinese labourers were recruited to Canada and the United States to build Pacific railways, to crack the Asin-Wati, or Rocky Mountains, with dynamite and pound spikes into them at the peril of their own lives.

"One dead Chinaman for every mile of railway," explained the tour guide as he led my group through the woodlands, past hoofprints and scatters of deer fur across Waskahigan Watchi, Mount Rundle. I dawdled when the tour was over, after the rest of the group had dispersed. I asked the guide to adjust his phrasing. "One dead *Chinese man* for every mile of railway," I requested he report on his future tours. Kind-hearted, he agreed and thanked me for the feedback.

I'd been so convinced of my rightness. Now, cowed by these mountains, doubts crept in. I wished I had made a different request of the guide, one not focused on mere words. They didn't matter as much as the unfiltered truth. At least double that estimate of Chinese railway workers died due to accident, illness, and harsh climate. They were sent into harm's way first, weighed by debt and so many constraints. They were not considered men with inner lives and loved ones, and they were hardly even considered workers. They were hardly conceptualized as humans at all. They were clumped together as *Chinamen*, a horde valued only for its labour. They existed to construct greater men's dreams. White men's dreams. They were not distinguished, not teased apart from one another. They had little claim to outcomes of their labour. They are hardly to be found in those iconic photographs of bearded white men driving the railways' final spikes and popping bottles of champagne.

They were *coolies*. Ever alien, ever lesser, ever outsider.

In that go-between status are pains we cannot fully comprehend. It hurt those marked by it most of all, but it affected the people who delineated it and kept people there, too. This is the underbelly of racist dehumanization we rarely flip and take stock of. In the end, it robs everyone of some part of their humanity, culminating in what Toni Morrison refers to as "the severe fragmentation of the self." This thievery has stripped each of us.

As a descendant of labourers like those who built the railway, I'm not too concerned about explaining who I am. Not anymore. I don't worry much about bridging misunderstandings, nor am I overly troubled about sleuthing for some elusive sense of belonging.

I've come to appreciate Dionne Brand's point: "Too much," she says, "has been made of origins." Bridging and belonging are important, but they are not essential to my peace. Go-betweenness is a birthmark of the difficulties my ancestors lived through. I'm not itching to blot it out of my life. I'm not surprised it should anoint me as a child of the racialized indentured.

What's important now is reclamation. But I don't think that's always about driving stakes into the ground and grasping at things taken away. I don't think it has to be about shaking yourself loose from the things that have hurt you. I'm not sure any of that is possible. I'm not sure the pursuit of it always honours the atrocities of what happened, either. I've come to imagine reclamation as a simpler pursuit. I imagine it can be a tenacious proclamation of the humanity of the dehumanized. A stubborn kind of memory.

With the coolness of the wind on my skin amongst those mountains, those elders of the earth, I promised I would not forget the legacy I was born into. I promised I would keep it close, keep it clearly. As manifold and tentacled as it is.

Maybe reclamation can be the uncomplicated awareness that we are more than our allotted function in the nexus of the enslaved, the indentured and coerced, and the overseer tethered on Indigenous land. Maybe it can be our insistence that we are far more than our labour—and the distillation of human to labour is always most deadly for those most devalued, those most othered and ignored and unloved. Maybe it is, ultimately, the daily resolution to value and love.

GO-BETWEEN GIRL

"When you don't write about yourself,
you remain unknown."
— M.G. VASSANJI, *Nowhere, Exactly: On Identity and Belonging*

"What does a word mean? And a life?
In the end, it seems to me, the same thing."
— JHUMPA LAHIRI, *In Other Words*

~

I can't remember how it was spoken to me, but I know I heard it like a fairy tale.

The people celebrated with drums, but the kings and queens were cruel and jealous. They banned the drums. The people used bamboo instead, tap-tapping as they sang and danced. The kings and queens forbade those, too. They didn't want the people to play or laugh. They didn't want them to feel joy. They wanted them to work day and night.

But the people didn't give up. They searched for new instruments to make with their hands. They discovered empty oil drums, abandoned at the seashore and rusting in ocean-salted air. The kings and queens didn't know about those.

The people rolled the drums away. They heated them with fire and beat them with hammers. *Ping-pong, ping-pong.* The noises they made were the promise of music.

They worked in darkness, hiding away so no one would stop them. They heated and hammered, heated and hammered. They shaped and forged an ensemble of new instruments. They carried them out into the streets to play, and the people celebrated the sound. The musicians could not be stopped.

I was twelve years old when I learned to play the Trinidadian steel pan. I was too small for the multiple sets, the double tenors, triple cellos, and bass pans where the player, girdled by six full-sized oil drums, spins and volts to strike their mallets. I was placed on the soprano pan, the one traditionally called the ping pong, which hooks onto a rack. As its name suggests, the ping pong is known for its ring, its twenty-four sweet notes pounded as bumps over concave steel. That pan was designed to carry the melody.

Ping-pong, ping-pong. Walking the streets of Toronto, I hear the sounds of a skilled player on a regular basis. Those notes in the air, delicate and distinct, trigger a flutter in my stomach. I'm not sure how they manage to cut through the racket of engines and construction. Perhaps the pan's magic is how it attracts the listener like metal to a magnet. Perhaps my ears are paired to its chime like tuning forks.

My parents put me in piano lessons from age six. I had to play Bach and Mozart in recitals, and hymns at church, perched on the bench with trembling hands. I dreaded those performances.

But playing the pan wasn't like solo piano. I stood at my instrument in a row with the other players. We made music together. It made me bold.

Most of the other players in my northwest Toronto middle school's steel band were like me: immigrant children and children of immigrants, mainly from Jamaica, Guyana, Trinidad, India, Pakistan, Afghanistan, Bangladesh. The room where we practised had big chalkboards mounted to the wall, a dinged upright piano, and a stepped platform where our pans were arranged in rows. Soprano pans up front, cello and tenor pans in the middle, bass pans and a drum kit at the back.

Our instructor was Mr. Pat McNeilly, a musician known as the Legendary Panman Pat. He wore colourful collared shirts and a neat fedora, angled just so. He regaled us with the tale of how the pan had been invented, its West African roots.

The musicians could not be stopped. The story stayed with me, and steel band class became my favourite subject. I caught on to the instrument quickly, striking my mallets too enthusiastically, getting too loud. *Ping! Pong!*

Calm down, Mr. McNeilly would gesture at me, patting the air with his palm as the band played the calypso arrangements he taught us. *Blend with everyone else.*

My scalp tingled with embarrassment every time, but I didn't stop playing. I loved sounding those *ping-pongs* too much to stop.

Sometimes, my school booked the band to perform at community events. We wore our yellow and green phys-ed T-shirts as uniforms. The audience would cheer us on as if we were famous. One day, a reporter and photographer from the local newspaper visited the music room ahead of one of these events. We played a soca hit as the photographer paced and crouched, capturing action shots. Afterward, we crowded the reporter in a clump at the chalkboards.

She pointed the tip of her pen in my direction. "How about you? What is it that you like so much about playing the steel pan?"

"I like that it's not the piano," I responded, thrusting my thumb at the upright, a battered version of the one I practised on at home.

"You don't like the piano?"

"You can't play calypso on the piano."

She chuckled and nodded, scratching in her notepad.

At the end of class, Mr. McNeilly pulled me aside. "I like what you said. You're right. You can play things on the pan you can't play on anything else." He smiled. "You're a good musician, you know."

My cheeks grew warm. That morning, I felt as if I had accomplished something monumental.

"Those boys like playing in the steel band, don't they?" I heard one teacher murmur to another as I hunched over my desk. Homeroom would begin in a few minutes.

The teachers, two men, stood at the front of the class, leaning close to each other. They wore sweater vests over dress shirts and slacks. They were both white. I understood they were referring to two of the boys in my class, a pair of cousins from an Indo-Caribbean family.

"Yes," the other teacher answered. "Seems so."

"They're—what? West Indian or something?"

"That's right."

"I would've never guessed that before coming to this school. I've never seen boys like that before in my life."

The teacher shook his head slowly, brow furrowed. "*East* India. I would think *East* India if I saw them anywhere else. Just look at them. They're so Indian. They're so *dark*."

Caucasoid, Mongoloid, Negroid. I'd already learned about the three races. My grade five teacher presented them to my class with anthropological diagrams, a sketch of a man of each race pasted onto a map. The square-jawed *Caucasoid* floated over Europe. The wide-faced *Mongoloid* covered Asia. The muscular *Negroid* spanned the continent of Africa. My teacher didn't explain that this trio was a postulation published in 1940, near the start of a world war, a half a century before he had taught it to my class. He didn't tell us it was speculative or contested. He presented it as self-evident, immutable fact.

What were those cousins in my class, those two dark boys? What was I, exactly? We weren't *Caucasoid* and we weren't *Negroid*, that much was clear. All that remained of the threesome was the *Mongoloid*, but that didn't seem accurate either. The race map didn't leave space for North and South America or the Caribbean. They had been cropped off the end. Could we be found anywhere in the world?

My throat prickled with an urge to clear the teachers' confusion. I wanted to patter up to them and translate what I'd learned of the race map in a way that included us. I wanted to act as the go-between girl, bridging their puzzlement and our existence, closing the gulf between their lives and ours. I wanted to explain that our families were indeed West Indian, our parents born and raised there, birthing and moving us here or else moving here and birthing us. But our great-grandparents, maybe our great-great-grandparents, or someone even before them, travelled not from Africa but from India. I wanted to explain that our fore-parents had gone to the Caribbean as indentured labourers, doing something different from but somehow related to what the enslaved labourers were forced to do.

I stayed right where I was, staring at the gouges on my desk. I had no idea how to go about doing such a thing. Even if I did know what to say to them, I didn't see why they should believe a word from my mouth.

I pictured Mr. McNeilly directing the band, hands swinging and toe tapping to the music as we ping-ponged away. He had no need of such whispers with the other teachers, I was certain of that. He was not stumped by who we were.

That was the first time I understood that white people were perplexed by people like me. That was the first time I realized the conundrum our unforeseen presence created for them.

"Swell getting worse, sir."

"Noticed that in here," muttered Captain MacWhirr. "Anything wrong?"

Jukes, inwardly disconcerted by the seriousness of the eyes looking at him over the top of the book, produced an embarrassed grin.

"Rolling like old boots," he said, sheepishly.

"Aye! Very heavy—very heavy. What do you want?"

At this Jukes lost his footing and began to flounder. "I was thinking of our passengers," he said, in the manner of a man clutching at a straw.

> *"Passengers?" wondered the Captain, gravely. "What passengers?"*
>
> *"Why, the Chinamen, sir," explained Jukes, very sick of this conversation.*
>
> *"The Chinamen! Why don't you speak plainly? Couldn't tell what you meant. Never heard a lot of coolies spoken of as passengers before. Passengers, indeed! What's come to you?"*

Joseph Conrad's 1902 novella *Typhoon* tells the story of a British steamer imperilled in the Pacific as it transports workers indentured back to China, the *coolies* and *Chinamen* Jukes and Captain MacWhirr speak of. MacWhirr refuses to change course to avoid imminent danger.

What the devil did the coolies *matter to anybody?* the boathands swear at Jukes while he worries over their state as the vessel shudders and threatens to break apart in the roiling waters.

In contrast to the seafaring Jukes, MacWhirr displays a banal dismissiveness toward the circumstances of the indentured. That's probably a sign of the ordinariness of their circumstances. After all, none of the *coolies* of *Typhoon* are given names. Conrad writes them as thinly as he writes the crew of cannibals in his 1899 novella, *Heart of Darkness*.

Never heard a lot of coolies *spoken of as passengers before.* Pejorative and complicated, used by European indenturers to degrade millions of racialized workers in the global indentured labour migration of the nineteenth and twentieth centuries, the word *coolie* might be equal parts reclaimed and reviled in places where descendants of indentured people live.

Hey, coolie *gyal.* Despite its derogatory connotations, I've always enjoyed being called a *coolie* by those I love—my family and friends in the pan-Caribbean community—and only them. For a second-generation immigrant in North America like me, the word spoken in warmth and intimacy with a stroke of the arm or soft kiss on the cheek is a wink to precious—if precarious—shared knowledge. It's an invitation I find myself in need of, even now.

Not everyone and every community feels the same way, and they have the right to respond as they will. Not everyone has heard it the way I have. For many, the maligning history of *coolie* is more present, more lacerating. They are to be protected. I can only be grateful that I have been so buffered from the cruelties of the way the term has been and can be used. Most of my experiences with *coolie* have been affectionate.

Rooted in classical Dravidian languages of India, including Kannada, Malayalam, Tamil, and Telugu, and neologized in other languages, the term has faded from European and North American parlance, just as it has slunk out of Western literature and stage and film. I'm not sure how many white supremacists, even the ones who claim to be expert historians, still use it. They carouse in mis-castings, dredge up all sorts of mantras and slurs, but *coolie* is not one I often hear from them.

That's not a bad thing. But it does serve as a signal of how forgotten the *coolie* has become.

Wherever they were in the world, racialized people in indentured and coerced work acted as go-betweens: across the realities of forced labour and ideals of free labour, flailing industries and fantasies of boundless capital, beliefs of race-based inferiority and superiority, and unrealized ambitions and mark-making careerism of European powerholders.

But where exactly has the *coolie* disappeared to? Where the term has vaporized and the people themselves have been overlooked, the *coolie*'s go-betweenness has been transplanted into everyday capitalism: gigging, jobbing, temping, contracting, piecemealing, patchworking.

Perhaps they haunt popular culture, infused in the symbol of the underpaid immigrant and the exploited and illegal migrant. They are the ghost in the machine, the disembodied global tech and customer service workers coding and moderating as so-called cyber *coolies*. They possess sweatshop workers in the music video for *The Hamilton Mixtape*, the immigrants sewing American flags at the midnight hour, getting the job done. They slog in the backdrop of the glittery Singapore of *Crazy Rich Asians* and the breezy Abu Dhabi of *Sex and the City*.

Free but not free, compensated but never well enough, agreeing with little alternative, essential but disposable, felt but not seen, always on the move. The modern-day *coolie* has likely multiplied tenfold, the go-between linking worldwide profiteering and the unacknowledged grind required to succeed in it. The *coolie* may have reproduced into billions of hands. They are still the cash-strapped and racialized—but, of course, racism and poverty aren't the only factors to account for in the *coolie*'s struggles today.

There is no indentured apart from enslaved, and neither is separate from the overseer. Bondedness and indebtedness in our past shaped the chain gangs, sharecropping, domestic work, caregiving, farmhanding, and export processing zones that followed it the world over—so much underpaid, underprotected, and disrespected labour on usurped land. Amid the layering of endless trade hookups and breakups, of novel technologies and artificial intelligences, ancient justifications echo down the corridors. Exploited labour seems a must in our minds, no matter how poetic we get about the future. We keep reinventing it.

Across the globe, from Europe to Asia to the Gulf to Africa to America, work seems designed to fracture the scrabbling worker from the component parts of their labour, splintering them into the cheapest, most inert shards. Hardly anyone can claim immunity in our gig and temp economies. Not when the terms of work for those long left outside of the smorgasbord of capital seem to have become the model for most jobs today.

Who needs to protect a worker obliterated into bits? What rights or compassion can fragments expect? What the devil does a *coolie* matter to anybody?

For me and my family, the who, what, where, why, and when of our indentured ancestors are hazy. The only story I remember hearing was about a pair of young Indian boys tricked onto a boat by a white man. He lured them onto the gangway with treats, with tales of a fantastical far-off land. Months later, they landed on the shores of British Guiana, their parents and family presumably never informed where they had disappeared to. The boys never set foot in their homeland again. They laboured on a plantation along with hundreds of other indentured adults and grew up to become the great-grandparents of my cousins. I didn't have a story about my own grandparents.

Traces of unreliable rumours were all that were left of my ancestors. The barely vocalized plight of my foreparents felt to me, as a child, too far removed for true and worthy recall. What is a memory that isn't cherished, that isn't handled carefully enough to repeat? Is it not a memory destined for disintegration?

The act of trying to remember that far back seemed foolhardy to me. The way adults in my family spoke of their Guyana homeland made it sound like a land of food and love and music and play. When I imagined them as children, I saw them amongst palm trees and sunshine, running and plucking fruit, mouths wide with laughter. There were times I wanted to ask them for more information about our Indian origins, but I wasn't sure what the purpose of knowing was. We were not even in the West Indies anymore; we were not likely to return to our Asian motherland. My friends and school and neighbourhood in Canada felt far more real to me. My immediate family went to a Western Protestant church, not to a temple or mosque. Whatever connection I had with what I presumed to be Asian religions and cultures and languages felt theoretical. And the little information I could piece together was enough to confirm that our ancestors' journeys were not happy ones.

Why would I want to remember misery? Why would I attack myself with a long-gone past and injure myself for the future?

Poor and desperate. Deceived and tricked. Nowhere to turn. No idea what they were getting themselves into. I wonder if my parents' generation had little to share about our foreparents because their own parents and grandparents didn't want to remember what happened, either. I wonder if they worried the old tales of hardship would blight them, that remembering too much would cast a malignant shadow over their lives in colonial South America, the only home they had ever known. Maybe the memory of indentured servitude seemed best forgotten.

I've been told that weak recall amongst descendants of indentured labourers is not unique to me and my own. Friends who share this ancestry have told me that their families seem to have become amnesiacs, too. They haven't been told enough and aren't sure where to turn for answers.

It's easy to blame such forgetfulness on fear and self-preservation. On the avoidance of intergenerational shame. But I've come to understand that the problem isn't a simple matter of familial fallibilities. Why should the act of remembering be left to us, all on our own? This amnesia afflicts everyone.

Leaving high school, anticipating university, I became troubled by my inability to situate my lineage. It seemed wrong that, even in adulthood, I had no answer for the murmurings of those two elementary teachers I had overheard in the classroom. I decided I needed to learn more. I selected courses in Caribbean and Latin American studies, expecting them to fill every gap.

From the very first lecture, the professor seemed to presume that his students had a foundation of knowledge about global colonialism and labour exploitation to build on. I felt hopelessly behind. I had no basics to ground myself in. I glanced at the faces of students around me. Wrinkled brows and frowns had spread across the room.

In time, these classes would review some elements of Caribbean indenture: oceans crossed, misrepresented work terms, exploited bodies, disappeared homelands, reinvented identities. But the information was partial and the narratives were fractured. I left university with more questions than answers.

I knew I would need to keep learning on my own. What I didn't know was that the experience would stretch into a two-decade journey, that I would tunnel through analysis from around the world. It has been nothing short of a revelation. A heavy excavation, too. I would've lived and died with none of it if I hadn't committed to my own investigation to reconstruct the memories that had disintegrated.

This is the understanding I have come to: in the 1600s and 1700s, British, Scottish, Irish, and other European people performed indentured labour in burgeoning American and Caribbean colonies such as Virginia, Barbados, and Jamaica in the form of manual, agricultural, and domestic work. They were mostly impoverished and criminalized, though some sought adventure and opportunity. They journeyed across the ocean with contracts that spanned four, seven, or more years, beholden to their masters by debt and legal penalty. After their terms of servanthood were completed, many of them stayed on in the colonies as citizens.

Their work was strenuous, their conditions were difficult, and they were subject to physical punishment. But European indentured labourers retained key entitlements and standards, such as allowance to petition for rights and argue against unfairness in court and an expectation of adequate food, clothing, and shelter. They gained freedom dues at the conclusion of their contracts.

Histories are woven together with tangled threads. At the same time that Europeans were indentured, every major European power was kidnapping and trafficking Africans to Europe and their overseas colonies. These fibres of the world's tapestry of unfree labour may be more familiar: European merchants, nobility, and investors partnered to occupy faraway lands, displacing, enslaving, and decimating Indigenous populations. They pined for abundant, cheap labour to generate wealth in perpetuity. Enslaved Africans brutalized into captivity became this workforce in the colonies.

Emerging laws marked clear distinctions between servitude of white people and enslavement of Black people. Indentured Europeans were not stateless, nor was their bondage all-consuming and intergenerational. They were not to be punished so harshly as to be permanently wounded, nor were they to be raped, whipped naked, or killed. They were not to face the horrors enslaved people faced.

Over the next two hundred years, transatlantic chattel slavery ascended as the preferred source of colonial labour and exploded profits from staples like sugar, rubber, tobacco, rice, and cotton. It was a bloodsoaked spiral of war and degradation. The hellish foundations of our modern markets.

Mechanization, economic shakeups, and uprisings dovetailed with moral concerns to bring the transatlantic slave trade to a staggered end around the globe, starting around the early 1800s. Colonialists were anxious. They still wanted cheap labour to keep economies running to their profit.

Over the period that the slave trade expanded, white

indentureship receded. After three centuries of enslaving African people, hardening white supremacist values, and systemizing ways of conducting business, colonialists considered undervalued colony work largely the domain of racialized populations. Now, indenture and indenture-like arrangements would be revived with a racial bent.

Indentureship from China began with the Portuguese colonists shipping workers to Trinidad. The movement of indentured Indian workers, including my ancestors, began with French colonists shipping them to Réunion, but the British quickly became the biggest exporters of Indians. British, French, German, Danish, Spanish, Portuguese, and American leaders and business owners relied on indentured and coerced labourers for plantations, mills, mines, and infrastructure construction across the Caribbean, eastern and southern Africa, the Indian Ocean, South Asia, Australasia, and the Americas.

In the case of nineteenth-century Britain, failing sugar production in its colonies meant rising prices for British consumers. In the thirty or so years between Britain abolishing importation of enslaved people and the U.S. doing the same, British-run sugar companies needed to boost output and slash costs or face tariff cuts that would put them in direct competition with slavery-based sugar producers. In 1837, Sir John Gladstone, British plantation owner and spokesperson for West Indian sugar planters, secured permission from the British government to start recruiting Indians through contracts they named "girmits," a Hindi-style pronunciation of the word "agreement."

Sugar planters of Mauritius were more proactive than that. They arranged for indentured Indians to arrive on the island's shore on August 1, 1834, the very day Britain's Slavery Abolition Act—in full, the *Act for the Abolition of Slavery throughout the British Colonies; for promoting the Industry of the manumitted slaves; and for compensating the Persons hitherto entitled to the Service of such Slaves*—went into effect. Mauritius's Aapravasi Ghat heritage site in Port Louis, an unassuming grey block structure once referred to as the *Coolie* Ghat, was a key locus for British ships from India. The ancestors of over 70 per cent of Mauritius's current population arrived at this depot. Half a million workers passed through. Some remained in local cane fields, others continued to worksites in Réunion, Africa, Australia, and the Caribbean.

As it had been in the past, indenture and indenture-style arrangements still meant that a worker was bound to their masters, overseers, and employers. But the varied terms and conditions of racialized incarnations were harsher—more constricted, punishing, and dehumanizing than when largely white people performed this servitude. Some have described it as *indentured paraslavery*.

For Indians working for the British, their contracts usually lasted five or ten years. When they were done, workers could go back home or try to make new lives on leased or government lands as seasonal labourers. Given famines in India, and given the ways colonial administrators encouraged workers to abandon their right of return, the majority stayed. My ancestors stayed.

Racialized indentureship to far-flung colonies dominated labour politics after abolition, but many forms of it existed before and during the time of the transatlantic slave trade. Chinese and Indian workers were the predominant workforces in indenture and indenture-like contracts, but they were not the only ones bonded into this type of labour. The first known mention of the term *coolie* comes not from nineteenth-century Britain, referring to Chinese or Indian workers, but from a Portuguese letter penned in 1581, referring to workers from Japan. Long before the Slavery Abolition Act was passed, the British imported indentured Chinese workers to Ceylon, St. Helena, and the Mascarene Islands, and forced Indian convicts to build infrastructure of their colonies in Singapore, Malaya, and Burma. The Dutch imported Chinese and Javanese *coolies* through both indenture agreements and convict labour arrangements in nineteenth-century Indonesia. Indian domestic workers across the colonies and within Britain itself may not have had indenture contracts, but they were indebted to and controlled by their employers all the same. Thousands of indentured Indians worked within the borders of Ceylon, Malaya, and India before and during the time Indian workers were shipped to Atlantic colonies. And from the 1860s on, Indigenous Pacific Islanders were abducted and enslaved in the Australian "blackbird" trade. White people referred to them as "kanakas," a Hawaiian word for "man" that became a blanket reference to labouring women, men, and children. Indenture work terms and regulations set up in the blackbird trade's later days reduced incidents of outright kidnapping. But the Islanders still faced discrimination and were paid only six pounds per year, a poor wage even for that time. Many died in the harsh conditions of the fields, mines, waters, and railways where they worked.

What is common to all of these racialized workers is the marinade of white supremacy they're soaked in, the notion that racialized populations are best suited to work for white interests. In remaking indentureship and indenture-like arrangements into a distinctly racial form, more restrictive than it had been, in constructing the *coolie* as a status, a whole class of people to juxtapose with free whiteness and enslaved Blackness, colonial leaders invented what they needed to maintain their power in new economic, legal, and labour landscapes. No matter the shape of unfree racialized labour over the centuries, colonialists saw themselves in possession of a natural claim to it. They found their way to continue subjugating racialized populations, to continue undervaluing their work and lives.

Tallied across time and borders and empires as they rarely are, racialized indentured workers represent a massive migrant movement. Between 1830 and 1930, the most active centenary for racialized indentured labour, an estimated forty to fifty-five million people were transported by European powers in varying arrangements.

Their descendants, people like me, are legion, whether or not we're entirely conscious of that fact. The stories and motivations of racialized indentured ancestors, expressed in their own words, remain obscure.

During my search for my ancestors' experiences, I located all kinds of artifacts documenting the movements of racialized indentured people: work agreements, ship rosters, letters, adjudications, photographs. But official documents offer limited insight into their choices, conundrums, and daily lives. There is no grand autobiographical tradition amongst them that compares to that of enslaved memoir writers like Solomon Northup, Olaudah Equiano, and Harriet Jacobs.

There are just a few precious accounts. One is the testimonio of Totaram Sanadhya, an indentured worker or *girmitiya* who arrived in Fiji as a seventeen-year-old boy in 1893. As a pandit, activist, and Indian nationalist, Sanadhya recorded his story to provoke governmental action and compel a freedom movement. The poverty of his widowed mother drove him to leave his household in search of work. He describes the recruiter who enticed him as a villain. "Look brothers," the recruiter said to him and the other recruits, "the place where you will work you will never have to suffer any sorrows. There will never be any kind of problems there. You will eat a lot of bananas and a stomach-full of sugar cane, and play flutes in relaxation."

He describes his three-month boat journey of "cramped sleeping spaces, a meal of dog-biscuits, sugar, rice and dried fish, the dead thrown overboard." He recounts exhausting plantation toil and terrible living conditions, meagre sustenance and severe punishment, all manner of abuses with no recourse. He calls the plantation overseers and headmen evil and heartless.

In a dream, he finds himself with the loved ones he has left behind. "One of them asks: 'Where have you been all this time?' I reply: 'Fiji'. My eyes opened as soon [as] I uttered that word. I was crying. I realized that I was all alone, not in India among my friends, family and familiar surroundings, but in the haunted line in Fiji, ruined and helpless."

I can conjure tales. I imagine a young man in British-ruled India, fifteen years old. His village is struck by famine after famine, one outcome of the Indian economy's decimation under the exploitative command of the British East India Company. There is no food, no rice that anyone can afford to buy. His skin is ashen, slack. His head throbs; his calves spasm. It is the sight of the children, the babies too lethargic to mewl, that compels him onto the road in search of work with a band of fellow villagers. They haul sacks on their shoulders and pull carts southward, toward Calcutta. Sun batters down. They soon come upon others who had departed their villages in the same condition. Over days and weeks, the knot of travellers balloons into a straggling, hungry mass.

Nearing Calcutta, the young man breathes the trace of salt in the breeze. He has never journeyed so far from his home. He has never seen the ocean. Men loiter at the sides of the road, calling out to him and his fellow travellers. They don gleaming sarongs and turbans. They are not dirty and exhausted like the villagers. They have been eating. They stand tall.

You will work, one of these men calls out, smiling and gesturing. *You will go to a land of plenty. You are needed only for a short while. You will have more food than you can dream of.*

I imagine a young Indian woman, married and widowed before she can have her own children. Her husband's family will not let her stay with them. She decides to leave before they kick her out, paying a neighbour to help her steal away at night. She travels to the only place she can find work, a Bombay textile mill. She spends her days and nights in the swelter of the factory floor, feeding raw cotton into the gin, stretching threads around spools.

Along with the other women, she is paid much less than what men are paid for doing the same jobs. She, along with the other women, is treated as spoiled goods. They don't have households or husbands and families; they have nothing to cover them. They are leered and jeered at. Her supervisor has already told her what she expects of every woman who works under her: she will have to sleep with men and hand the money over to the business. She is unprotected, employed by bullies. She cannot quit. They make sure women can't say no.

The woman learns of the recruiters from another widow at the mill. They are anxious for women to board their boats, unable to set sail if they can't find enough. She will tell them that she has no husband, that she is abandoning no family by approaching them. She is warned that they will be suspicious of her and hold her in their barracks for months to confirm she's telling the truth. To confirm she is a woman of good character. She decides to be patient. She has run away once. She will find a way to run away again.

I imagine a man in China, a day labourer farming wealthy men's land. Between jobs, he frequents a village bar. He meets a couple of men he has never seen before. They make breezy conversation with him, chattering about the rich foreigners they work for. They offer him liquor well into the night. Dizzy, he rests his head on the table. When he awakes, light pierces his eyes. His hands are tied. He has been tossed into a moving cart with a half-dozen other men. He is dazed and bruised, bleeding from the head. As horses bump them along, he chokes his nausea and understands he has been drugged. The men at the bar were the crimps he had heard rumours about.

He is held in a camp in Macau with dozens of other men. They are tied together. They sleep on the dirt, pressed for warmth to the captives next to them.

Their captors treat them like criminals. When the man resists their blows, they beat him harder. When he demands they let him go, they taunt him. *You're swine*, they say. *Pig in a pen.* They tell him they will hand him over to the Spaniards, who will force him to toil in a mine. They tell him they will kick him into the belly of one of their "floating hells," banishing him millions of miles away. There's nothing he can do but try to survive, unaccounted for by his lost family and friends. Alone on the open waters.

In my search for stories of racialized indentured people from their own perspectives, I found text from a pamphlet circulated by early-twentieth-century Indian nationalists in the Uttar Pradesh and Bihar regions. It warned locals away from "depot-wallahs," one of many names they used to refer to indenture recruiters in search of people to sign onto the boats. "Don't hear sweet talks," it says. "They are your enemies."

European officials employed Indian recruiters and scouts who could then subcontract out to secondary agents, paying for every individual they signed on for indenture. They competed against one another in the escalating demand for workers, spreading rumours about their rivals. *They'll chop off your arms and legs if you go with them.* They spied on and undercut one another. Locals referred to them as liars, crooks, and kidnappers who oversold the protections and riches of indenture to the colonies. They made it seem as if the jobs were nearby, lasting over only the shortest of seasons.

In 1838, when outcries against recruitment abuses and poor labour conditions from abolitionists who called indenture legalized enslavement grew too loud, London officials halted the flow of Indian workers and launched inquiries. They implemented reforms like installing protective agents in ports and colonies to suppress criminality and unrest and keep an eye on women. As passionate as some protectors may have been about preventing flagrant abuses, their job was to smooth the path to more *coolies* scooped for colonial use. Many harms persisted, but the British restarted Indian migration in 1842 anyway. In the end, their investigations served to neutralize dissent and re-establish the rightness of their regime, undoubtedly fed by the fact that British officials trusted Indians only when they spoke in the presence of their overseers. *Coolies* continued to serve as assets for empire.

Recruitment in nineteenth-century China was known to be especially brutal. Abductions were common, as were total misrepresentations of pay and terms. With bounties paid per head, many recruiters acted like criminal traffickers, signing labourers onto ship rosters by force and lies. From their thuggery emerged the notion of getting "shanghaied."

In any port, however regulated it was or was not, those profiting from indenture and indenture-like recruitment would not have been particularly motivated to seek full and informed consent. Many of the indentured, likely my own ancestors, signed contracts with a fingerprint because they were illiterate. The root of the word "indenture" partly comes from the act of marking indentations on a tally, a practice to track the work of people unable to read. These arrangements had a built-in imbalance. There were those who knew far more about its terms, risks, and troubles and those who knew far less. Power holders surely banked on this.

Did European champions of the *coolie* trade view it as a business innovation? As the future of colonial money-making? The pro-indentureship influencer John Gladstone certainly seemed to see it that way. His negotiations amongst his merchant peers, as well as with magistrates and lords, sanctioned it as distinct enough from slavery to be legal in the heyday of British abolitionism but close enough to maintain the clout and wealth of the plantocracy. For him, the whole thing was a win-win. He was ardent that racialized indentured workers had clear and free choices to make. But that seems an impossible assertion when desperation, exaggeration, lies, fraud, and force were so infused into the recruitment process.

I'm not sure what the quality of decision making can be when you are pressed, impoverished, unprotected. I'm not sure exactly what choices refugees pushed and pulled by the ruthlessness of life can fully call their own.

Perhaps my ancestors, if not directly deceived by recruiters, fled widowhood, debt, hunger, hyperinflation, conflict, abuse, pain, or some barbed combination of the above. Perhaps, at the same time, they might have chased promises and hopes and dreams. Their unique reasons for boarding the boats have been lost to time and neglect. To the winds of our forgetfulness.

Not all survived the perils of their journeys. Latin America–bound indenture ships from China were similar to slave vessels: overcrowded, unhygienic, poorly ventilated. Many Chinese workers who boarded them died along the way. Ships from India adhered to higher standards, but the travel was by no means safe. In 1837, one of John Gladstone's first ships set sail to British Guiana with 419 Indian workers from Calcutta. Thirty-eight died en route and at least seventy were stricken by illness, presumably cholera. Between 1856 and 1857, 12 per cent of Indian men and 19 per cent of Indian women on British ships to Trinidad and Guyana died. Children fared worse. Twenty-eight per cent of the boys, 36 per cent of the girls, and over half of the infants perished.

For workers who did reach the colonies, indenture conditions were often constructed on the scaffold of enslavement conditions. Indentured people typically worked in the same fields and mines and lived in the same quarters enslaved people once did. Toil was backbreaking; pace and hours of work were gruelling. Sickness, infection, and risk of harm were ever-present. On Fiji plantations, for example, workers were chronically attacked by dysentery, tuberculosis, malaria, and other diseases. Regular accidents, violence, and suicide meant high death rates. Indentured women suffered uniquely. For instance, on those same Fiji plantations, women were outnumbered from the start, with about one woman to every four men. They were regularly mistreated and subject to assault and harassment by overseers and fellow workers. Given their lower status and pay, they had little recourse against the abuse.

Authorities rarely stepped in to temper the whims of overseers, an outcome of what Philip J. Stern, in *Empire, Incorporated: The Corporations That Built British Colonialism*, calls "venture colonialism." Kingdoms were not primarily amassed by royalty and armies but by force of joint-stock corporations: ragtag investors who pooled resources to win profits. European authorities were partial to the ideals and desires of business leaders, granting them charters and patents, and relying on them to operate the mechanics of settlement, control, and expansion. In many cases, colonial governing officials and colonial entrepreneurs were one and the same.

By virtue of their definition as free people volunteering labour, workers in indentured and indenture-like contracts had legal cover on paper. They could, in theory, issue complaints about violations and poor treatment. In practice, their rights and freedoms were scant, they were often blocked from formal remedies, and they faced significant discrimination. For example, in nineteenth-century South African gold mines, the movements of Chinese indentured workers were strictly controlled to prevent contact with white settlers. Workers were considered too "cunning" to be allowed beyond the gaze of colonial officials. In Mauritius, vagrancy legislation, a pass system, and punishment for labour organizing applied to both those with active contracts and those who had completed their contracts, ensuring command over every Indian on the island. British Guiana adopted vagrancy and pass laws, too, which heavily criminalized all manner of worker infractions.

Indentured workers faced severe corporal punishments, like beatings and whippings, and they could be imprisoned if they didn't do as they were told. Wages, set to a minimum, were withheld and clawed back for any number of transgressions or to pay fees. Months and years could be added to contracts for missed work, illnesses, injuries, and missteps. Overseers in the colonies were often stand-ins for absentee owners across the ocean, and many developed a reputation for brutality, corruption, and incompetence. They were put in place to wring out the most profit from the *coolies* for the least consideration.

Sweltering heat. A film of sweat that can't be wiped away. Sleeplessness in overpacked, barebones quarters. Soiled and torn clothing. Coughing that lasts for weeks and months, that burns in the throat and lungs. Skin pitted by bedbugs, mosquitos, ticks, fleas. Limbs marred by unhealing bruises, the old and new slashings of whips. Bushes for bathrooms. A lingering stench of sewage. Water pulled from stagnant streams for washing, drinking, and sooty cooking fires. Joints aching from overwork. Back stiffened by hours of bending to drive a machete into cane stalks, to bundle cuttings, to hoist and stagger and heave them onto heaps. An empty and cramping belly, never full enough, never able to take in enough. A throbbing skull. Memory maimed by the sight of floggings and molestations, of fellow workers laid down for deterioration and death.

Meagre hope of rest, care, or respite for myself and those around me. I try to envision the difficulties of what my ancestors witnessed, touched, tasted, and smelled in the plantations. I try to teleport my body into their bodies, fitting my form into their forms. Just the beginnings of such an exercise, and I am overcome.

The indentured revolted. Chinese workers staged mutinies, sabotages, and strikes. Indian worker uprisings and protests peppered the colonies. In 1872, at British Guiana's Devonshire Castle plantation, a crowd of Devonshire workers walked into the nearby town. They had been promised an opportunity to bring their complaints of poor treatment to the magistrate. What they discovered upon entering the courtroom were constables armed with rifles. I imagine them, men and women bustling out of the court, doubling back on the road that had led them into town.

Coastal breezes billow the fabric of their clothes, the ends of their head coverings, kurtas, saris. Some hold staves. I hear them lamenting the display of force to one another, maybe in old dialects of Hindi, maybe in newfound English, maybe in some blend of these. They are incredulous. They had allowed themselves to slip. Allowed themselves to believe they had a chance of being heard. They shake their heads, kick the dirt under their feet. They know that they should have known better.

I see them slowing at the road turning into the estate. They cannot simply return to the fields, swallowed by the cane, never to be heard from again. I see narrowing eyes. Tightened grips on staves. They choose to stand up. They will block the way of the overseers and magistrate into the plantation. They will hold their own court where they stand. They will make themselves heard.

When the magistrate arrives to confront them, he is accompanied by two dozen constables. After more than an hour of rising tension, of arguments and shouts both ways, the magistrate gives the order to seize the man at the front, the Indian they view as the ringleader. The constables advance into the crowd with cocked rifles. There is tussling, shoving. A shot rings. Then nine more.

Screams and scattering, bodies collapsed onto the road. The five workers killed at the sugar planation are listed in the record as Maxidally, Kaulica, Baldeo, Beccaroo, and Auckloo. Beccaroo was eighteen years old.

The incident was recounted in an official inquiry. The resulting report was soaked in colonists' anxieties over racialized uprisings across the empire, including Jamaica's 1865 Morant Bay Rebellion and the notorious 1857 Indian rebellion against the British East India Company. Authorities were certain that the actions of

Devonshire Castle's indentured workers were the genesis of a riot and proof of Indian propensity to violence instead of British maltreatment. The magistrate and police were exonerated, celebrated for their suppression of violent sedition that would have surely devastated the order of British Guiana and the West Indies. Perhaps the order of the global colonial project at large.

But the sharp awareness of those indentured people, their enduring concept of their own rights as workers and their own ideals of due process, sparkles through the report. They pushed for what they wanted an ocean away from their homeland, in spite of the way they were treated, regardless of the danger. They believed in fairness, a sense of shared responsibility that ran deeper and truer than the terms of their indenture contracts. Their complaints were to be listened to, no matter what the authorities must have told them. They carried a conviction of their own worth and dignity. If human beings have innate propensities to speak of, this conviction must be the biggest one.

What would I tell those elementary school teachers about the things I've learned, if I could speak to them now? I'm so much more protected than my indentured foreparents ever were. I often wonder if this ancestry is one I can fairly lay claim to. Their binds are a million miles away from me—at least 4,500 kilometres away, in the most literal terms. A few years before I was born in the late seventies, my parents immigrated to Canada under new policies that opened doors to highly skilled, British-educated English speakers. They moved far from the Guyanese plantation landings of their grandparents, perhaps their great-grandparents, perhaps their great-greats. I was raised as a second-generation immigrant myself, a Western urbanite lavished with amenities and options unimaginable to my ancestors. I know little of the stolen Amazonian land where they forged a life. I know even less of the hardships of their time and place.

Over the years, I've found myself tripping into guilt as I've discovered the details of global racialized labour exploitation. If I'm honest, I worry there's something trivializing about me taking a place next to my ancestors, pretending we have anything in common. I remain unconvinced that a go-between girl like me has anything, past, present, or future, to latch onto at all. If I'm honest, I've occasionally found my efforts perverse.

There's at least one connection between me and my ancestors of which I am certain. Most of the world's unfree racialized workers never set eyes on the lands where the wealth they generated was siphoned to. And even that's an oversimplification. It's not just that they amassed riches they would never touch. Their circumstances are carved into the contrivances upon which my easy Western life is built: currency and credit, stakeholders and shareholders, speculation and valuation, branding and marketing, shipping and supply chains, refining and manufacturing and borders and ownership and entitlements and the law and statutes written into it.

The sustenance in my mouth. The clothing that wraps my skin. The purchasing power and protections assigned to my name. The assets and access we persecute and storm and murder one another for. None of it would be what it is today without the suffering of these racialized ancestors. In this sense, not one of us has the right to opt out now.

In their go-betweenness, cast across strange lands over the span of a century, what did my indentured ancestors feel about their ordeals for someone else's profit? Will we ever uncover a way to know?

Gaiutra Bahadur writes in *Coolie Woman: The Odyssey of Indenture* that indentured Indian women's absent voices reflect their lack of power. But she wonders if that might be too thin an interpretation. Perhaps they would not share their secrets with us even if they could. Perhaps they would hold back the details of what pushed and pulled them onto the boats.

When she was alive, the racialized indentured woman's consent wasn't as respected as it should have been. It must be respected now.

This may be the only grace I have to offer to my lost ancestors. This may be the only grace we have for anyone who endured the horrors of our centuries, no matter who they are or where they were. The option to have held their own words to themselves and still be remembered. Still be mourned and cherished.

I was a suburban kid, overprotected by my parents in my childhood and teenage years. I was hardly allowed to do anything but attend school and church: few parties and extracurriculars, few hangouts at malls and friends' houses, no dating and hardly any dances or sleepovers or camping experiences. I did my homework and exams and pursued the grades expected of me, all along wishing for the nebulous freedom other kids my age seemed to have, foggy and thrilling as it was inside my own head.

Fresh and blinking in the corridors of higher learning, things changed. I was bewildered and spoiled by possibilities in my first year of university. I could read anything I wanted and meet new people. I could explore buildings at every corner of the campus, browsing library collections I'd never need for my assignments, sampling seminars and panels and fitness classes at all times of the day and evening. None of it was particularly adventurous for a regular nineteen-year-old. For me, it was an utter frolic.

I didn't set out to become a new person, but I was thrilled to have the option. I decided I should start by getting to know my fellow students. I stalked the floors of my college building, skimming the notice boards advertising film festivals and trivia nights, debates and town halls, parties and pub crawls.

A recruitment poster drew my eye. *Calling all South Asians on campus!*

I had never defined myself as South Asian, never strongly sensed my life as a product of long-ago ancestries I barely understood. Could I refine my senses? Explore the person I would've been if it hadn't been for some boat that had set sail long before I or my parents had been born? Would I visit this club and be delighted to discover I could indeed be the child not only of Indo-Guyanese people but also of an Indian motherland?

A few days later, I turned a corner in the hallway and stumbled onto a bunch of students. The South Asian student club banner was tacked to the brick above their heads. Club representatives chatted and laughed, bustling and shouting greetings. A pair of boys, jackets slipping off their shoulders, jostled each other in a play-fight.

"Hey," a girl standing near the display table called to me,

waving. "Are you interested in joining?" Her hair draped over her black sweater, blending into it.

I realized I'd betrayed my interest by slowing my stride. "Yeah, maybe," I replied over the commotion. "What's it about?"

"We do movie nights, parties, that kind of thing. A lot of socials. Sometimes we fundraise and volunteer. Only sometimes." She grinned. The jewelled node of her nose ring shone.

She's such a pretty brown girl. I wondered if she thought I was, too. I wondered if she saw me as Indian, just as I had presumed she was.

She handed me a pamphlet. "Doesn't matter what your language or religion are, it's fun stuff. You'll make a lot of friends."

I thumbed through the folds of the paper. Would I visit the club and be delighted to discover I'd been South Asian all along? "I guess I should check something with you," I said. "My family is from Guyana. I mean, we're Indian, but we're not from India. Would it still be okay for me to come out, you think?"

What happened next was so fast, so blasé, that loosening of her expression and the glazing of her eyes. Her pupils skidded to the left of my head and fixed on something beyond me. I stood there smiling, waiting for her answer, expecting it to match the openness of her reception. *What a friendly, pretty Indian girl.*

But her attention had withered. She angled her body, squeezed past my shoulder and the cluster of people next to us. She began speaking with someone else.

The noise of the students bouncing over those brick walls might have buried my question. Perhaps I hadn't noticed a fellow club member beckoning her away, compelling her to take care of another need. Intentional snub or not, being left suspended without an answer in that hallway, that place that was not really a place, was a mortification. It prodded the shapeless bruise of my identity, who I was and was not, who I would never really be.

I had been rejected. There was no room for somebody like me, somebody who hadn't visited the right places, who ate unfamiliar foods and had learned alien stories. An anomalous sibling set across a vast ocean, adrift on a separate block of land.

The moment evaporated into bitter residue in the kettle of my insecurities. I felt a prickle of perspiration under my scarf. I felt silly for toying with the hope of being South Asian. I should not have expected a university education to perform sorcery. It couldn't transmute a whole vanished history onto me. It didn't have the power to ferry me to bygone shores. I was wading in the murk between East and South and West. I was a go-between who would stay between.

I placed the pamphlet on the table and walked away.

I wish I had known of Haruki Murakami's *The Wind-Up Bird Chronicle* back then. In the novel, the two narrators, Toru and Lieutenant Mamiya, get trapped in dry wells. If these two characters aren't supposed to be read as younger and older versions of the same man, Toru and Mamiya are certainly twinned by loneliness and haunting memories.

Toru's well is situated in a Japanese suburb. Mamiya's well is bored somewhere in the wilds of Outer Mongolia. Both wells are dark and depriving. Both feel too real and dreamy at the same time. Stuck inside, the men seesaw between a hyper-awareness of their mortal pains and a surreal feeling of floating outside their bodies. When their purgatories end, they both climb to the overground world forever changed. They live as if a remnant of who they once were has been left underground.

Soundlessness for the ears. Acidity for the nostrils. Sparse light, no shadow for the eyes. Airless but oxygenated. Pinprick stars above. Invading shafts of ethereal, fast-extinguished sun. Padded, contained, cramped. Knees to chest, elbows to flank.

Ever since I read their stories, impressions of what Toru and Mamiya survived have burrowed into me. I often find myself trying to match them to a feeling, rotating and refitting them together like puzzle pieces. I wonder if my sense of go-betweenness is anything like the liminality of those dry wells. Tumbling into them makes you reconsider whether your pasts and presents and futures are real and worth believing in and hanging onto. You are suspended in life and death, buried and breathing all at once. The sense lingers, no matter what. No matter how you distract yourself, it's there.

I wonder if I share what Toru and Mamiya share, if I might be their forgotten triplet. I wonder if all descendants like me possess a sense of permanent liminality.

Murakami's dry wells are not pleasant, but they're not all bad. They allow for contemplation and reconstitution, as disquieting as the process might be. That's why Toru climbs into his well, seeking it again and again. It is not always an unchosen state.

Liminality becomes an opportunity. The liminal spaces of our lives—echoing stairways and empty back rooms, zombie malls and abandoned halls, train stations and airport terminals—are described as unnerving by some and strangely comforting by others. These are the uncanny places between places where we can simply be, where the expectation of something better, of something at least different, drifts as unfading vapour. What we make of them, what we do in them, is up to us.

Is there a glimmer of possibility in liminality for the liminal person? Does being liminal enable our ill-ease to settle into a peculiar kind of peace?

I believe we have to do everything possible to create that peculiar peace. I believe it starts with our own understanding of our breathtaking human interconnectedness. A passionate belief in it and love for it, right down to the marrow.

That the core figures of Western colonialism—settler, Indigenous, enslaved, indentured—were never "sealed off hermetically from each other" should be obvious, says Paul Gilroy in *The Black Atlantic: Modernity and Double Consciousness*. But the implications of their coexistence are "systematically obscured by commentators from all sides of political opinion."

The rise of the *coolie* trade can't be teased apart from the rising ethos of its day: liberty and individualism, fantasies of endless profit, conviction about man's journey from strength to strength. The *coolies*, under-remembered as they are, were contrasted with the enslaved Africans and free white men to lay out the terms of modern personhood, ideas so taken for granted in our collective imagination that they're invisible to us today.

In *The Intimacies of Four Continents*, Lisa Lowe explains that the Asian *coolie* was conceptualized in the thick of these ideals "to define and obscure the boundary between enslavement and freedom, and to normalize both." The *coolie* was less a person and more a symbol of what colonial powers salivated for: an abundant supply of free but boxed-in workers, compliant and sustaining, slotting into and upholding the fundamental hierarchy of the races. *Caucasoid, Mongoloid, Negroid.*

White dominance partnered with white saviourism. Imagineers of the *coolie* insisted these racialized people were victims of their backward cultures, better off labouring for empire, even if subject to its excesses. Migratory work was a grand edifying project, not unlike the way enslavement was seen as a civilizing sieve for Africans.

The spectre of the *coolie* never sat singularly or rested easy. Such is the nature of its go-betweenness. European leaders eager to benefit from the *coolie*'s presumed freely chosen labour vaunted it. British abolitionists and Indian nationalists asserted the *coolie* was a reinvented slave, steeped in misery and miscast as free. For Gandhi and his fellow Indian nationalists, indenture contracts were another example of British injustice and hypocrisy. They embarked on anti-indenture campaigns that fed into their tactics to decry the empire at large. In America, early enthusiasm for Chinese workers in coercive contracts gave way to hostility against *coolie* labour, clasping hands with anti-Asian discrimination and white nationalist rhetoric. Opponents successfully petitioned for the advantage of white workers and excluded and suppressed the racialized migrant.

Political pressures and campaigning, along with the bloat and bust of colonial mercantile power, spelled the end of most formal indentureship schemes—in 1917 for Indian workers and in 1949 for Chinese workers in general, although some *coolie*-style arrangements lasted longer. Up to the 1950s, for instance, colonial powers kept indentured Chinese workers in the Pacific via minor adjustments to their contracts, evading regulation. Australia continued to import indentured workers for its pearl-shelling industry into the 1970s.

Has it ever truly vanished? Aren't the factors that pushed vulnerable people into unfree labour arrangements then still driving billions today? Don't economic and state leaders uphold the conditions for bonded and indebted labour, profiting from impoverished and subjugated people's limited choices? Aren't racialized indentureship and unfree work arrangements, as much as any other exploitative historical force, an ever-living template for so much of how the world runs now, whether or not we can stomach that fact?

I've claimed the *coolie* has been forgotten, but I've overstated. We don't always say much about what happened, and we may not be fully conscious of the details, but I'm certain that millions of descendants like me at least have a sense of their go-between legacies. I've only touched the shores of the Caribbean sporadically myself and have never journeyed to my Indian ancestral homeland, but I know enough to know the offspring I am, removed from India, removed again from Amazonian land. Our kindreds and countrymates know us too, grafted relations as we all are.

This knowingness is highly influenced by postcolonial, civil rights, Third World, and Black consciousness movements that set the world alight from the 1950s onward, sparking a renewed sense of identity, solidarity, and pride. But fires can burn. In their quests for independence, unadulterated destinies, and accountability, formerly colonized nations like Uganda, Guyana, South Africa, Fiji, Mozambique, and Trinidad were ripped by political and social tensions between the once enslaved and blackbirded and the once indentured and migrated. At times, the tensions have escalated to exclusion, violence, and expulsion. At times, the truces have been uneasy.

You didn't strive hard enough, one side is accused of saying. *You didn't get where you should have.*

You colluded with the colonizer, the other is accused of saying. *You conspired and will always be a foreigner.*

British historian Hugh Tinker labelled Indian indentureship *A New System of Slavery* in his iconic 1974 book. There's a sense in which the lens has merit. But indentureship and indenture-like arrangements did not strip and castigate labourers as mercilessly as chattel slavery did the enslaved. Indentured people were not defined and treated as property the way enslaved people were. A level of mother tongue, faith, and family cohesion remained intact amongst the indentured. The enslaved were purposefully and cruelly ripped apart. Over the years, indentureship has had the effect of extending the shuffle of unceded Indigenous land and resources into limited hands. That is the grotesque reality of stolen land and labours.

One of the tragedies of the baseline bigotry of European colonialism is the way it smears racialized peoples' shared legacies and sours the possibilities—the aching need—for alignments. *We have more in common than we think*, much of the impetus behind unflinching re-examinations of history seems to say nowadays. *Don't forget how we have suffered differently. Don't forget how we have suffered together.*

I find hope in this insistence on holding different truths together at once, in an avid buffing away of the smear. Any voice that refuses to do so is not to be trusted.

Time is forever transitory, in and of itself, an eternal go-between. Five hundred years and seventeen generations have passed since feet first staggered onto boats in unfree racialized labour. It's easy to sketch people as tropes. It's harder to slow down and meditate on the humanity of history, our ancestors' seasickness and exhaustion, how they shook with fever, cringed under lecherous stares, and raged at abuses. They lived our past in their present bodies. How much they inevitably lost. How hard they had to fight to live.

And what of the enslavers, planters, overseers, owners, merchants, investors, lawmakers, law enforcers, and beneficiaries? They were humans, too. They stoked their entitlements and pressures, made their choices and repressed their empathies. They let their arrogance, fear, and ambitions lead them. How much they determined to overlook. How much they will never answer for, at least on this plane of existence.

It's overwhelming to carry the weight of ruptured humanity in retellings of our past. But let us be willing to try, in any event. Let us refuse to forget that every single person in our history was, indeed, a person.

Je t'aime
Te amo
Ya tebya lyublyu
Ani ohev otach
I love you
The sounds are all as different
As the lands from which they came

And though the words are all unique
Our hearts are still the same

"Love In Any Language" is a single from Sandi Patty's 1986 gospel album, *Morning Like This*. The record went platinum and ignited Patty's stardom, stewarding her to sound stages and stadiums across the United States. The song also altered my little eight-year-old life.

My class was amongst those at my school selected to perform it in a music video. We learned the song over the span of months, singing with the cassette over and over again. We became breathy and sweet when Sandi was breathy and sweet; we belted when Sandi belted. Our teacher taught us choreography to pair with the chorus. American Sign Language for *love in any language.* Chest pointing for *straight from the heart.* Fanning palms for *pulls us all together, never apart.*

On the morning of filming, I chose a green sweater with a yellow pear across the belly to wear, a shirt inherited from my cousin. I imagined it would stand out best.

When we filed into the gym, we tittered and squealed at the sight of the crew awaiting us, their cameras aimed at the stage. The director arranged us in meticulous order on the bleachers, swapping students from back to front and front to back. I landed down on the first row. I twisted around to survey the faces behind me. *Caucasoid, Mongoloid, Negroid.* The races were assuredly present, briskly stirred into one another.

The track echoed through the gym. We sang and gestured and the cameras panned. The director instructed us to smile and do it again, to open our mouths wider and broaden our hand motions so the cameras could capture our zeal. We did it again.

"This is beautiful," more than one member of the crew gushed. "This is what the world needs."

I'm not sure how many rounds of "Love In Any Language" we cycled through in the end, and I'm still not sure who we sang it for. I can't locate a trace of the final product, though there are countless videos online of children performing the song the world over.

Recordings of the song from the era when the album was popular are earnest, often hokey. The original mix, its tinkling synthesized piano and lilting MIDI strings, bears its time and place. So does its poetry. *From Leningrad to Lexington, the farmer loves his land/ And daddies all get misty-eyed to give their daughter's hand.*

But even in the grainiest concert footage, Patty's pitch is beguiling. It is sparkling and crisp. More satisfying than her vocal aptitude is the radical climax her lyrics meander to in the bridge. *Though the rhetoric of government may keep us worlds apart/ There's no misinterpreting the language of the heart.*

There's no misremembering either. I can still sing the whole thing by heart.

"Love In Any Language" glued itself onto me—not only the lyrics, but the kitschy thrills of its feel-goodness. I understood these sentiments would win the day, no matter where I took them with me. They pushed me to first place in short story contests and to top marks for presentations and posters during Black History Month, Indigenous History Month, and International Human Rights Day. They compelled me to trace sketches of Dr. Martin Luther King, Jr. and Mahatma Gandhi from a library book and pass them off as my own art in grade five. I was rewarded with prime real estate for their reprint in the school yearbook.

Love in any language fluently spoken here. Even then I suspected that the impression of fairness might be more desirable than its actuality. That humans caught in the calamity of history didn't matter to us as much as how we rearranged their predicaments to believe we had ascended to something better. I can't be certain, but I doubt I learned what the songwriters had intended.

What did I know of history and humans? Most of what I was taught in elementary and high school revolved around Europe and two world wars. Hardly any attention was spared for Indigenous and African legacies—even less for pan-Asian civilizations. How can a child hope to understand the wholeness of the world when most of the world is wholly absent?

These omissions may be on a plodding course to correction, prone to backsliding as it is. But I wonder if the fates of the enslaved, the indentured and coerced, the Indigenous, and the overseer will ever be treated as an interconnected lot. Is it only at a post-secondary level, in esoteric and partial reading lists, that some of us have a chance to conceive them together? To one day knit the elements relegated to the edges of the cloth into one big quilt?

Oh, maybe when we realize
How much there is to share
We'll find too much in common
To pretend it isn't there.

Why have we made it so difficult to conceptualize our histories as one? In failing to fuse them together, we don't believe ourselves to be obligated to communicate them together. We don't compel ourselves to look forward to the future together. The answer is that we mean to pretend our entwined destinies aren't there.

THE FAILED MODEL MINORITY

"Like my mother, I am drawn to the sea.
It can hold complexity and paradox in its blue throat."
— RAJIV MOHABIR, "Why I Will Never Celebrate
Indian Arrival Day," *The Margins*

This may be a difficult read. I write it in the belief that sharing these stories helps more than it harms. I encourage you to read as you see fit, in a manner that allows you to take care of yourself.

~

My mother got sick even before I knew her. Before she got married and had children, she developed a life-threatening sickness. By the time I was in elementary school, she had her first experience with cancer.

These illnesses became more than discrete diagnoses, more than segments of time managing her body's dysfunctions. They blended into a blot that always hung over her, that seeped down and saturated her, its edges watery, expanding and disintegrating.

Please help my mom feel better, I would pray in bed as a child. I would wake the next morning disappointed, having fallen asleep before reaching *In Jesus' name, Amen.* I wanted the prayers to stick and get answered, but I could never execute them right.

I prayed for my mother to feel better because I wasn't sure it was possible for her to actually be better.

The labels were as mysterious as spells. I had memorized them and could incant them, but I had no idea what they were meant to conjure. They were affixed to my mother's pill bottles, along with a rainbow of tabs that served as tacked-on admonitions. *Take with food. May cause drowsiness. Do not use while breastfeeding. Do not exceed recommended dosage.*

The bottles multiplied in drawers and cupboards and loitered on her dresser top. I thought of them as siblings that lived together in their houses, the musty insides of cabinets and side tables. At times, they seemed to grow into standing armies, dozens strong.

Some pills were of saturated hues, blue and red and yellow. They were manufactured and jolly, like beads and candy. Other pills were white and brown and beige. These ones were serious, like forms that emerged from nature. Rocks or bark or insects.

I would pinch bottles top to bottom between my fingers. I would shake them next to my ear like maracas.

Tss-tss-tss, the tiny smooth pills intoned.

Clack-clack-clack, the big coarse pills complained, chalky and grating.

My mother would collect these bottles after visiting neighbourhood family doctors. During the summer months, when school was out, she would take me and my sister with her to her afternoon appointments. Sometimes, she visited more than one doctor's office a day.

I remember the East Asian doctor with glasses and freckled cheeks most of all. He was the one she took me to when I got sick, too. One day, I sat side by side with my mother in front of his desk. I fixated on the spider plant on the windowsill, the slats of the blinds, the jar of tongue depressors paired with a jar of cotton balls, neither of which ever seemed at risk of running out. I imagined their refilling by supernatural force, contents dropping in like manna or else multiplying themselves like loaves and fishes.

I hadn't been listening to what my mother and the doctor were going back and forth about. The breath he puffed in my direction snapped me to attention. The two of them had been arguing.

"She doesn't listen," he said, shaking his head at me. "She only wants what she wants and she doesn't listen."

He bowed and scratched a pen over his prescription pad.

Then why don't you actually help her? I thought. My own question made me flinch. I was surprised and confused by it.

I couldn't have been older than twelve at the time. Did I truly think my mother wasn't getting what she needed from the doctors? How could I have known something wasn't right if it was all I'd ever seen? Did I really sense something amiss?

I knew other mothers didn't go to the doctor as much as she did. I knew other mothers didn't seem so tired and aching all the time. But other mothers didn't cook the way she could cook either, on special occasions, hosting get-togethers for twenty and thirty guests, so many of our aunts and uncles and cousins.

Other mothers weren't praised for their sweet hymn-singing voice and compassionate ear for anybody who needed it the way my mother was.

To me, she seemed somehow both more and less functional than other mothers. More capable and less capable. As I got older, the incongruences of who she was flustered me more and more, the disjuncture between what she could and couldn't manage, her low and high moods, her darkness and her laughter. Her care and overprotectiveness and pride for me, her irritation and disappointment in me.

Of course I would become aggrieved and despondent. Of course she and I would argue.

When my mother's kidneys failed at the top of my first year of university, I thought it had to have been the result of the cocktail of pills she had needed for so long. I pictured her kidneys as crimson twins tucked in her body, mirrored in fetal position in the small of her back. They were under aerial attack, I thought, shuttering and shrinking in the battery. My mother hoped the pills were fighting for her, but they turned on her. They stormed and flattened the body they were supposed to liberate.

We would learn that the cancer had come back, now advanced to inoperable renal cancer that intertwined with failed kidneys. What exactly came first, the cancer or the failure, the failure or the cancer, we couldn't untangle. Perhaps they had both led to the debilitating strokes that would follow and render my mother ineligible for the kidney transplant she had hoped for from an anonymous donor. Not an organ extracted from one of us. She refused to let us offer a part of our bodies to fortify hers.

About seven years would pass between her fraught diagnosis, dialysis treatments, palliative care, and death. Still, I see those pills as the culprit, as at least a colluding factor. As spies and traitors. I still circle around the problem of those pills in her body, the problem of her need for them. The problem of a body and mind infested by an ever-growing blot.

"Visit 'Chinatown U.S.A.' and you find an important racial minority pulling itself up from hardship and discrimination to become a model of self-respect and achievement in today's America." This 1966 *U.S. News and World Report* contained the first American media mention of a "model" group of minorities. "At a time when it is being proposed that hundreds of billions be spent to uplift Negroes and other minorities, the nation's 300,000 Chinese-Americans are moving ahead on their own—with no help from anyone else."

The report was published at a time when Canadian and American immigration laws were in flux. Even with the complexities of its time—distinctions drawn between "bad" Japanese and "good" Chinese immigrants in the aftermath of World War II, for example—policies trended away from exclusion and internment. In *The Color of Success: Asian Americans and the Origins of the Model Minority*, Ellen D. Wu calls the creation of model minorities a race-making project, in which supposedly inherent traits of racialized people are flexed to suit the needs of white supremacy. East Asians were transitioning from *coolie* to role model, contrasted against Black, Latin American, Indigenous, and other communities who clamoured for civil rights, fairer conditions, and compensation, battling the particular barriers they faced.

"Still being taught in Chinatown is the old idea that people should depend on their own efforts—not a welfare check—in order to reach America's 'promised land,'" that backhanded *U.S. News & World Report* reads, right near the top.

In *The Karma of Brown Folk*, Vijay Prashad says the extension of East Asian model status to American Desis was a "godsend." The media registered no understanding of these immigrants as a curated community filtered in during the 1960s, the "cream of the bourgeois South Asian crop" with advanced degrees and capitalist values suited to upward mobility. Like East Asians, South Asians were heralded for superior family stability, low divorce rates, and bootstrap ambitions, never mind the fact that immigration rules disincentivized family breakdown, never mind the ongoing experiences of discrimination and the disparities of wealth and well-being across lumped-together Asian populations.

Never mind the tenuousness of modelhood itself, how it's swiftly granted and snatched away, again and again. The model is presumably blessed, Prashad says, the result of culture or genetics or both in a serendipitous blend. The model accepts fitful congratulations for these traits, sometimes hesitantly, sometimes happily. Dissenting and otherwise questioning voices in model communities get swamped out.

Searching the term "model minority" leads to all kinds of articles with the word "myth" in their titles. Addressing modelhood without the qualifier can indeed camouflage the flattening power of the term, how it downplays the experience and harms of anti-Asian racism.

And where do descendants of racialized indentured people, those who worked fields, mills, and mines and built the infrastructure of European colonies, fit into this model schema? Legacies of indentureship are not a conscious component of model minority status, even though millions of South and East Asians in the West descend from indentured workers in one way or another. The racialized indentured descendant slips under the obscuring blanket of Asianness by virtue of their forgotten and ignored ancestral migrations.

Of course, this is only the case from the outside looking in. Within and between people of pan-Asian descent, there is far more awareness of indenture ancestry. Sometimes, it can take the form of prejudice. One sociological study addresses the invalidation Indo-Caribbean Americans can feel from those in Indian American communities, making special note of gendered nuances. As nineteenth-century Indian nationalists fought for an end to indentureship by pointing to harms and dishonours indentured women suffered, so can Indo-Caribbean women today be treated as if their Indianness is tainted by their double-diaspora backgrounds.

In these complexities, what is clear is that model minority status was propagated to complement whiteness and evade association with the conditions of non-model populations, particularly Black communities. That's where its attractiveness to whiteness resides, more than anything else. *They are not like the others.*

The model doesn't have to do much of anything to affirm or deny such a sentiment. The model horde's thoughts on these racial tensions are regularly assumed. *The other ones are always so unreasonable, so hard to deal with, so rude, so ungrateful. These ones know what we're talking about.*

What operatic gaslighting it is for any racialized person to be told they've just about achieved whiteness, regardless of how they're truly perceived and treated. What mental gymnastics it takes for any racialized person to just about believe it, too.

"Asian Americans inhabit a vague purgatorial status: not white enough or black enough; distrusted by African Americans, ignored by whites, unless we're being used by whites to keep the black man down," says Cathy Park Hong in *Minor Feelings: An Asian American Reckoning*. It results in racial self-hatred, in "seeing yourself the way whites see you, which turns you into your own worst enemy," she says. "Your only defense is to be hard on yourself, which becomes compulsive, and therefore a comfort, to peck yourself to death."

Most doggedly tied to Asian immigrants, the model minority stereotype affirms illusions of basic racial fairness. Takeo Rivera describes its purpose as "to provide evidence for the prominence of meritocracy over the structural barriers faced by nonwhite peoples" and "implicitly blame less 'successful' minoritized populations for their own subjugation (most notably, but not exclusively, those racialized as Black)." Contradictory and ever-shifting, the model minority stereotype is a racist tool designed to undercut and deny the potency of racism.

I have never been invited onto a stage to muse about my life. But I have noticed that children of model minorities who are so invited often tell tales of their childhoods, heaping praise on the efforts of their parents and caregivers. For some, it is their loudest and proudest story. *They came to this country with nothing. They worked hard every day, sacrificing for me and my siblings. They taught me everything I know. They were resilient and tenacious. They are my best friends, my protectors, my advocates, my heroes.* They gesture at them in applauding audiences. They wave them up to the stage to embrace.

I try not to doubt their sentiments. I myself had good parents. Still, I'm a restless, vulnerable bird with tales of immigrant perfection, jabbing my beak at a mysterious nut. I'm fascinated and flummoxed, pleased to hear them, hopelessly mistrustful of them. I'm prone to distraction. I flit off to the children with unsettled stories about who their parents and caregivers are.

It is the offspring of model minorities with hard-to-love parents that I flap around. Their parents can be morose and noncompliant, unhappy and unwell and unfair, and, at times, barely functioning. Their parents may be diligent workers and excellent members of society outside of the house. But that's a slipshod narrative, strung up like streamers at the edges. That's the perspective of the skimming eye that relies on assumption to furnish what's inside.

These children speak of model minority parents who aren't particularly successful as caregivers, who perhaps don't even want to be models or whose non-modelness pokes out in spite of their best efforts.

Theirs are the households cloaked in mesh. From a distance, the cover might appear unbroken. Get up close, set yourself at the right angle, and you start to perceive the holes. The imperfections show through.

"With limited English and little Canadian work experience," writes Jen Sookfong Lee of her mother in *Superfan: How Pop Culture Broke My Heart*, "she watched as she was whittled away, layer by invisible layer, until the only part that was left was her hard, immovable, fiery hot anger." As a girl in Hong Kong, Lee's mother dreams of becoming a singer. In Canada, she is a mother of five, grieving the early death of her husband. She is prone to depression, to rages against her daughters. She is a providing mother, not a nurturing one.

"In the beginning, the invisibility was forced upon her," Lee says. "Later, she retreated into it. It was what she knew, the only space that felt designed just for her."

In *What My Bones Know: A Memoir of Healing from Complex Trauma*, Stephanie Foo recounts her childhood with parents who immigrate from Malaysia to pull off the American dream, the house and car and careers. Her parents' physical and mental abuse against her is relentless. They beat and berate and threaten to kill her. They are reckless with their lives and hers. They are impossible to please, despairing, and, many times, suicidal. When Foo reaches her teenage years, their abuse turns into absence. They both move away to start new families and live their own new lives, abandoning her in the home where they raised her.

Prachi Gupta describes herself and her father, mother, and brother as an immigrant Indian family of achievers in *They Called Us Exceptional: And Other Lies That Raised Us*. It is their model successes that expand to choke them, to push gender-based violence and mental illness to the airless margins. In so many ways, it is their familial connection and fervent love for one another that makes it so hard for them to put a finger on their pains and alienations, right to the point that it splits them apart.

"But I want you to know when I think of you," Gupta pens to her estranged mother, "I feel your warmth."

This is the real trouble: there's often no lack of love, no lack of worthiness. But even as the model parent may do well, they are not well. Even as the model parent is not well, their unwellness is tucked away. The veneer of modelhood is too amenable to dismissal and camouflage.

Sometimes, models are incapable caregivers. Sometimes, they are deluded about it. Sometimes, they outright lie.

Smothered in the heat of these narratives, my body melts into a puddle of outrage. I am angry. I am glad. It's a twisted pleasure, the way I salivate to witness the misdeeds of the model minority parent brought to light.

I align myself to the confessions of the children. I want the blanket presumption of sacrificing only for the good of the children to be yanked off the table. I want racist stereotypes to be debunked in every way they can, up to and including supposedly positive myths of respectability, even when the grit of the truth left behind is ugly. I want us to concede that the very best in model minority citizenry can be fantastically bad at caregiving. That they, like any- and everyone else, can be indifferent and ill-intended toward their children. That they can fail miserably, too.

But still, a river streams through me, cool and urgent, my instinct to protect the failed model parent. Many are hurt and embattled, traumatized and weakened and sick. Many want to love and, for so many reasons, simply cannot. Modelhood forged many of the bars of their prisons, locking away their unmet needs for care and consideration and visibility. Modelhood is part of the calcifying chemistry that distills them to flint.

How could anyone in their position live up? How can any

fallible, breakable human being be expected to be anything but fallible and breakable?

These contradictions, the failed model's and my own, reduce me to a shudder. My arms tremble as I type.

"This essay is a roller coaster of guilt," says Jen Sookfong Lee as she writes her relationship with her mother into her book for strangers like me to read. How agonizing it must have been for her and Foo and Gupta and every other writer who makes the effort to do the same.

Because the truth is that our parents are always so much more than they seem on the page. So much more alarming and perturbing, so much more loving and proud, so much more aggravating and thrilling than we children could ever convey. We know them beyond the limits of written language.

And when we meditate more deeply, we recognize that we know only pieces of their lives, the crumbs of their backstories, thoughts, and feelings. Mere flashes of their blazing drives and dreams. We know speaking of who they are as parents can be an injustice to the fullness of who they are as whole people.

Gripping highs, devastating lows. Wonderfully, frightfully human. I think any child of a model minority parent, if they can find space to reflect, buckles themselves into this roller coaster when they share their experiences with any measure of honesty. Guilt may be our truest commonality.

Is it possible that this racial purgatory plays out differently for those of us conscious of our indentured ancestries? In our go-betweenness, never quite footed on any single shore, are we more likely to hold presumptions of our modelhood at bay? To keep it at arm's length, to carry it in loose fingers?

Is it possible that we indentured descendants own weaker illusions about belonging and acceptance because we don't fit into whiteness, don't fit into Blackness, and don't quite fit into pristine Asianness, either? Might we adhere to softer notions of permanence, citizenship, and "making it"? Do we understand more intimately the fluidity of human identity? Are our expectations of being perceived in any single, fixed way muted? Does the sense of being somehow spoiled or lost serve us, in the end? Does digging into our go-betweenness, not wrestling with it, hiding or mourning or resenting it, in any way help us to find ourselves? Does it in any way help to free us?

I consider racialized people working in Western colonies in indenture and coercive contracts the very first model minorities, imported with high anticipation for their labour. They were not educated or professionally trained like some of the model immigrants who would follow much later. They were not invested into by their families and home communities as some models were in the latter part of the twentieth century. They were construed as ideal labourers: governable, mouldable, and hard-working, especially compared to once-enslaved people. *Coolies* bound by contracts and shipped on boats were ultimately imported for similar purposes as the model minority of the sixties: to keep the order of capitalism and colonial economies running.

And *coolies* not only laboured on the farm, mill, and mine. They toiled in the symbolic fields of monied imaginations, protecting the morality of white overseers and employers and their beneficiaries and descendants. These largely Asian migrants of the nineteenth and twentieth centuries affirmed the rightness of the white colonial system and its leaders. Some colonialists considered the enslavement industry an evil because it drove white people to dishonour and sin. The impact of enslavement on inherently noble whiteness—not its brutality to the enslaved—was their overarching concern and motivation for abolition.

As Nell Irvin Painter explains in *The History of White People*, thought leaders like Thomas Jefferson, Alexis de Tocqueville, and Ralph Waldo Emerson wrote of their anxieties about the project of keeping slaves, especially the chattel enslavement of the American South. They considered it degrading to the ascendant character, customs, and work ethic of people of mythological Anglo-Saxon lineage. Painter notes that, as an advocate of self-reliance, Emerson himself viewed slavery as "a relic of barbarism that was bad for civilization, that is, bad for his kind of white people." The suffering of the enslaved did not figure into his equation. "The absence of moral feeling in the whiteman is the very calamity I deplore," he wrote in his 1851 journal. "The captivity of a thousand negroes is nothing to me."

Coolie labour could address this conundrum. No longer would upstanding white people subject themselves to the bloody and generally unsavoury subjugation of Black people to maintain their exploitable workforces. No longer would high-stock white men, women, and children risk their own moral, spiritual, and sexual uprightness to extract the labour they believed they were owed. They would wash their hands of the defiling affair. They would get work they desired—free and racialized and bonded, all at once—from the *coolies*.

But exploited labour is never trusted labour. Akin to the enslaved African evoking perpetual fears of insurrection, the indentured and constricted Asian evoked perpetual fears of domestic peril.

It was in the legislative and cultural changes of the 1960s that, as political scientist Jane Junn writes, "the dominant trope for Asian Americans . . . shifted dramatically from *coolie* to model minority." Modelness certainly reads more optimistically, but it is not an uncomplicated story. Junn says that "the simple take away in drawing the line from *coolie* to model minority is that Asian Americans remain racialized, distinctive, and threatening."

More than a shift, I picture it as a sheathing. Modelhood sits within a wider historical vista, dawning long before the 1960s-era admission of professional-class Asian immigrants. Inside of the frame of the model minority lives the new world *coolie,* a body within a body. The modern model is reiterated from that *coolie.* And the stories and symbol of the *coolie* are intrinsic to the contemporary racialization of the Asian. It is within the *coolie* that so many of the model minority's multiplicities and conflictions lie.

In 1990, economist Louis Winnick called modern pan-Asian immigration America's "golden blunder." He described these immigrants as a flood of rivals with an "unappeasable hunger for jobs," many of whom held "eminently marketable skills, advanced education, and unbounded career ambitions." They would revitalize the labour force and renew urban life in floundering cities, yes, but they posed an ever-present foreigner's danger to the beating heart of America, never granted a chance to join the fibres of that heart. "It seems that the Law of Unintended Consequences, so malign in most of its workings," Winnick writes, "occasionally displays a benign face."

The *coolie* transforms to model through a recursive rework, a Fibonacci computation of stereotype, a golden ratio that is simultaneously golden blunder. The *coolie* is the nested doll in the model minority. The model is crafted through racial *mise en abyme* or Droste effect, the technique of painting a copied figure within a figure.

The *coolie* is the earlier narrative written into the later narrative. The earlier is echoed but, in the end, it is willfully erased from the page. It becomes a spiteful haunting of the story.

For me, locating the *coolie* within the model minority feels revealing, but it is not in any way affirming. It feels like a breakage. It's like cracking into one of those ancient nested Egyptian coffins, golden box within golden box. You imagine you'll uncover treasure. You only find bones.

Was my mother strong or was she weak? This question lingered for me over her years of cancers, strokes, illnesses, and disabilities.

At her funeral, an answer emerged from the pulpit as I and other mourners sat in the pews below. She faltered on earth like every human being falters on earth, the preacher said. But she trusted God. In the wake of her mortal death, she would no longer falter. She would no longer be weak.

At the kitchen table with my family after the funeral, the answer was different. She was a survivor, they said, battling her way through countless treatments and setbacks.

"People didn't see how strong she was," my uncle said. "She kept fighting and she lasted through it for years. It takes real strength to fight like that. The preacher was wrong."

My aunts agreed. That my mother had made it as long as she did was a marvel. They had seen her fight with their own eyes.

I remained quiet.

"You two are lucky you had your mother for as long as you did, you know," another aunt I didn't know well told me and my sister at the wake. "My children lost their father when they were too young to handle it. I saw them suffer so bad. You two don't know that suffering."

This kind of bluntness, it's familiar to me. I know this aunt meant it as a better offering than the bland truisms of mourning. That didn't make it easy to hear.

Still we nodded, our heads cocked and our brows knitted. I'm not sure we meant to agree that losing a mother in early adulthood is luckier than losing a father as a child, but that's what we did.

I thought of the man I was going to marry, who was only seven years old when he lost his father. I thought of how he had described the day it happened. He walked into the kitchen and his mother told him that his father would not come home. His father had collapsed at work, dead of heart failure.

"I can't remember what happened next, but I guess I must have hid in my room," he had told me. "I guess I must have cried."

No, my sister and I responded to this aunt of ours, *we don't know the suffering your young children knew.*

A few months later, I attended the funeral of a co-worker's father. "This must be hard for you," another co-worker murmured in my ear as we waited in a line of well-wishers that snaked up to the family. "You must be thinking about your mother's service."

The grieving family stood shoulder-to-shoulder with the lacquered coffin at their backs. Our co-worker's eyes were glazed with tears as she embraced a visitor. Her hair had become staticky with the heads pressed against hers, one after the other. With the soft fingers of her family and friends combing through it.

"I had my mother for longer than a lot of people have their parents," I answered. "I can be glad for that."

My co-worker frowned. "We don't expect to lose our parents in our twenties, do we? We expect more time." She rested a hand on my shoulder.

Was it a matter of fortune or misfortune? Was it too little time, or more than most? Had my mother's life been marked by strength or by weakness?

I had seen too much. My mother was terribly ill and entirely strong-willed all at once, defying the expectations and prognoses, again and again.

I had felt too much. There were days I missed my mother as if I hadn't had enough time with her, but I couldn't deny that her passing felt like a relief. There were times my mother fainted and fell to the ground in her last years. There were times I bent to feel for her pulse in the startle of her collapse, with desperation, unvoiced, for the suffering to be over.

I was trapped in these incongruences, unable to reconcile them. I mistook grieving as sewing together mismatched cloths of memory to forge a tapestry that would make sense. I imagined the ironing of contradictions to amount to healing. If I couldn't find a way to make the pieces fit, if I couldn't find a way to smooth the wrinkles, I worried I wouldn't ever feel okay.

It took me years to understand that contradictions of our past and present exist together. Fortune and misfortune, strength and weakness, too little and just enough. They're a matter of perspective. Of elusive wisdom.

Some contradictions do straighten in time. Others will persist.

"I knew your mother was depressed, you know," that same aunt whose children had lost their father too young went on to tell me and my sister. "Even back then. I told her to try to get out there. Try to do things that would make her feel better." She shook her head. "'I don't feel to,' she said to me. 'I just don't want to do it.' Didn't you see that yourself? Didn't you see your mother was having a hard time, even before she got so sick?"

I had seen my mother stay in bed for hours. Sometimes, I heard her sniffles, her tears. I heard her wordless whispers to herself, her groans. She would get up to go to the bathroom, sometimes hardly able to lift her slow, scuffling feet. Her physical and mental ailments, tangled and impossible to tease apart, were not lost on me.

Many times, I resented having to be privy to them. Many times, I wanted to escape them, to shut myself inside a peaceful box when they overtook her in our house. I wanted her to stop feeling what she felt, to at least dam it away so I wouldn't have to live with the sights and sounds of her pain.

Depression and trauma, right alongside disorder and distress. These were not the words they are now. The parlance of chronic illness and mental health was not traded so knowingly or generously. *Caring upstanding mother* and *unwell struggling mother* seemed hopelessly misfit against each other. They seemed impossible to snap together.

We knew, yes, my sister and I nodded again. *We knew something was wrong.*

How was it that this aunt, this woman I wasn't certain I'd even met before, could speak something so unspoken so easily? How was it that she was compelling us to agree with her so late in time like this, after my mother was already gone?

How was it that no one had ever seemed able to truly help my mother? Why couldn't our care and love save the day and make her well?

I disliked this unknown aunt for voicing such things. I wanted her to go away. At the same time, it was a solace to hear her say what she said. I wanted her to keep going, to tell us more about what she had perceived in my mother long before I was conscious enough to see it myself, long before anybody had had the language to commit to it.

I was enraged and thankful for what this woman was doing, allowing chaotic truths to tumble from her mouth. I was perplexed at how such conflicting reactions could feel so sharp, so scraping inside the hollow of my chest.

In the routine immigration processes of many countries, Canada and America and the United Kingdom included, would-be newcomers are screened for communicable disease, for mental and physical incapacities, for all manner of problems and dysfunctions and unpredictability. They are to disclose their conditions, prescriptions, and diagnoses. They are not to be accepted as residents if they stand the chance of clogging examination rooms and emergency departments, if they might clutter the waiting areas and occupy the beds. They are not to pass the threshold of a border if the costs and hassles of keeping their persons intact exceed the revenue they generate.

There is little point to the body and mind of an immigrant that drains more money than it gains. First and foremost, immigrants are to serve as net benefit. They solve problems, cover holes, and fill cracks in periods of widespread anti-immigrant sentiment and pro-immigrant gusto and anything in between, when immigrant-attracting countries need doctors and caregivers and drivers and fruit pickers and exotic dancers and office workers and tradespeople and entrepreneurs. Whether or not receivers begrudge them, immigrants are caulk and spackle and putty. They are here to be useful.

To become a model immigrant, you must work. Work is your logic and motivation and reason for being. Work is the spirit of your existence. You are not to be sick or disabled or addicted or in any way underfunctioning or underproductive in the economy. Your body and mind are not to be broken.

British medical officers examining Indian workers for indentureship in the 1800s were not only tasked with ensuring that recruits were free of illness and could survive their monthslong boat journeys. They were also to assess their suitability to the station of *coolie*, preferring men of particular classes and castes, of certain heights and weights and builds, with developed chests and calloused hands. Hernia, anemia, diseased eyelids, enlarged testicles, and varicose veins were grounds for rejection. Also grounds for rejection was evidence of opium eating and tobacco or ganja smoking. Medical officers afforded greater flexibility to women recruits because of their scarcity in the indentured population, given the domestic, familial, and sexual duties they were expected to fulfill to nourish *coolie* men's needs. Records show officers were directed to accept women who had "reasonably hard hands" and were not "beggars, devotees, dancing girls or prostitutes."

Fitness for labour—for the role of labourer—has long been of fundamental importance to border crossing. But clearing a checkpoint doesn't mean a body is truly and forever fit. Foreign bodies are always risky, as sites for and sources of contagion. This has been the situation across the globe for at least five hundred years, especially at times of outbreak, from syphilis and cholera to tuberculosis and Ebola. The foreign body, however long it remains within borders, is an eternal problem.

And forever foreignness is readily ascribed to the racialized body. People of East Asian descent and their offspring in Western countries were punished for foreignness in the 2020 coronavirus pandemic, even if they had been born and raised in those countries and never in their lives set foot on Asiatic soil. Over half of respondents of Chinese and East Asian descent polled by Angus Reid across Canada in 2020 reported being the target of name-calling and insults. Forty-three per cent reported being personally threatened or intimidated. From government offices and boardrooms to basements and backyards, the "yellow peril" trope of the 1800s was readily revived and slapped on anyone who seemed Chinese.

Even if they're declared fit for labour, even if they've long ago become citizens, racialized immigrant bodies, even the models, even the children of models, carry within them the germ of destruction.

Off the coast of British Columbia in the Salish Sea, between the San Juan Islands and Vancouver Island, D'Arcy Island was established in 1891 as a quarantine site for Chinese labourers who contracted leprosy. Workers had arrived from South China to build the Canadian Pacific Railway or else populate the fish canneries and mines. Between 1891 and 1924, forty-nine men were exiled to the island.

Conditions on D'Arcy were described as "deplorable." Once every quarter-year, a steamer arrived at D'Arcy's shore with a health and sanitary officer. They left food and clothing on the beach and gave the men with leprosy a quick lookover, supplying them with opium. An armed guard stood by to make sure no one tried to escape.

For fifteen years, the City of Victoria and the federal government quarrelled over who should have to pay for and manage the colony's operation. Quarantined men were left to the ravages of their infection in the meantime. Some were deported. Others died with only one another as witnesses, their bodies disposed of in unmarked graves.

D'Arcy Island is now part of the Gulf Islands National Park Reserve, a rustic landing for boaters and kayakers. It's favoured as an ideal spot for birdwatching. Back then, it was the "Island of Death" for *coolies* too afflicted to work. *Coolies* whose bodies nobody wanted to be responsible for.

In the week after she died, I worried about my mother's body constantly. I would jerk awake in the middle of the night, blinking and breathing hard, remembering that she had been carried to the funeral home and was not in her bed on the other side of my bedroom wall.

The body is there, I thought, attempting to reset myself to the new reality, *not here*.

When my mother had been sick in bed, there were times the house was so silent that my ears ached, eardrums wincing without a noise to vibrate to. When she died, the house got loud, strained with the voices of visitors and clinking dishes, with memories told and retold. So many sounds and sights and smells. Such overwhelming, misty-eyed sympathy.

That week, I asked my fiancé to steal away with me. We drove off, him at the wheel, me in the passenger seat. The windows were down; the breeze found our faces. Just six months before, we had decided to get married. I didn't tell her about the decision. I didn't want to confirm that there was someone new to pledge myself to. I didn't want to hurt her. Put her second. I let her meet the grave without knowing.

After the funeral and wake and gatherings were over, the cacophony of mourners shrank to me and a handful of close family members, clumped in the narrow crematorium. The air we breathed was humid. The floor under our feet was concrete. The furnace in front of us, stainless steel.

I rested my forehead on the shoulder of the aunt in front of me. It was warm.

None of us wanted to press the furnace's button. The cremation technician explained some things about what we should expect, the length of burning, the collection of remains, the storage of ashes in plastic bag inside cloth bag inside wooden box. He pushed the button for us.

I heard stifled sobs when the machine roared on.

The body is here, I thought. *And now it's gone.*

I dreamed of my mother's body for years after that, just about every night. In my dreams, she was usually in a state between life and death. She died and somehow came back to life, came home to be sick in bed again. Sometimes, I didn't even see her in the dream, but I felt her body's presence in the house. In these dreams, my extended family was often with me, aunts and uncles and cousins. We were in the kitchen, waiting for her to die. Waiting to have the funeral and wake and cremation all over again.

They used to be anxious dreams. I used to feel my heart thumping. I used to wake from them with a tense, sweaty neck.

These days, dreams about my mother's body are quieter, less frequent. They are not peaceful, not exactly, but they're muted.

"My mother was my mother," Amy Tan says in *Where the Past Begins: Memory and Imagination*. "There were many times in childhood when I wished that were not so." Her mother dealt with mental illness her family could not name. "The main problem, as I saw it growing up, is that she was negative in her thinking."

I, too, remember thinking this way. I remember blaming my mother for her moods and thoughts and for sharing those moods and thoughts with me. I was unprepared for them, too young and self-centred and unobservant. I hardly knew how to respond.

You'll be happy when I'm gone, she would sometimes say.

You're making me sick. I can't remember the exact frustrations and difficulties and pains that led my mother to say such things to me. I do know she repeated them so many times that I stopped thinking they could've been true. I stopped believing that even she believed them to be true.

How could she think this? I remember wondering as a teenager when she had said it to me, yet again. *This is so much bigger than any of us.*

Amy Tan hadn't yet written her book, but I would've been stunned to see myself in her words if I had read them at the time. I didn't know these unnamed things could be shared between people who never knew each other, who lived miles and years apart. I would've been shot through with recognition of the disgruntlement she felt toward her unwell mother when she was young.

Perhaps I would have been intrigued by the turn that came for Tan, too. "But when I was grown, she was inextricably part of the way I thought and observed," she writes, "and to wish she were not my mother would be like wishing I were a different person."

I wouldn't have believed such a mentality would ever become true for me. But perhaps I would have clung to a nub of promise in Tan's shift in perspective.

Children of model minority parents unfit for their labour get familiar with a particular kind of strain. I know it well. It seems to pulse through Tan's words, too. It's the contradictory stress of disguise and overattentiveness. We are aligned to our parents' plights. But we distance ourselves from it, some of us through rebellion, some of us through diving into achievement, some of us through willful ignorance of our pasts. It is an exhausting brand of overcompensation, a grasping for worthiness in a context that doesn't recognize our worth, either way.

Deep down, we feel this strain even if we can't speak it. We feel it in our bodies. Deep down, we know this howling feeling of a hole.

Conceding that model minority-ness is not designed for our well-being or wholeness has to be a part of our paths forward. We have to appreciate that as much as we post-mortem the details of exactly how we and our families struggled. We need to consider what failure means in a scheme so rigged. We need to understand that a falsehood was weighing on our heads from the very start.

A model is an ideal, an excellent example of itself. Modelling is a series of activities that build and maintain and replicate the ideal.

But the creation and preservation of a model minority is not a fixed action on an inanimate object. Modelness is not a status merely attributed. Model making is a dynamic enterprise, both ascribed to and indwelled by people.

The unquestioning model minority, if such a person exists at all, is often written off as chasing modelhood for the pleasure and privileges of white acceptance. Those of us who proudly declare ourselves to be non-models can be their brashest belittlers. *I hate math and science, I hate shutting up, and I hate following the rules*, we say. *You should too.*

But who's to say a model's strategic self-positioning is an easy stroll down the path of conformity? Who's to say choosing to live as a minority model, if it can be considered a choice at all, is not a form of resistance to racism itself? Who's to say that joining them to beat them, to at least survive with them, is innately wrong?

These are sticky questions for those of us who worry about getting sucked into racialized modelling ourselves. Is the desire to be a model and the active pursuit of modelism valid or invalid? A fair compromise or a form of selling out? A selfish, unethical chase or an understandable reaction?

How should we live, really? Are we good or bad people?

Takeo Rivera sets these questions aside and explores model minority racialization as masochism, a "model of subjectivity that often embraces rather than eschews its status of otherness and subordination." It is a "self-inflicted incoherence" embodying "an internal logic of accommodation and subversion at once." Instead of seating them at opposite ends of a see-saw, Rivera appreciates the striving for and rejection of modelhood at the same moment in a double pull: enjoying the casting of stereotypes and assimilation and punishing yourself for enjoying it.

The dissonance of pleasure and pain is built into what it means to be a model minority. So, too, are the incongruencies of bargaining with gendered ideals and biases. A paper overviewing several studies highlights contradictory stereotypes Asian American women face: they are hypersexualized but seen as passive, exoticized and othered and tokenized and criticized and over-scrutinized, all at once. The studies tie this mixed messaging to a host of mental health concerns like high levels of body shame, disordered eating, depression, and suicidality.

But the situation amounts to more than bad input equalling bad consequences. More than garbage in, garbage out. A sociological study finds that for South Asian women, there can be an inner battle over being considered a good worker and good mother, that women can accept and resist the ideals at the same time. Feeling like a "super parent" can become a point of personal pride, a way to cope and feel a sense of control with the pressure of labels and expectations.

Pan-Asian and Pacific Islander people in America are less likely to seek help for mental health, substance use, and addiction issues. Model stigmas and cultural values certainly have something to do with it. But I wonder how much of the hesitance is due to the reality that mainstream programs, treatments, counselling approaches, and therapies haven't proven they have the bandwidth to deal with the complexities of model life. The fighting and the feigning of it, all at once.

Pleasures and pains of modelness will indeed be elusive to disciplines with a history of disregarding racialized people, of barely listening to what they have to say about and for themselves. I think we can spot the ignorance a mile away.

And what in the world do these disciplines have to say about the unkempt modelhood of those of us with indentured ancestries? Of those of us living as racialized nesting dolls, *coolie* body within model minority body within *coolie* body? I have seen little evidence that it even registers on the scale.

"How do people from your culture view the concerns you're telling me about?" the older white man asked me, squinting and leaning toward me in his chair. "How do you think their standards for women play into it for you?"

We sat together in the small room in the community centre. The door was closed behind his back. I could feel my muscles begin to shake at his question. After my mother died, I was without much health care coverage. I had visited this man, a volunteer mentor in my neighbourhood who made himself available to provide counsel in informal sessions to anyone who needed it.

I had been exhausting myself from the beginning of our conversation, battling my defensiveness to every suggestion he offered to help me manage the stress and anxiety I told him I was feeling. The thrum of my pulse became a soothsayer. *Try as you may, you won't change a thing,* it told me, drumming at my neck. *You can't handle this counselling stuff. It's messed up and you're messed up. And look what's happening to you now.*

"Culture has nothing to do with it," I replied. "I don't want you to think I'm coming to you with some kind of cultural problem. It's not." I heard the quiver in the back of my own throat.

His eyes skidded to the papers in his lap. "Oh, okay. I understand."

I left the building feeling as if I had achieved a victory for the greater good. But by the time I arrived home, my triumph had soured. I wondered why I couldn't allow myself to entertain any notion of a cultural dimension to my problem. Why that man asking me for my thoughts on it so inflamed me.

After a few months, I wondered why I had to dismiss the experience altogether to feel better, to mock it and write it off as xenophobic nonsense.

I knew my reaction was more than irritation over the reality that racialized people's needs get rendered exotic, generally nonhuman, which has a way of neutering or at least tainting the help we get, sometimes from medical and therapeutic sources, sometimes from friends and co-workers and volunteer mentors alike. My mother had not always been given the care and consideration she needed in medical and hospital settings. I had worried over the ways discrimination factored into her treatment countless times.

But sadness and sensitivity about medical racism would have been the easy explanation for my behaviour.

I had assumed a train of thought on that man's part. I assumed he conceptualized my culture as some kind of stereotypical South

Asianness, a crass television brand of Indianhood that had nothing to do with me, nothing to do with real people living real lives. *Land of the Taj Mahal and forced marriage and Sati. Land of the unfortunate, disempowered, broken-down woman.* I believed he had no concept of me as a second-generation immigrant woman of Indo-Guyanese heritage born and raised on the very land we met on, of what culture truly meant and didn't mean to me and my family and the situation I was in.

I had assumed his assumptions and I hated every single one of them. I had been run ragged by them my whole life, skin chafed translucent by them after so many years of friction. I was all buzzing and sparking nerves. Every breeze had the power to trigger burning and make me scream.

I felt I had to stand up to him. I felt I had to fight for us, for myself and every racialized individual he had ever talked to, believing he owned the answers to our alien cultural dilemmas. I thought the man was arrogant. He didn't know as much as he assumed he did, I believed, nor did he truly care to know us. I had to protect myself. I had to protect us all.

What I needed was simple. A kind ear, a warm smile, a referral to a competent mental health professional I could feel comfortable with, perhaps the suggestion that searching for some kind of diagnosis for myself wouldn't have been an insurmountable barrier.

I needed to seek and find for the sake of my own well-being so I wouldn't always have to fight so hard. Because I worried the same blot that had troubled my mother was oozing its way toward me.

That generous neighbourhood volunteer, stuck in a room with my complicated neediness. Neither he nor I had the capacity for it. In the end, I didn't have a chance of getting what I was looking for that day.

⁂

It's the disasters of modelling that alarm me most. The news stories where things seem to go terribly wrong in a seemingly model family, where the children of those families do awful things.

A woman stabs a young woman, someone she had never met before in her life, in the heart and kills her. She is deemed not criminally responsible due to untreated schizophrenia, symptoms of which had probably begun to show up in her teens. A man slaughters his mother, grandmother, father, and sister in their home the day before he's supposed to graduate, after lying about attending university. He plays video games in between his gruesome crimes. Another woman allegedly hires men to shoot her parents in their home after dating a man her parents disapprove of and lying about being in school.

Reportage of these cases references high immigrant family achievement and expectations, signs missed and signs ignored. They point to hard work and hard sacrifices of parents, deferred and unrealized dreams, the dismay that springs from disappointment over wayward and underperforming children. These narratives spell out silent suffering, polite grins to hide agony at school and work, a sheen of perfection that narrows and intensifies to sickly spotlight.

Is the model pathology attributed to these cases accurate or fair? I consider the people whose lives were needlessly robbed from them. I think about their surviving loved ones who feel barred from justice and care in the lonely aftermath. Is failed modelhood a truthful explanation or reasonable description to apply to any of it? Or is it a distraction from or a perversion of the real nature of the horror?

I don't have the answer. But I suspect that modelness gets in the way of what needed to happen in these cases to avert catastrophe, on some level. That signs of distress or malice would have been perceived sooner if the haze of the high-functioning immigrant family didn't smoke everything over. That early problems would have been treated more seriously and urgently if model respectability wasn't a clouding factor. That people might have otherwise gotten the tools and treatments they needed to take responsibility and prevent the worst of outcomes.

I worry that model minority-hood and its inevitable breakdowns are far more dangerous than we've ever conceived them to be, not just for the individual affected by model standards but also for everyone around them, for even the innocent bystander. I worry that perhaps the most harrowing stories could end differently, if only we paid attention.

I've read books and listened to commentary by racialized coaches, trainers, and consultants designed to help the racialized Westerner, model minority or otherwise, heal. They take a peer perspective and focus on embracing authenticity, cultivating belonging, and building appreciation of self that has atrophied or gotten snatched away. They encourage the harmed racialized

Westerner to reclaim their culture, eat their foods, and insist on the correct pronunciation of their names at work. They advise them to find joy in their melanated skin.

This help is certainly valuable, but I get morose in its presence. Just about inconsolable. I'm distracted by pessimistic thoughts and dispirited questions I haven't heard many ask.

What if the racialized does not heal?

It's only in fiction that I find a semblance of answers. Franklin Hata in Chang-Rae Lee's *A Gesture Life* is an upstanding small business owner in a small American town, a Korean born into the Japan of World War II. His neighbours know him as Doc Hata, a mannered near-retiree enmeshed in his daily routines. Years ago, he adopted a girl he found himself incapable of parenting—a re-enactment of his earlier ineptness as a young officer in the Japanese army. Back then, he was tasked with monitoring a group of Korean women systematically sexually abused by the soldiers. He fell in love with Kkutaeh, one of these so-called "comfort women," convincing himself that she loved him back. She longed for the mercy of death. He longed for an impossible romance.

Years after she is raped, murdered, and dismembered at the hands of the soldiers, Hata having made no attempt to stand against them, Kkutaeh materializes in his suburban home. She is at the foot of his bed, a midnight spectre of his cowardice. By the end of the book, Hata's efforts at reconciliation with his adopted daughter and his past are furtive, hardly more than gestures themselves.

What of the racialized who refuses to heal?

Mohun Biswas of V.S. Naipaul's 1961 *A House for Mr. Biswas* scrabbles to establish his individuality, even as he unwittingly marries into an influential Indo-Trinidadian family and moves into their house. They threaten to swallow him whole. He fantasizes about independence, antagonizing his wife and resenting his children. He falls short. He tries to build a house but it is blown apart by a tropical storm. When he does secure a house, it is rickety. When he sinks into his own career, he is laden with debt.

Age and illness mellow Biswas; he himself makes few motions toward wholeness. "Roving reporter passes on" is the headline he imagines the newspaper he writes for will publish as his death announcement. "Journalist dies suddenly" is the headline they print.

Like Hata, Biswas is an old man at the conclusion of his story. Both men are twitchy over the fates of the children they have barely parented. They don't have much to offer the people in their lives. Like Hata, Biswas is never completely relieved of his alienation. Both novels finish at death: Hata's anticipated, Biswas's actualized.

That these men are cursed from the start is plain. Hata is adopted into a family of apothecaries for villages struck by disease. His Japanese surname means "black flag," and in his visions, Kkutaeh drapes that flag of crisis over her reassembled ghostly form. Biswas is born blighted by a pandit's prophecy. He is warned about water and bears a sneeze that makes bad things happen. As a child, his father drowns searching for him in a river. Biswas is found hiding on the bank, given away by his sneeze.

Contemporary racial self-help material is sober and optimistic, designed to uplift and unchain the suppressed self. These novels, formative classics for me, are designed to disquiet. At times, they punch unhappy laughter from the gut. Neither Lee's nor

Naipaul's stories read as hero's journeys in my eye. The men they birth on the page are too dissatisfying to be heroes.

Beyond their failures and misbehaviours, Hata and Biswas beg a thornier question in my mind. What if the racialized model Westerner is doomed from the start?

For years, I told myself the story that I should not have gotten married when I did, just four months after my mother's death. For years, I told myself I had gotten married so hastily to divert myself from the inevitability of grieving. I told myself I should've taken the space and time to process everything on my own, that indeterminate brand of mourning while living that happens when someone you love is unwell for so long. I told myself and other people that I should have focused on finding real therapy, that I should not have been so anxious to latch onto somebody else.

I told myself I'd been reckless, repeating this conclusion again and again. Who knows what could have happened? Who knows the disaster I could've inflicted on the person I promised to love? What if he wasn't who he is? What if I had been a little more self-destructive or nursed a little more self-loathing than I did? What if, after all that time pretending I was okay, pretending I was perfect, I'd become as despondent as I worried I'd become?

My story had no other variables, plotted only with high-wire stakes. What if I were the daughter of Hata and Biswas, unable and unwilling to heal, a force of catastrophe for myself and everyone around me? What if I were doomed?

"Maybe you shouldn't have gotten married when you did," my friend told me when I said this to her. "I thought you could've chosen another way at the time, too. But I think you did it because you needed to. I think you did it because it was a safe space to deal with everything you were dealing with."

It was as simple as that, my story's quiet, close revision in the voice of a friend. It is her compassionate read that enabled me to rewrite it for myself, for the better.

There's a defiance in not healing from racial harm. As dreary as it seems, I find something admirable in it. It's an acknowledgement that something bigger than you is broken. It's an awareness that the racism that frames your life, casts you into somebody you're not and gets in the way of who you want to become, is itself entirely sick. It interferes with so much—your laughter, creativity, aspirations, sense of beauty and worth and humanity, and, yes, even the way you grieve and hold the memories of your loved ones. No amount of self-help can fix that.

It's an understanding that, as ill or as broken as you are, as failed as you feel, the experience of racism is not your fault.

But not healing is a frightening thing, too. Racism is a process of rendering the racialized body and experience both too visible and invisible, all at once. The racialized's suffering is seen too much. The racialized's suffering remains unnoticed too often.

Being so seen and so unseen is an awful discordance to live with. Sometimes, it's nothing less than lethal.

Perhaps not trying to heal from racist harm means that your defiance, too, is likely to be overseen and, paradoxically, not seen at all. Maybe refusing to heal, to admit that you need healing, in the end only wounds you and those you love. Maybe you need to seek healing, as incomplete as it will be in so sick a context, because you need and want to love better.

And every person in the world, without a single exception, needs to love better. I am convinced of this.

Yes, then, please do what you can to heal. And in your own way, oh so carefully, in your own time and amongst the people you so choose, share that story. As difficult as the sharing might be. You might find it rewritten for the better in ways you never could have imagined.

Much more than the complexities and contradictions that lived inside her, that live inside each and every one of us, my mother loved me with her wholly human love. Perfect and imperfect at once. That's what is here for me now. That I had her love in all her pain seems to me nothing short of a miracle.

Twenty years ago, on the very day I type right now, my mother died. Only a few weeks back, I dreamed of her again. I suppose anticipating the anniversary and writing these things is what triggered it.

We were in a rowboat on a river. The air was clean; the sky was clear. The water was calm but flowing fast, its surface flashing like a turned crystal. I saw fish swirling around the boat, orange and pink koi. I saw the billow of underwater flora, green leaves and impossibly large peony blooms. Sunbeams warmed my skin.

I wasn't thinking of my mother's body on that river, if it were sick or well, if it were alive or dead or dead then alive, only to become dead again. I was just trying to understand what she was saying to me. I was trying to listen as she chattered and laughed and gazed around at the grass and trees and wildflowers.

I didn't catch her words. The wind rushed around me and muffled them. I laughed with her all the same, the way I do when the music is too loud, when the conversation is too boisterous for me to take it all in. When the gladness around me is unmistakable but the details have become unclear.

I never mind laughing in those circumstances. I don't believe that kind of laughter to be untrue. Quite the opposite. I believe in laughter that is partly unknowable but wholly felt in the body, in the limbs and the chest and the belly.

I often wonder what that kind of laughter really is. It seems to me a laughter of faith. Of hope. I wonder if it has anything to do with the afterlife at all, with a better place. I wonder if it has anything to do with glory.

This laughter in my dream, I felt in my face. I felt it in my cheeks.

I didn't know how to steer our boat. I don't remember it having oars at all. I wasn't worried and neither was my mother. I simply rested as I was and let the shimmering water carry us along.

BETTER LIVES

Wind braced my body. I had to push against it with every step. A few yards ahead, the sandy soil under my feet plunged into a cliff. Water roiled at its base, cresting and foaming and colliding. Birds zigzagged overhead and slipped into nooks in the rock face.

Cabo de São Vicente in Sagres, Portugal, is the southwestern-most tip of continental Europe. Here, the North Atlantic crashes against the craig, churned by clashing gales from the north, west, and south.

From the bus that ambled here, I had watched the trees disappear. Only wildflower and scraggly grass remained when we pulled up to the red-and-white lighthouse at the cliff's edge, where land compressed to a point. In the ocean beyond the lighthouse, a nub of rock jutted out of the waves. Cracked off the mainland, it seemed as if it was fighting to keep its chin above the torrent. Bobbing for rescue.

I'd been eager to visit this *fim do mundo*, the "end of the world." Seeing it with my own eyes, shivering in the blow, I understood why the Portuguese called it that. Black clouds in the distance met the horizon of the sea like a curtain dropped to the floor. It seemed as if nothing could exist beyond it.

The Portuguese were not the first to be sobered by this vista. Neolithic menhirs erected across the region hint at its significance before recorded history. The name Sagres itself evolved from an older Latin name: Promontorium Sacrum. Holy Promontory.

Penned around 17 CE, Strabo's *Geographica* says of the cape that it is not lawful "to offer sacrifice there, nor, at night, even to set foot on the place, because the gods, the people say, occupy it at that time." It is the spot where the divine roots itself to earth.

Sacrum is also the name given to the thickened triangular bone at the base of the human spine. From this apex, wings of the pelvis unfurl. Into it, the spine implants. The root of the body, too, is called sacred.

Why the earliest humans migrated out of Africa in the first place remains a mystery. Was it the result of climate crisis, food shortage, epidemic? Curiosity, restlessness, boredom? The factors that compelled our ancestors' uproot, jolted them out of the inertia of staying put, is hotly debated.

Why did the Portuguese themselves, led by Prince Henry the Navigator, venture past the end of the world, kickstarting what is nicknamed the Age of Discovery? What led to hundreds of years of seafaring and war, land theft and enslavement, riches and disparities, technological explosions and environmental degradations, and even greater migrations? I've heard the motivations cast so confidently: nation building and greed and power playing and delusions of dominance.

But struggling on that cliff to stay grounded as the wind threatened to hoist me over the edge, I wondered about the fourteenth-century pandemic. It had reduced the European population by half and scattered people into small settlements. I wondered if they felt a push of destruction at their backs, too. I wondered how many loved ones plague survivors had watched succumb to infection. Perhaps they felt the pull of life, of at least something better than decimation, beyond the cape's stormy unknowns.

I live in the same city where I was born and raised. The absence of push or pull to uproot me from my place is a privilege. I am no navigator; I am no adventurer. Consistency has always represented comfort to me.

What would happen to make this land I've settled on too uncomfortable? What would condemn it and make it impossible for me to stay?

Cabo de São Vicente is the namesake of Vincent of Saragossa, the third-century Spanish deacon. His story is recounted in a lyric poem by Prudentius describing persecution at the hands of the Romans. Vincent of Saragossa refuses to subject holy scripture to flame, so he is tortured and martyred and cast away on a boat that shipwrecks at Sagres. Ravens of the cliff, swooping and fluttering, protect his body.

He is the Saint Vincent behind the name attributed to that rainforested isle in the Caribbean six thousand kilometres away. Before Christopher Columbus docked at its shore in 1498, before the colonizers warred with Kalinago people who lived there and shipped enslaved and indentured people to labour on it, that seed-shaped land of hardened lava was known by its Indigenous name, Hairoun. Land of the blessed.

Is the process of uproot a condemnation or a blessing? I'm prone to dread the push, the disasters that would force me away from my safe place. What it would mean to leave everything I have ever known for the pull of possibility is just about unimaginable.

I. CASTES

I don't remember what we'd been reading or watching when the issue of caste clattered into my grade eight classroom. My teacher, a short white woman with permed hair who, to my child's eye, looked like a grandmother, stood in front of us to explain the ancient order in her own words.

"India has *varnas*," she said. "*Varnas*. Levels everybody in the country fits into, no matter what." She turned to scratch a pyramid on the chalkboard. "Brahmins are the ones at the top. They do the religious ceremonies. Regular people, workers and such, are under them."

She looped an oval under the base of the triangle and scrawled the word *untouchable* in its centre. "Untouchables don't even belong in the triangle, you understand." She prodded the board with the nub of her chalk. "They're the lowest of the low. You're not supposed to talk to them. They do the work no one else wants to do, like garbage collection and cleaning refuse. You're not even supposed to look at them. The untouchables live terrible, terrible lives."

She slapped the chalk onto the chalkboard ledge.

"This system has been around forever. Thousands of years. It'll never change. It's organized and terrible."

Levels everybody has to fit into? And it's been around forever? Words jumbled in my mouth. This blueprint was entirely foreign. I couldn't understand why no one had told me about it before. *There are people you're not supposed to look at? What happens if you look at them by mistake? How would you know who they are? Do they look different than everybody else?*

My mind answered by conjuring a man with a crooked back in rags and a turban. I saw him muttering, shuffling down a dusty road, broom in hand, cheeks soiled. I thought of *Indiana Jones and the Temple of Doom*, the monkey brain–eating extras sweating through bronzer as a man's beating heart is ripped clean from his chest. *Om Namah Shivaya, Om Namah Shivaya!* Even at that age, I understood the depiction to be racist.

By the time I untangled my questions and reactions, my teacher had turned away from the class. She had moved on to another subject. I waited for the chance to stretch my hand over my head and ask her to tell us more, but she never returned to the *varnas*. She erased the pyramid from the chalkboard and never spoke of caste in the classroom again.

What caste would we have been if we were in India?

I was bothered by the question. I brought it to my mother and aunt. The three of us were in the kitchen, probably on a Saturday morning. I was in my pyjamas and my mother and aunt were in their slippers and bathrobes.

"What did that teacher tell you?" my mother responded with furrowed brows, standing at the stove as she cooked something. "Why would she say those things to you kids?"

"Don't worry about old-time things like that," my aunt said to me with a softer voice. She sat at the table next to me. "That's a long way from where we grew up and a long way from here. People don't think that way anymore. Thank goodness."

I gazed into the steaming cup of tea that one of them had set on the placemat in front of me. I blew to ripple the milky brown liquid. I had a sense my aunt and mother were protecting me from something. I fingered the corner of the placemat, indenting crescents on it with my fingernail. I didn't push them for more.

By the time I reached high school, I had learned, likely gleaning the term from something I saw on television, that so-called "untouchables" were more appropriately referred to as Dalits. But I hadn't learned much else about South Asian history or cultures or the Hinduism of my ancestry. I knew just as little about Guyana and the Caribbean where the adults in my family were born and raised. Being brought up as a Westerner and a Christian meant the direct experience I could absorb by osmosis was scant. Still, I convinced myself that I had deduced the truth about my family's caste ancestry all on my own. It was a matter of simple logic.

"I'm a Dalit," I informed my friends from Indo-Caribbean and Indo-African families who, like me, were descendants of the indentured. "So are you. Think about it. If you had money and servants and houses and you were at the top of the pyramid, why would you get on a boat? Why would you need to leave India at all?"

Eyes narrowed; heads pressed into slow nods.

I recall one or two of my friends protesting, repeating something their mothers had told them about their grandparents and great-grandparents, something an auntie or a pandit at their temple had claimed about their lineages.

I slammed their arguments against the blunt force of my reasoning. I was smug. I told them I understood why they would have a hard time admitting their Dalithood to themselves. My presumed untouchability had turned into a point of pride. Those who cap pyramids don't know about real struggle or suffering, I told my friends. They don't know how the world really works. Privilege renders them foolish. Living at the bottom is nobler. More in-the-know.

I dragged this resigned, self-righteous, and wholly invented knowledge into my early adulthood. *If everyone treats you well as a matter of birthright,* I reasoned, *why would you need or want a better life? Why should anyone who came from indentured labourers imagine they're anything other than untouchable?*

When I read about the complicated truth of caste in Indian indentureship years later in a library, I was chided by it. My view floated off the pages of the book to the sunlight on the windowpane beside me. I realized how wrong I had been. I was overwhelmed by how much these hidden histories have to teach me about humility.

British colonists spoke of the earliest Indian indentured workers as casteless tribal wanderers partially or completely outside major cultural and religious hierarchies. These workers originated from the Indo-Gangetic Plain, a swath of land that includes northern and eastern India, eastern Pakistan, Bangladesh, and southern Nepal. Their true identities and diversity, difficult to parse now, were compressed into the crass signifier of *hill coolie*, a term that camouflaged their heritages and practices and presumed their backwardness, rootlessness, and bottom-rung existence on the ladders of labour and civilization.

For those opposed to nineteenth-century racialized indentureship, the inherent lowliness of *hill coolies* rendered them too vulnerable to consent to ocean-crossing work arrangements. These critics believed *hill coolies* to be devoid of faculties to understand what they were agreeing to. For champions of indentureship, the marginality of *hill coolies* was considered a plus. They reasoned that these unfortunates were already separated from mainstream society and religious traditions, serving as beasts of burden within the borders of India anyway. Outsiderness meant they were unbound by the duties, dietary rules, and cultural obligations of other groups. They were used to hard work and poor compensation. They were happy with stifling heat and punishing conditions, uncomplaining and innately industrious. They were free-floating, groundless natives without land and order.

John Gladstone, planter, slaveholder, and father of four-term British prime minister William Gladstone, saw *hill coolies* as the perfect working population to buoy up the declining West Indian plantocracy. Messrs. Gillanders, Arbuthnot & Co., the Calcutta merchant house Gladstone corresponded with to set up indenture arrangements, assured him that *hill coolies* were "more akin to the monkey than the man," with "no religion, no education, and in their present state no wants beyond eating, drinking, and sleeping."

Abraham Maslow's hierarchy of needs would not be published for another century. Still, in this assessment, *hill coolies* slotted into the floor of the pyramid as creatures of pure physiology, pure reactive impulse. No angst over self-actualization. No drive for transcendence. No illusions of peer-to-peer fellowship. These hardly-human workers were unburdened by the desires of real and true humanity.

By the mid-nineteenth century, Indian workers across many regions were signing indenture contracts. They represented a range of cultural and faith communities and high, middle, and low castes. Examinations of indenture contracts of workers who landed in Fiji and British Guiana, for example, reveal that about 15 per cent of labourers came from higher castes, 40 per cent came from middling castes, 30 per cent came from low castes and outcastes, and the remainder were Muslim. Census records from 1881 show that the caste and religious breakdowns of labourers on indenture boats around that time were not so different from those of Indian society itself.

Ground-shaking proximity to one another meant that many elements of caste separation were undermined in the workers' journeys to the colonies. From airless holding ports where they awaited departure to cramped boat quarters where they slept and ate together to the landing sites where they performed similar work, caste faded as a distinguishing trait and governing principle like a photograph bleached by sun.

Crossing the murky ocean itself—the *kala pani*, as they called it—meant damaged status for the indentured, particularly for those in higher caste positions with more to lose. It opened the door to new kinds of allyship and familyhood, too. Some thought of themselves as *Jahaji Bhai* and *Jahaji Bhahins*. Brothers and sisters of the boat. On plantations, authority of the Brahministic order and validation of ancient traditions were physically and mentally miles away. The practices and precepts indentured people clung to in the colonies were only what they remembered and chose to act on in their new circumstances.

But any suggestion that caste completely vaporized across the waters, caught and whisked into fog, would be an overstatement. Distinctions did not disappear in indentured Indian populations across colonies, though they reformatted themselves in different ways. In Mauritius, for instance, some indentured Brahmins took on functions, ceremonies, and rites in their plantation landings beyond what they would have performed in the communities they left behind in India, which may have bolstered their standings. In Suriname, Brahmin men were often referred to with the honorific *maharaj*, their wives, *maharajin*, a practice not necessarily maintained in other colonies. A comparative analysis of the cultures and practices of indentured Indians in Fiji and Guyana observes that caste disintegrated as a system of ritual and work categorization in both places, remaking itself into marriage preferences and serving as a source of identity and pride. Similarly, another analysis notes that in the decade after indenture was abolished, caste orders across Indo-Caribbean communities may have morphed into class orders, unscrewing from birth status and bolting onto educational and economic achievements.

For the individual indentured Indian labourer, caste allegiances shifted in intensity and purpose. Some plantation owners didn't want Brahmin or Muslim workers, believing them to be unsuited to field labour. Some indentured workers had to downplay or hide their affiliations, even where those affiliations would have been an asset in their home communities. Those born of lower castes were generally less likely to return to India after their indenture period than their higher caste counterparts. For higher caste labourers, their returns might have hinged on their ability to shoulder the cost of pricey purification ceremonies to reinstate lost status.

Transformations of intertwined gender and caste status for indentured women were particularly dramatic. Across many colonies, indentured women exercised all kinds of novel agency: intermixing with people of different castes, entering and exiting romantic relationships across divides as they saw fit, remarrying as widows, and gaining money and the respect associated with it in their new landings.

Artist and researcher Andil Gosine says that while careless transcription by colonial clerks may have damaged the status of workers with high caste names, for others, throwaway record-keeping may have been an opportunity for self-reinvention. "It's hardly surprising," he says, "that many indentured discarded names that marked them as less and chose ones that offered a notion of more worthy status."

Crossing the *kala pani*, as painful as it must have been, was not a monolithically agonizing journey. It may have had the power to turn alter egos into reality. It may have vaulted dreams into the air.

My old question circles back: why indeed did the racialized indentured get on a boat, whether in ports of India or China or other places around the globe? Yes, of course, trickery and kidnap and flight from misfortune, destitution, volatility, hunger, widowhood, debt, hardship, abuse. For me, these feel like the obvious motives to imagine for such an onerous migration.

And some of these motives would have weighed more heavily on some heads. Indentureship may have been a special draw for widowed Indian women of higher castes, given the stigma they faced in the prospect of remarriage and their dearth of opportunities to secure an income. The very shortage of indentured women workers across the colonies enabled those of lower status to ascend the caste ladder through typically frowned-upon relationships with men of higher castes. Women's transgressive choices in love on the other side of the *kala pani* would have acted like a hammer striking the sculpture of caste in everybody's minds.

Still, I wonder if force and desperation are overly safe explanations for everything that happened. For me, misty human longings hover around the bloodied stones of utilitarian escape. To what degree were the indentured attracted to the promise of gaining something more in life? How many relinquished themselves to unscrupulous recruiters, transporters, and planters expecting their suffering to only last for a time? How many believed the pain would be worth it?

For labourers who did make a meaningful choice to board the boats, what did they hope and pray would happen during and after their indentureship? What kind of new life might they have imagined for themselves and their families?

The humble baggage of the indentured might offer a clue. British indenturers allowed Indians to carry onto the ship a cloth handbag, a *jahaji bandal*. This is where they may have stored their copies of the Ramayana and the Qur᾽ān, texts many couldn't read themselves but which would serve as a reassurance in unknown territory. The indentured also carried seeds, cuttings, fruits, and herbs with them: mango, fennel, cumin, lotus, pumpkin, pomegranate.

Many were agriculturalists from agrarian communities. It makes sense that they would take tools of their trade with them. I envision them cupping saplings in their palms, wrapping them in strips of cloth, tenderly placing them in their *bandals*. I can't help but wonder if there's more to this act of swaddling, if what they brought with them alludes to a desire to sow and nourish themselves anew. Perhaps they were finding ways to make their stays familiar until they returned home. Or perhaps they wanted to discover a new home altogether. Either way, it seems that they wanted to cultivate their own gardens, risky and fitful as the attempt might be.

Were they hoping to sow gardens of paradise for themselves for a short while? For the rest of their lives? For their sisters and brothers of the boat, too?

Records of labour resistance offer another clue about the new life the indentured may have hoped for. Desertions, vagrancy, uprisings, and rebellions in the colonies certainly prove the mistreatment and oppression people suffered. But resistance also stands as evidence of a clamber for change, the workers' basic understanding that they deserved better. They show their objection to the dismissiveness and sneering of colonial overseers and leaders. Perhaps the indentured intended to make the new world they were helping to craft their own, too. Perhaps they intended to be actors and not simply to be acted upon.

At this point, the question of what exactly pushed and pulled the indentured may have been exhausted. Maybe we have to embrace abundant possibilities in an unresolvable debate. Influential Fijian historian Brij V. Lal shifts his attention to the children of the Indian indentured around the world instead, the people who became "individualistic and pragmatic," he says, "self-oriented, more egalitarian, more alone, sometimes extravagantly proud of their ancestral culture and heritage but not enslaved by its rituals and cultural protocols." He says they were "torn between two worlds, one which they had left but to which they could not return; the other which they adopted but which they could not, or were not allowed to, embrace."

That tension, "the sense of transience, alienation and uprootedness and general ambivalence, animated their existence," Lal says. "They were a people caught in-between."

And still, I wonder how much of the in-betweenness of my indentured ancestors is a matter of circumstance and how much of it might be a matter of design. Of unabashed dream.

II. CULTS

Your family is from Guyana? The Jim Jones place?

I'm likely not the only person of Guyanese heritage who has met people aware of Guyana solely through the 1978 murder of more than nine hundred Americans in the Jonestown settlement, once situated in the northwest interior region near Port Kaituma village.

Don't drink the Kool-Aid, they usually tell me at some point in the conversation, with a wink.

Without the green-and-white sign at the settlement's old driveway, and the stained memorial stone crawled over by foliage, pinpointing Jonestown's location on this Amazonian land would be a challenge. Cottages, dormitories, storehouses, and meeting places the Jonestown residents had erected have been broken down. The plots they farmed in that mutinous, barely fertile soil have long overgrown.

The story of Jonestown and Peoples Temple, on the other hand, persists in public imagination, mined again and again in books and film. Stories of people who sequester to remake and reposition themselves are endlessly compelling. As the central antagonists, Jim Jones and his inner circle of leaders have been exhaustively analyzed, their psyches and tactics over-plumbed. Jones himself has claimed a great deal of mental energy and creative and cultural resources. Almost fifty years later, audiences remain attracted to him and the salaciousness and nihilism of what he did.

Jonestown met its dreadful demise the year I was born. I can't help but wonder what it would've been like to be a Guyanese citizen back then, a journalist or public servant or emergency response worker charged with some aspect of the aftermath. Combing through books, articles, documentaries, and archives on the topic of Jim Jones and Peoples Temple, I find few personal accounts from those voices.

The voices of the everyday people who accompanied Jim Jones to the Amazon are also often unheard. These were the congregants enlivened by the prospect of building a new life together with their families and children. They were largely African American, nursing ambitions to shape a universal brotherhood free of discrimination and race and gender distinctions, thwarted in that mission by the realities of American bigotry. Like other movements of their day, they set their sights on interracial farming projects, including one in the Guyanese interior.

And like many groups deemed cults after their heydays, Peoples Temple attracted an array of dedicated and gifted individuals. They thrived in the face of marginalization and anti-Blackness. They achieved brilliant successes and won thousands of supporters and donors to their vision. In *The Road to Jonestown: Jim Jones and Peoples Temple*, Jeff Guinn details the talent and resources congregants dedicated to operating affordable care facilities and providing training and employment opportunities, clothing, food, and meals for community members; free tuition and boarding for low-income college students; and health services for elderly, ill, and recovering people. He shows how Jones and Peoples Temple were primary drivers of the desegregation of the city of Indianapolis, their strategies rendering opponents frankly foolish in comparison. The church's achievements were openly praised by civil rights leaders like Angela Davis, Dennis Banks, and Laura Allende, sister of former Chilean president Salvador Allende.

The reach of Peoples Temple cannot be read as a narrow American misadventure, either. In the 1960s, Guyana was led by Prime Minister Forbes Burnham in a Black-majority government eager to solidify itself internationally. His party had ascended during an election split between the Indo-Guyanese and Afro-Guyanese populations, after years of racially charged interference by the U.S. government. What happened in Guyana remains a lesser-told chapter of America's global anti-communist fervour and manipulations.

The Guyanese government did not just provide land to Jim Jones and Peoples Temple. They also offered it to David Hill and the House of Israel, an American-based Hebrew Israelite movement that incorporated Black Power ideology and New Age beliefs common to the era. Such acts of refuge to American sojourners allowed the Guyanese government to increase its visibility and stakes in world politics. The presence of American settlers in the country's western territory, which was coveted by the Venezuelan government—an active conflict today—served as a buffer.

Whatever Jones's and the Burnham government's motivations were, regular Peoples Temple congregants themselves weren't simply in it to create an insular, perfect life for themselves in the

Amazon. They didn't uproot themselves from everything they knew for mere escape.

They migrated for utopia. In his analysis of Jonestown as a communal farming project, E. Black says the initiative and others like it functioned as "primordial schools, wherein early humans learned, honed and fundamentally and dialectically both taught and learned cooperative communal skills to and from each other, irrespective of age or gender." Peoples Temple aimed to offer "samples and examples" of a promised Land, "a way to make their envisioned non-racial, non-sexist, non-classist utopian future into an actual and realized present." They didn't mean to retreat from reality or fall off the grid or be absorbed into the jungle's foliage. They cordoned themselves off from the world but also meant their utopia to serve as instruction for the world.

Of course, Jonestown didn't work out as they had planned. Farming yielded poor and unsustainable harvests. Jones's paranoia and megalomania intensified, hurtling the settlement toward horror.

Perhaps showy utopias, whether concluded in whimper or bang, can't last. Perhaps quarantining yourself from the contagion of the world is no way to serve as an example of how to live in the world. Still, so much of what most Peoples Temple and Jonestown members desired was worthy. Their sacrifices, skewed and toxic as they became, began as a hope for greater good.

They won't be the last to try and fail at better lives. Dreams of utopia endure. Better is meant to be shared, and no one is deterred from searching for it for long.

III. CHOICES

"Answers about caste are elusive," Thenmozhi Soundararajan says in *The Trauma of Caste: A Dalit Feminist Meditation on Survivorship, Healing, and Abolition*. "So much is hidden. So much is unspoken. There is so much shame, secrecy, complicity."

As had happened to me, first exposure to a Western definition of the "untouchable"—hers in the pages of an encyclopedia—snagged Soundararajan's child mind. Her family's rootedness in the Indian subcontinent meant that her question about caste was definitively answered in her mother's whisper.

"We're untouchable."

It pierced a light through her parents' secretiveness, her father's avoidance of his full name. Their fugitive fear would fuel Soundararajan's questioning of caste in the face of hatred and threat as one of the first openly self-identifying Dalits in an American institution.

She tackles the opinion that India's caste order is a colonial invention, an argument I've heard many times. The British certainly harnessed the ideological weight of caste and collaborated with caste-privileged people in their domination strategies. This is clear in their presumptions about *hill coolies* and their definitions of them as preferred indentured labourers. The British layered their own racist logic onto their Indian exploits, deepening divides, firming up the idea of dark skin as low and light skin as high, even as the spectrum of melanin within caste groups is a diverse reality.

But Soundararajan confronts Indian caste order on its own terms, apart from the workings of European colonialism. It was established long before British arrival, rooted in interpretations of Vedic texts that date back to 200 BCE. She demonstrates its doggedness, its penetration of traditions beyond Hinduism and Vedic beliefs, right through to Buddhism, Sikhism, Islam, and Christianity.

Amongst Indo-Caribbean friends and family in Canada and the United States, I've heard about avid searches for marriage partners with direct continental Indian background. Living in the realm of rumour and whisperings more than in confirmable facts, I wonder how much of this drive for a "legitimate" South Asian spouse represents a desire to reconnect to cultural and religious roots, to unearth lost histories, to pursue caste-grounded promises of compatibility, and, yes, to refill caste status drained through the legacy of indentureship.

For me, the voices unmasking hidden caste-based assumption and discrimination are the most gripping evidence of caste as remade reality amongst children of the indentured. Fijian writer Esha Pillay, also known as Izland Kuli, speaks to the indentured descendant laying claim to Dalitism without real knowledge of their ancestry, as I once did. In such careless acts of reclamation, we can unwittingly uphold casteist practices, even as we claim to be post-caste. "To not know is okay," she assures, "because there have been a lot of erasures."

In *Caste: The Origins of Our Discontents*, Isabel Wilkerson expands the prism of caste, defining it as a "universal form of human division that could be applied to many hierarchies in the world." Slotting into the footsteps of thinkers like W.E.B. Du Bois and Michelle Alexander, she addresses Black Americans as the United States' "untouchable" class. She demonstrates how the specificities of anti-Black racism and racialization are malleable, ever-updated for contemporary applications, the last-born child maturing in the shadow of first-born caste.

Whether in Indian, German, American, or other contexts, Wilkerson draws common lines across caste hierarchies. They're legitimized by deity and nature, encompassing those determined to be inherently superior and inferior. Caste is transmitted through birth, threaded by apprehensions about mating and pollution. Caste orders circumscribe suitable occupations for the people inside of them. They're rationalized as benign yet infused with dehumanization. At times, with sheer terror.

The degree to which caste systems interrelate with one another, and the tightness of their symmetries, are matters of debate. Even the inference that the bottom rung of the ladder exists to contrast with the top rung can be interrogated. Making the case for caste hierarchies to be examined as unique entities as much as they are compared to each other, Diana Kim explores how "untouchability" can be experienced outside of the interpretive lens of strict hierarchies. Surveying histories of Korea, Yemen, and Nigeria, she advocates for sideways views in addition to up and down views, attending to the complexity of how people in outcaste groups define themselves and interpret their positions. As seductive as comparisons of worldwide caste orders can be, she advises that they are to be measured against one another with a delicate hand.

But caste groupings are persistent. They endure in the wake of policies and punishments to undermine their power. That point cannot be argued. Caste is also endlessly negotiated and wrestled with by those sorted into its categories, despite the enthusiasm and violence of those who tend to benefit most from the ordering. Status quo caste apologists do not rest unresisted.

Soundararajan traces roots of Shramanic traditions like Jainism and Buddhism as reactions to Brahmanistic supremacy itself. She showcases "caste abolition ancestors" of the subcontinent—notably, Dalit icon and revolutionary B.R. Ambedkar, intellectual contemporary of Du Bois and author of the provocative 1936 *Annihilation of Caste*. Dalit activism has only grown since then, proliferating across digital and social media, art, politics, and public spaces, more present and expansive than ever, catching and critiquing gender and economic and caste oppressions all at once.

Even as our caste systems persist, even as they shapeshift to sustain themselves across generations, we find ways to challenge their abuses and register them as traumatic, harmful, and unjust. More than our cycle of creation and re-creation of caste orders, more than investigations into their intricacies and the ways they converge and diverge, this eternal urge to frustrate caste oppression is what fascinates me. Not only to improve the lot of self and kin, not merely to win top spot, but to de-create caste hierarchy entirely.

That, I believe, presents us with a basic mystery of our humanity.

To what degree do we dream of bursting out? Not only from our personal caste positions but from the bounds of caste hierarchies, period? To what degree might we choose to traverse social lines and borders, to cross rock and water in search of freedom from them, personally and collectively? Might this desire, even the buds of it, have sprouted in the hearts of the indentured?

I first learned about Hugh Tinker's *A New System of Slavery: The Export of Indian Labour Overseas, 1830–1920* when I was an impressionable nineteen-year-old. He was a British historian and professor of Commonwealth studies, and the book title alone seemed to clarify the past for me, this straight-as-an-arrow view of transatlantic enslavement reformatted into transatlantic indentureship after abolition.

I latched onto it because chattel slavery was the only form of labour exploitation I'd been taught about. It was the only form of labour exploitation that had been frankly labelled exploitative. No one said much about unfair compensation or criminalized labour or the sneaky terms of all sorts of compelled, coerced, and unchosen forms of work. No one spoke of the countless ways people get pushed to the precipice of life and death through their labour and left there. There had been few other formative stories to help me conceptualize such binds. The endless chores of the orphans of *Annie* and *Oliver Twist* were the product of cruel, unfeeling adults, not a matter of institutions profiting from child labour. The Oompa-Loompas of *Charlie and the Chocolate Factory* were already rewritten by Roald Dahl, edited from "African pygmies" to small white hippies pleased to be smuggled to England to work for Wonka. I knew of no other prisms through which to view the legacy I'd been born into. Indentureship seemed to lock into enslavement with a satisfying and familiar click.

Comparisons between transatlantic enslavement and transatlantic indenture do have their value. They highlight the race-based mercenary thrust of both systems. They illustrate how modern race hierarchy is crafted to make stolen land and stolen labour seem inevitable. But comparisons of slavery and indentureship can overemphasize the Atlantic situation headed by the British and discount other unfree labour traditions that fed into the mechanics of racialized indentureship and coercive labour arrangements. They can miss the roots of all kinds of bonded work practices that tunnel deep across the globe, stretching centuries before the launch of the transatlantic slave trade, before the explosion of European colonization itself. They do little to compare and contrast with other influential coercive labour approaches, such as the *engagé* style of indentureship utilized in France and its overseas territories, including Louisiana, Nosy Be, and Réunion.

Like my low-caste-only fable, the indenture-as-new-system-of-slavery paradigm had been my narrative for years until I started to pay attention to those who questioned it. Their writing opened a trapdoor in my Tinkerian floor.

Coming to terms with the distortions of the indenture-as-new-slavery paradigm has been more than an intellectual exercise. It has meant that I'm confronted by the agency of the indentured, bonded, constricted, and coerced, something I find energizing and troubling at the same time.

The energy of it is its humanizing power. Humanhood, to me, is a desire to choose, even where meaningful choices are blocked. Conceptualizing desire to choose in the inner lives of dehumanized people is an exercise of empathy. And empathy is an exercise of love. Remembering the desire to choose helps me love and relate to my indentured ancestors more than ever.

But trouble floats in choice. To the degree that my ancestors chose their fates, did they choose any of it for my benefit? In that case, did they choose wisely?

A legacy of chosen suffering is a sobering responsibility. I'm shaken by the thought. I'm not sure I live in a way that makes the choice worth it.

This is where history once again proves itself a lens that swivels to those of us doing the remembering. If the idea that indentured ancestors at least in part may have dreamed of de-creating caste hierarchies seems too ambitious or fanciful, we have to ask ourselves why. Why do we allow such narrow space for audacious desires?

Do racist assumptions prevent us from conceiving utopian visions in the heart of the racialized migrant? Or are we afraid of the implications of our foreparents' human choices for us, right now?

For both questions, I think I have to answer in the affirmative.

Every so often, my cousins and I muse about what our parents had to do to leave Guyana and go to white-majority countries like the United States, Canada, and the United Kingdom. We've found it difficult to parse. Investigating and filing applications before the internet was a glimmer in anyone's eye, before racialized immigration was widely seen as a virtue, a plausible answer to national taxation, birthrate, talent, and revenue conundrums? Scraping and accounting assets, purging yourself of the ones you couldn't bring with you? Telling everyone you knew, everyone you grew up and worked and worshipped with that they might not see you again? Telling your children they'd leave their schools and friends forever? Explaining your plans to aging parents and siblings with no intention to follow? Packing up and shipping belongings, lying in sleepless wait for a flight through tropical breeze into frosted air?

Our parents were in a better situation than many. They had Commonwealth education and English fluency. But the building blocks of their departures still pile up and trap us. We doubt our competence to find our own ways out, our own steadfastness in uprooting our lives the way they did.

I act like I'm strong, I always end up telling myself in these mental exercises. *I act like I can figure out how to do the things other people do. But I'm not strong. I couldn't have figured this out. I wouldn't have left.*

I feel bewildered by every immigrant I meet who makes the choice to leave their homes, no matter the circumstance, no matter the pushes, pressures, and promises of why and how they made it here.

They come for a better life for themselves and for their families. The politician's line about the tough choices of the immigrant—especially the racialized immigrant—centres on personal drive. Perhaps it's a shortcut to sympathy in staunchly individualistic, white-majority receiving countries, always at risk of collapsing in on themselves for fear of aliens in the ranks. Perhaps it most effectively dampens protectionist tendencies. *Wouldn't you want better for yourself and your children, too?*

But I'm troubled by how this *better life* story can stitch in the desires of the racialized immigrant, stuffing them inside of the self. What is this *better life* they seek, exactly? Does it have to be so entirely insular, nuclear, personal, and bottled? Is there any room for a *better life* to contain multitudes?

To desire a better lot for yourself and your children is uniquely human. So is the drive to desire a better lot for somebody unrelated to you. Could the immigrant's choice of a *better life* also be a choice for *better lives*? For all its merits, the singular *better life* mantra might steal a slice of humanity from the immigrant because it sets them afloat to strive for themselves and their own, robbing them of their peers. Of their love and affinity for fellow human beings. It might deserve our resistance.

TheDream.US, the United States' largest educational program to support undocumented immigrant young people, leaves acres of green field open for the pursuit of *better lives*, beginning with the name of the organization itself. This understanding of the undocumented child as a dreamer is an innovation. A cursory scan of the organization's website shows just how many of these scholars are driven to become health professionals, educators, social workers, and more. So many of them dream of the opportunity to give.

Are these dreamers extraordinary? Most would probably not ask to be called such a thing. They might prefer being seen as normal students with normal hopes who simply need the chances status-holding young people have. They didn't have much of a choice in their statusless state. Still, I can't help but call them extraordinary, if only to myself. At the very least, I do need to be thankful for them, the way I appreciate anyone so motivated to choose *better lives* at the same time as they strive for a *better life*.

In *Everybody: A Book About Freedom*, Olivia Laing surveys the great minds of modern freedom movements. They are unlikely companions upon first glance: eccentric orgone accumulator and cloudbuster inventor Wilhelm Reich, musician and civil rights activist Nina Simone, modern artist Ana Mendieta, second-wave feminist Andrea Dworkin. The worlds they dreamed of and grieved over, societies with no fear, never materialized. But they collectively hoist Laing toward a conclusion. "If I'm certain about anything at all," she says, "it's that freedom is a shared endeavour, a collaboration built by many hands over many centuries of time, a labour which every single living person can choose to hinder or advance."

She points to Angela Carter's critique of the Marquis de Sade's misogyny: "My freedom makes you more unfree if it does not acknowledge your freedom also." Laing suggests the opposite must be true as well: freedom that acknowledges the freedom of other people makes everybody more free. Surely freedom that not only acknowledges but chooses to chase after the freedom of other people is even better.

Perhaps this is the wildest, brightest, most divine brand of freedom: the act of choosing to build a world where everyone can live without fear. Perhaps this is the noblest human dream.

The Jonestown Memorial in Oakland, California, is a pink granite slab inlaid by four grey tablets. It is carved with the names of every Peoples Temple member who died in Guyana, including, not uncontroversially, Jim Jones himself. It lies open to the sky in Evergreen Cemetery, its burial grounds spiked by palm trees and tombstones. Four hundred unclaimed bodies of the over nine hundred who died in Jonestown are buried here.

In 2018, a gathering was held at the memorial site to mark forty years since the massacre. Watching videos of the event, I expected the traffic noise and camera clicks, the rustling winds and cheeping birds. What I didn't expect was the peppering of friendly conversation, greetings, and laughter amongst the survivors and family of survivors. I didn't expect the sounds of happiness.

Jim Jones Jr., one of Jones's surviving sons, is the master of ceremonies. "Can we all just look to our side and just say welcome?" he says. "I miss you, it's nice to see you, thank you for being here?"

Attendees chuckle and chatter off camera, on cue.

"The children, the senior citizens, the youth, the idealistic intellectuals," survivor Jordan Vilchez says during her time at the microphone. "I'll always cherish the incredible feeling of unity that I had, that I remember feeling. There really was nothing like that. And I have not really felt that since that time."

She ends her speech with a heavy breath, with an exhortation for enduring love amongst the survivors in honour of those who died. They would, she says, "want us to be aware of the tremendous—and I really mean tremendous—value of our connection with one another. And that that connection between us remains loving, sustaining, and, above all, enduring."

"We were a mixed and a mixed-up bag," Stephan Jones, another surviving son of Jones, says during his address. "Compassionate, mean, passionate, depressed, courageous, cowardly, faithful, paranoid, vivacious, dull, and so many of us were heartbroken. And they taught me so much about the soul and sacrifice."

More than all the books and shows and articles about Jonestown, it's these glimpses into community bliss that shake me most. People of Jonestown who are still with us, so saddled by dreadful memories of what happened, dearly and tenderly love each other.

Being in a cult is never about being in a cult. "Human beings are really bad at loneliness," says Amanda Montell in *Cultish: The Language of Fanaticism*. "Our behavior is driven by a desire for belonging and purpose. We're 'cultish' by nature." That's why the linguistic manipulations of high-control leaders and groups work so well, the love-bombing and buzzwords and thought-terminating clichés. These concepts intellectually applied to closed communities seem nefarious, but in practice, in the weary and worn ear, cult talk doubles as healing words. It nourishes, sprouting the seed of hope. It convinces people that they have found other people to entrust themselves to, to belong with, to know and be known deeply and fully by. Cult talk is a portal through which everyone in the community can share the experience of euphoria at the same time. Cult talk is our collective and connective idealism put to words.

That's what I think we all want in life: something good, together. That's the desperate heart of utopia we can't shake, even if utopia has a way of disappointing us.

The tension between dream and disenchantment is something we have to contend with soberly, given the trembling mass of spoiled utopias we've constructed one after the other. The whole thing tilts, looms over.

"Nearly all of us would rather have helped than done harm," Stephan Jones says of Peoples Temple. "To have made this world a much better place. And yet so many of us helped Dad and his circle do great harm, either with a direct hand or by feeding the temple's unhealthy appetite in some other way or by looking the other way when someone else did these things."

Not every utopia is created equal. Creepy sects and isolationist communes aren't the only examples to be wary of, either.

A few years ago, hiking with friends amongst the mossed trees of Oregon, while spellbound by rocks splattered with green fluorescence along the trails, I was interrupted by the thought of just how successful unworthy utopia can be. The state of Oregon was designed as a white-only haven, at one point boasting the highest per-capita Ku Klux Klan membership in America. It was not the only region in the United States built on a vision of white paradise in its early statehood, but it did distinctly document it. Today, Oregon's population is 86 per cent white, and Portland is considered the whitest big city in America. These outcomes, two of many that stretch beyond skewed demographics, are in part consequences of a corrupt and rather successfully realized dream.

But utopia has captured us many times and it will do so again. Utopic reverie is the natural future state of any attempt to account for the past and present. *Long live. God save. Glory to. Power to. Death to. Take back. Up with. Down with. No more. Say yes. Great again.* There's a kernel of utopian longing vibrating in every one of our slogans, those coined by activists and political factions, congregations and corporations and terrorists alike, as radioactive and carcinogenic as they may be.

And there's little to be gained in warning anyone away from utopia itself. Maybe we lose too much in losing our dreams. Perhaps we need them, at our core, to motivate living in the first place. We want something good, together. Maybe that's the deep-down base we share, even if we don't have language to vocalize it. From onerous migrations to misfit communities to unexpected alliances, utopic dreams inspire human choices that don't necessarily get registered or recorded. They are the tug over the cliff, beyond the *fim do mundo*, that pulls us all.

"Freedom doesn't mean being unburdened by the past," Olivia Laing says. "It means continuing into the future, *dreaming* all the time."

If we are to do well in our dreaming, if we're wise to dream in the thick of our disillusion with wide-open eyes, then we must reconsider human motivations. We must afford new space for the migrant, the undocumented child, the idealistic community-builder, and, yes, the indentured labourer to dream of and choose utopia themselves, too. To want a *better life* and *better lives*, all at once. We have to allow fresh opportunities for the bloom of many desires in the inner lives of people too easily and regularly dismissed as desireless. Perhaps it will help us move forward in worthier ways, dreaming of and choosing to build more worthwhile utopias.

Something good, together. Perhaps it starts with acknowledging the multifaceted dreams of others.

WHITE FEMINIST WHISPERER

"If the rider shows a lack of confidence in the horse and acts as if she were suspicious of him, the horse will soon know it, and will do exactly what the rider fears that he will. A horse has a mind which very readily receives impressions from the rider's mind."
— *Riding and Driving for Women*, Belle Beach (1912)

When I was about a decade into my career at a feminist non-profit organization, representatives from a trio of sister charities, the one I worked for and two others, met to discuss a new partnership project on systemic racism and its impacts on racialized women and communities. The representatives from the two other organizations were white. The representatives from my organization were racialized.

We sat at a table together and talked through what the project could look like. Tea and snacks were set out between us. Every so often, someone would stand at the flip chart, jotting our ideas down with a marker. By the end of the meeting, it seemed as if our partnership was going to happen. Everyone in the room agreed our efforts were timely. Of *critical importance.*

A day after the meeting, the representatives of the other two organizations sent a joint email to my organization expressing their intention to pull out. They called our expertise and connectedness to other organizations into question. They wondered if the issues we told them racialized women expressed concerns to us about—police brutality, immigration troubles, young men killed by gun violence, over-targeting by child protection authorities, and more—were the most *critically important* ones a partnership like ours should tackle.

In fine feminist form, my colleague and I decided to respond by formal letter.

Your organizational mission statements assert that you prioritize the needs of marginalized women including those who experience racism, heterosexism, transphobia, ableism, et cetera, we wrote. *But you withdrew your support and endorsement when we asked you to work with us to actually do something about those needs.*

You are white women. We are women of colour. We wonder why you decided to treat us this way.

One of the women we had sent the letter to swiftly emailed back. She asked me and my colleague to meet with her at her office.

When my colleague and I arrived at her building, our conversation faded away. The receptionist who greeted us led us into the boardroom. My colleague walked straight-backed and poised. I was well-acquainted with her confidence and competence.

I tried to match her stride. My legs were unsteady, muscles quivering with nerves.

A young South Asian employee entered the boardroom and offered us coffee and tea. She sat at the table with us, her notebook open, our letter pressed flat in front of her.

"This is a big misunderstanding," she said. "My colleague wasn't being racist to you. She didn't mean it that way at all." She began talking through the points of our letter, explaining what the colleague on the project had really meant to say and do.

I was confused. This young woman hadn't attended the meeting in question. She hadn't sent us that offending email afterward, and she wasn't in charge of partnership decisions at the organization. Why was she explaining what the white woman had done or not done to us?

"Excuse me," my co-worker interrupted, hovering a pen over the empty page of her notepad. "Where's your colleague now? Is she on her way here? Why isn't she speaking for herself?"

"A problem came up. She had to leave. She asked me to take care of this with the two of you."

The young woman kept talking about the letter on behalf of her white colleague. *She asked me to take care of this.* All three of us, all younger women of South Asian descent, dithered and debated what an older white woman in a position of leadership had intended by her words and actions. It was a fruitless exercise.

At some point, sound faded into a hiss. I can't remember where the conversation went. I don't know in what state my colleague and I escaped that building.

I do remember wondering how we had gotten ourselves into such a laughable situation. How that young brown woman, pleasant as she was, had gotten into her position, too. Racialized apologist for an absent white woman's misdeeds.

Mikki Kendall's *Hood Feminism: Notes from the Women That a Movement Forgot* hadn't been published yet, but I wish I'd had her clarity of vision. "Erasure is not equality," she writes, "least of all in a movement that draws much of its strength from the claim that it represents over half of the world's population."

I remember a time when intersectionality wasn't evoked in mainstream non-profit or activist mandates, but there's been a whole lot of intersectionality talk over the last two decades. It has spread beyond its Black feminist legal roots into all kinds of charity, philanthropic, and political discourses, absorbed into government, academic, civil service, union, and corporate circles, too.

"Intersectionality isn't a convenient buzzword that can be co-opted into erasing Professor Kimberlé Williams Crenshaw, who coined the term to describe the way race and gender impact Black women in the justice system," Kendall says. But it certainly gets treated that way when organizations vacuously aspire to help women achieve their potential without minding the progress and well-being of their families and communities or the broader forces that have blocked their potential. Intersectionality is taken too lightly when the feminism of minoritized women remains underfunded, under-noticed, and dismissible.

In *Against White Feminism: Notes on Disruption*, Rafia Zakaria describes Western white feminism as a colour-blind movement that couples whiteness with women's liberation. She says the legacy of white supremacy has meant that "the white gaze has never been disaggregated from feminism itself." It means that "most of the times when women speak 'feminism,' they unintentionally take on the cadence and color of whiteness." She links the tendency to suffragettes of the early twentieth century who, from the start, expected racialized women to align with their fights and abandon their own—especially if they called on white women to account for their abuses. Racialized women were suited only for white pity, validation, and benevolence, blighted by their own inferior cultures and religions and the barbarism of their men.

In this framework, the colonialism and capitalism that brutalize women and communities the world over at best remain unquestioned. At worst, they're trumpeted as progress. White feminism is handmaiden to white supremacy. And the white feminist whisperer is handmaiden to white feminism.

I define the white feminist whisperer as a racialized woman who minces words about the ugly facts of racism in white feminist spaces. She tenderizes it for them, makes it seem digestible—erasable—through minimal effort and investment. One-off celebrations and memorial days, quick-draw policies, short training stints, lunch and learns and panel talks, documentary screenings, poetry and performances and cultural ceremonies, personal reflections and sad feelings and kind thoughts.

She assures white-centric feminists that their suspicions are true: nothing fundamental needs to change to solve racism. No one has to be docked pay or miss a promotion or get let go. No one has to lose clout or face. She affirms that everyone is doing the very best they can with the limited resources available.

The white feminist whisperer acts as planted evidence that mixed demographics is all an organization or group really needs to aim for. That recruitment and hiring is where racism lives and dies.

We are committed to the principles of diversity and inclusion and strongly encourage applicants from underrepresented communities to apply . . .

She gets positioned as racialized spokesperson in all sorts of misleading ways. *In my community, women are treated like . . . Growing up, our families tell us to . . . According to our beliefs, we're taught that we should . . .* The white feminist whisperer has a way of universalizing these statements, freezing them in time and space, encasing them in glass as perusable and unassailable truths for anyone who looks anything like her. She may be holder of a vast array of cultural facts and scenarios inquiring white people want to know about but rarely risk asking for, lest they discover the faults of their assumptions. She makes her peers who beg to differ, who assert ideas and experiences and ways of seeing and being to the contrary, seem defensive and divisive.

She is the most grateful and gracious one. The fairest of them all. That's why she regularly seems to throw every other racialized person under the bus.

In white feminist spaces, change is less about identifying and breaking racist barriers and more about multicultural awareness. Accruing the world's panoply of food, song, costume, and dance. Eating sushi for lunch and curry for dinner and squeezing a yoga class or cupping session in between. *I don't have a racist bone in my limber body.*

A white feminist whisperer enables those working from a white feminist perspective to collect cultural artifacts in their pockets like marbles. *This is how you greet us. These are the spices we enjoy. Let me tell you about the funny ways we think. Why don't you try our practices, our art, our medicine?* Clink the colours together, win the anti-racism game.

But anti-racism has little to do with it. White feminist

whisperers help white-centric feminists feel justified remaining firmly at the centre of every conversation about rights, freedoms, opportunities, and lack thereof. You don't need to heed the insistent voices of those who are underheard. You won't endure the unsettling truth of what they tell you about your services, your approaches, your slammed doors, your foul attitude. You don't need to reduce your authority, access to resources, or decision-making allowances. You don't need to interrupt your own stream of consciousness, take a break from your posting and panels and keynoting. You don't need to make room for other experiences and perspectives, especially when they contrast or conflict with your own. You don't need to share the air.

> "Some horses are addicted to a very troublesome and vicious habit of turning round suddenly,—we do not here allude to shyness, but restiveness,—without exhibiting any previous symptom of their intention."
> — *The Young Lady's Equestrian Manual* (1838)

I tell people I'm a paid feminist. It makes me one of the lucky few. Over the past two and a half decades, I've had the privilege of building a career in organizations focused on gender equality and human rights, community service, and civic engagement, most of which explicitly label themselves feminist. It's been an education in matters pressing to the fate of humanity. It's been an opportunity to spend my days doing things I am passionate about. Things that make my brain and heart and belly tingle.

It has also opened my eyes to the banality of white supremacy infused into modern work and relationships. No corner is swept of its grime. Not even the most righteous, charitable, and feminist corners.

I've seen white-centric feminists' cluelessness about racialized women's needs and concerns. I've heard outright refusals to listen. I've witnessed tears interrupt the pursuit of accountability for such refusals. I've lived through powerful principles of anti-racism as they are misunderstood and misapplied, rendering them just about useless. I've sensed resentment at racialized women being too monied, too educated, and too vocal, for not sufficiently scrounging as the lowest and lowliest of the low. I've listened to exasperation at racialized women and families who didn't particularly need or want intervention.

I've seen white-centric feminists get irritated at women of colour for revealing racism exists, for asserting racism is a problem to contend with, for getting upset at them for discounting the impact of racism, for insisting racism is a problem they, as paid feminists, have a responsibility to address, too.

It isn't always deep. I've witnessed overblown annoyance at racialized women for having a point of view about just about anything a person can have an opinion on: books, film, music, food, leisure time, travel, cars, fashion, hair, perfume, celebrities, eye shadow, eyelashes, sports, nails, menstrual products, brassieres, pantyhose. Let alone political matters. Let alone gaps in the ways charities and businesses and organizations and activist groups operate.

I've experienced it directly. *Of course she enjoys working with you, you're just like her. A white woman like me doesn't stand a chance.* I've faced suspicion for being racialized and having racialized women managers, a relatively unusual occurrence in non-profit workplaces, even nowadays. *Why do you two go for coffee together? Why do you two always talk?*

I've been invited to serve as a racial installation at donor tours and exhibitions. *Come to the meeting; they'll want to see diverse people in the room.*

I've been encouraged to pay no mind to the unique troubles faced by Black and brown women and communities, likely because they made little mark on the quality of white people's lives. *We don't need to do anything about that issue; it's not in our mandate.*

I've asked what they would do if it were their children being harmed, their families and friends in distress.

It's mission drift, white colleagues have responded to me more times than I care to count.

Perhaps the most perplexing experience is the extraordinary reversals, the white-centric feminists locally known by racialized women to say and do racist things—at least racially insensitive, dismissive, or disingenuous things—transcending to new heights as equity and inclusion executives, advisors, coaches, consultants, trainers, enthusiasts, evangelists.

They trigger my double takes, to say the least. Sometimes, they trigger my migraines.

Whether such advancements are the result of miracle or mistake, of meaningful penitence or Machiavellian fraud, is not for me to say. I have little desire to debate it, nor do I care to spend too much time dissecting individual motives. I'm not so fussed that white women tend to get overpraised for doing equity work, especially if they're good at it, though the fact that they can get overpaid for it and claim the thought leadership of racialized women as their own is a legitimate problem to address.

I think it's more important to take umbrage at the ways white women have become the safe faces of inclusion on the whole. They're the ones corporations, academia, government, and human services are prone to turning to for equity guidance, and, more significantly, the ones they point to as proof of growing leadership diversity, policy improvement, and shrinking pay gaps. They enable workplaces to pat themselves on the back for gender-based advancements while achieving little by way of racial and other forms of equity. This tendency might very well worsen in modern backlashes against institutional diversity, equity, and inclusion initiatives. Efforts to reduce barriers for white women won't be first on the chopping block of disincentivized, mocked, and outright cancelled policies and activities.

Back patting for thin equity achievements is one of the reasons it's been white women who have tended to gain most from affirmative action policies and not Indigenous, Black, and other racialized women and communities. It's one of the reasons gender pay and leadership gaps have shrunken for white women over the past three decades but still yawn wide for racialized women.

Inclusion of white women is low-hanging fruit, the convenient unspoken end state for organizations that don't want too much change. White women's voices are the ones leaders seem most amenable to listening to when it comes to rights and fairness. The problem is that so much gets lost in such selective hearing.

In *Some of My Best Friends: Essays on Lip Service*, Tajja Isen says that white women's personal awareness of and apologies for these dynamics don't do much to rebalance power in and of itself: "White femininity is very, enviably good at this—metabolizing critique and converting it into a moral, political, or financial asset." It's a passageway for influential white women to venture through, that narrow margin between racial privilege and gender oppression, carved into the landscape just for them. Some set off on the journey ignorant of how bespoke it truly is.

A white woman I worked with closely in a feminist organization, an intelligent and good-humoured colleague, joked that she could always become a professor of white womanhood if she couldn't find other employment. "I'll write a book," she said, stroking her chin and studying the ceiling. "I'll get on the lecture and media circuit and get popular. I'll make a million dollars. When people start panning me for getting rich from racism and sexism, I'll spiral out. Not bothered by the white critics, but in a total rage about the racialized ones, you know? I'll blast out at them, tell them to get a life and be grateful for what I've done. It'll turn into a huge scandal.

"Then I'll make the news again by apologizing and writing a follow-up about white women's apologies. I'll make a million more, happy and sad because I became a martyr for anti-racism. Those mean women of colour who couldn't admit I was just trying to use my power for good. What do they want from me? I'll show them. I'll die and go to white lady heaven. Don't you think it's an amazing plan?"

I chuckled all the way. Tongue-in-cheek as she was, looking back, there's something prescient in her insights.

It's easy to home in on sins, the *caucasity* of this behaviour. It's juicy. It's irresistible. Especially when the pretenses of leaning in, barrier-busting, and ceiling-shattering get thrown into the mix. *Oh, they act as if they're on the cutting edge of freedom and revolution. They won't shut up about it.*

The more cognitive dissonance is stirred into the glass, sweet and syrupy as it is, the more cubes of hypocrisy are shaken into the cup, the more satisfyingly the cocktail of falsehood lands on the tongue. Resist as I might, my palate is unrefined. I crave and savour every sip.

Critiques of mainstream Western feminism are necessary and warranted. "White feminism in itself isn't particularly threatening," writes Reni Eddo-Lodge in *Why I'm No Longer Talking to White People About Race*. "It is a problem, because we consider humanity through the prism of whiteness." Feminism's susceptibility to the distortions of white supremacy, like so many burgeoning frameworks for social change, is inevitable. Eddo-Lodge says that the worthy potential of feminism as a movement that, at its best, seeks to liberate every marginalized person and community set up to fail is exactly why its inclusivity must be extended and defended.

The reality is that we've never gone as far with Western feminism as we like to think we have. Serene Khader states it well in *Faux Feminism: Why We Fall for White Feminism and How We Can Stop*. "The world where white feminism and other feminisms for the few don't really count as feminism," she says, "is a world we have yet to create."

Perhaps nothing human-made, even feminist action, can back up its claims of pure intention and pristine execution. Plus, the striving for extension and defence of the best of feminism, as irritating and exhausting as it can get, can sometimes be a whole heap of fun. Some of my fondest memories include breaking bread over it with other racialized feminists. There are many pleasures in shared exasperation.

And not all critiques are trustworthy or productive. Not these days. Bad actors have weaponized them as an indictment of all feminist and human rights action. Of the inherent duplicity of women and equity-seeking people. In the contemporary rise of authoritarianism, fascism, power mongering, and sneaky shape-shifts of old discriminations and supremacies, I get nervous.

Seyward Darby addresses a curdled "choice feminism" in *Sisters in Hate: American Women and White Extremism*, one that stands up for privilege "under the guise of individual liberty." Choice feminists, not uncommonly white nationalist women influencers and those adjacent and sympathetic to them, gnarl the precepts of feminism and rob it of its capacity to unmask patriarchy, systemic bias, and predatory capitalism. They wield their remake to justify whatever opinions they want to uphold. Claiming real freedom, they "demonize women's liberation as overly sensitive, aggressive, and hysterical" and accuse feminists of being "spoiled brats and selfish hypocrites, jockeying for cultural sympathy while looking down their noses at women whose lifestyles and politics they disagree with."

In our COVID-19 pandemic hangover, choice feminism pulses across digital media, camouflaging and bolstering misogyny. It can get nasty. It can get downright *manospheric*. Swapping one falsity for another nets no gain, and I'm not interested in careless criticisms that end up propagating it. "It's hard to be a woman, and at times it can be even harder to be a feminist woman," Ijeoma Oluo says in *Mediocre: The Dangerous Legacy of White Male America*. "And in the midst of it all, we still have to deal with dudes."

Beyond the misbehaviours of white feminism, I want to attend to racialized feminists stuck in white feminist circumstances. I wonder how they deal with it. I wonder how they make it through.

I can speak about what has happened to me in acute moments of racism in feminist places, that sensation of a kick to the stomach, my fantasies of getting sucked into the fold of a chair. Shakes, sweats, stutters. My natural weakness in the wake of conflict, my deep aversion to it, escalates to blaring red alert. The guilt that floods in is multi-pronged, the result of being thrown off guard, of not being nearly sharp or witty enough for an effective retort. There's longing in the stew, too: to be feckless, fearless, forthcoming. The things I fancy myself and every day prove I'm not.

To metamorphose into a hardier feminist. This is what I think I need in these moments that feel like stinging slaps. To vaporize the agitations of everyday white supremacy. This is what I can't help but wish for.

Because there have been so many unguarded moments.

Those people are so ugly, don't you think?

What are they protesting about this time? How can you stand their complaining?

Did you see what happened on the news? How barbaric they are.

My most deleterious tendencies can overtake me. The impulse to smooth over everything. To vanquish discomfort from the room, primarily for my own benefit. The inclination to please everyone and have everyone pleased by me, even when such a thing would be impossible if I responded with any level of integrity. The yearning for simple affection by any means necessary, any obscuration or suppression necessary.

Their aesthetics are just different from what we're used to.

We all have a right to protest about the things that concern us.

That was such a scary incident, oh my goodness. I did see it on the news.

Saving and pleasing. A sucker for flimsy camaraderie and hollow love. How could I not have become a white feminist whisperer?

"The fact is, horses are often very sensitive;
and while this one may never have been cruelly treated,
yet he has been misunderstood, and his feelings
hurt a great many times a day."
– *Horsemanship for Women,* Theodore H. Mead (1887)

My theory is that some of us feel more pressure to practise the art and craft of white feminist whispering. For feminists who are Black and Indigenous, their racial transgressions may often be too great as a matter of definition. Their positioning in racial hierarchy—on top of strong community traditions of confronting legacies of stolen land and labour—may more often work to disqualify them from white feminist whispering. They face the consequences, their outsider status and exclusion from white feminist circles, accordingly.

Model minority women, on the other hand, may more readily and commonly serve as candidates, for better and for worse. I believe the land of model minorities is where white feminism most readily seeks its endorsement and affirmation. It's a sunny spot to try to catch a tan. *The other ones are always angry and agitating, but thank goodness, these ones say we're doing okay on racism. We must be doing okay on racism.*

One-on-one, white feminist whisperers get pushed into and rewarded for keeping white-centric feminists in a cushy place. They become the racialized women anybody can handle in a gathering. They watch their own expressions; they monitor their own tones. They offer shoulders for tears and arms for embraces. They provide words of encouragement to carry on as-is. They just might become beloved oracles, gurus, prophets, psychics, shamans, and coaches for white-centric feminists. But their insight always has its limits. It doesn't rouse anybody to step outside the cocoon of the enlightened self.

The labour of the model minority to keep racial order intact is indeed the labour white feminist whisperers perform in white feminist spaces. They serve as racialized respites from the toughest challenges to white supremacy: liberation, not just charity. Land back, not just land acknowledgement. Reparation and reckoning, not just equal opportunities. Sustainability and protection, not just greenwashing and gig work. White feminist whisperers advocate for diversity of thought more than justice in communication. Representation more than barrier dismantling. Empowerment more than power sharing. Psychological safety more than perspective transformation. They don't often allude to anti-Black racism or the forces of neocolonialism, neoliberalism, and neoimperialism.

Those issues are serrated and implicating, floating outside appropriate scope. That's why white-centric feminists seek out the opinions and advice of white feminist whisperers instead of the opinions and advice of racialized feminists who don't put them on a pedestal, who are clearly skeptical of their motivations and methods.

White feminists and white feminist whisperers request no ongoing accountability or transparency. No meaningful interrogation of just how ineffective white feminist efforts have been in improving conditions or shifting fundamental power relations to benefit marginalized women, families, and communities. No meaningful critique of incarceration, law, policing, borders, social work, education, child protection, real estate, banking, research, medicine, disability services—all the institutions and their associated policies routinely harming Black, Indigenous, and racialized communities. International development bodies, philanthropic orders, human services, and non-governmental organizations don't have to consider the ways they uphold white dominance, either. Everybody is so well-intentioned. Real problems lie somewhere else, out in the foggy distance.

That's because, for white feminist whisperers as much as white-centric feminists, racism is a misunderstanding. A failure of civility and respectability. A gap in exposure to diversity, a lack of diverse friends. It's growing up in a mostly white neighbourhood, going to mostly white schools, dating mostly white people. It's limited exposure to the rapture of humanity's music and restaurants. It's mostly unintentional bias, mostly feeling cagey and fragile, mostly amygdala hijack. It's individual ignorance and fear, pitiable but not fatal. It's not orchestrated power imbalance, tested and refined and maintained over centuries. It is not a pillar of the way we've made our world work. It's not something we have a motive or responsibility to change.

Racism hasn't benefited any women anywhere. So the white-centric feminist and her partnering white feminist whisperer would have you believe. So white feminism as a global phenomenon, a finger in the invisible hand of mainstream white supremacy, would have you believe, no matter who upholds it.

"If you are a coward, your horse will soon find it out, and will laugh at you; for horses can and do laugh when they what is usually termed 'gammon' their riders."
– *Ladies on Horseback: Learning, Park-Riding, and Hunting, with Hints upon Costume, and Numerous Anecdotes,*
Mrs. Power O'Donoghue (1881)

I saw a woman hurrying down the front steps of the feminist organization I worked for. The hem of her dress billowed around her calves and an oversized handbag hung from her shoulder, tucked under an arm. Her hair was swirled into a messy bun. Sun speckled her blonde flyaways.

When her feet hit the sidewalk, she whipped about in my direction. I knew her—she was a partner who had been working with us on a violence prevention project. Her jaw was sharp; her eyes flashed. Red blotches bloomed over her neck.

My legs slowed.

My manager appeared in the doorway, propping the door open with her arm. She wore a suit jacket over the flare of a flowered skirt. Her salt-and-pepper dreadlocks were spiralled at the top of her head. She looked at the woman through thick-rimmed glasses. Her face, calm.

The woman glared up at my manager. "I am not a *race-ist!*" she screamed.

She marched along the sidewalk and pushed past me, breathing hard. I watched her stomp away.

My heart pumped in my chest. I scampered up the stairs. "What's going on?"

My manager's brow was knotted. "She's mad at me." Still holding the door, she stepped aside to clear a path.

She sighed. "Let's talk."

The office was located in a converted home constructed around the 1880s. The basement pipes were insulated by horsehair. Someone had told me it used to be a boarding house for wayward girls to practise domestic work. The room where I sat with my manager had once been the house's parlour, complete with fireplace.

My manager explained that she and the partner had met to discuss the project's progress. At some point, the partner told my manager she had been "too aggressive."

My manager, a woman many people admired for her forthrightness and fairness, told the partner that she didn't appreciate the term. It was a loaded and coded way to describe Black women's behaviour, she explained. She said it made it difficult for her to take the feedback to heart.

The temperature of the conversation between them rose. It began to steam. After a few minutes of back and forth, it boiled over. The partner grabbed her things and thumped out of the office.

"How could it have gone so bad so fast?" I asked.

"It can be like that. All gut reaction and offence. No time to process."

I had worked with that partner before. With me, her voice was paced and soothing, even sweet. She often talked about the need to make sure the project was inclusive. Equity had been her theme.

My manager shook her head. "It's just how it sometimes goes when you're a Black woman trying to challenge a white woman."

⁂

> "However frightened a lady may herself feel, she should never reveal her secret to her horse by speaking to him in a terrified tone of voice, or by otherwise displaying fear; and above all things, she should never lose her temper and hit him, no matter how obstinate he may be, as doing so will only make him shy on the next occasion, with a display of temper thrown in, and he will then be more difficult than ever to manage. The best way to act with a horse which shies from desire to 'play up,' is to take as little notice as possible of his antics, give him more work, and less corn."
>
> – *The Horsewoman: A Practical Guide to Side-Saddle Riding* (1903)

⁂

In white-dominant spaces, it's possible that most racialized women have carried some aspect of the white feminist whisperer inside of them. I'm sure our years of experience with racism attune us to the very particular set of skills the white feminist whisperer applies: unassuming body language and pacifying words, tilted head and tender smile. The ability to contain disaccord and choke her real voice down.

Over the years, with diligent training, I've managed to dissipate the white feminist whisperer's powers inside of me. And I'm realistic these days: racism in feminist spaces hasn't disappeared and won't remedy itself. Feminist sensibilities have been spun on the wheel over and over, moulded to fit just about any agenda and project, even exclusionary and discriminatory ones. Sculpting a mainstream, sustainable anti-racist feminism is going to take a lot of time and a lot more effort than we've put in so far. At least I've decoded the hacks to dismantle my most unhelpful whispering inclinations.

Still, there are times the white feminist whisperer coalesces again, filling out my arms and legs and claiming my faculties. The white feminist whisperer will not die.

Then again, I can't fairly suggest she's a possessing entity alone. Whether or not I like her, she is a part of me and probably always will be, an unpredictable quotient in the equation of normalized racism. She is the good *coolie* girl in me, the good child of good model immigrants doing our good duties.

She certainly materialized when that very white woman who screamed at my manager called to explain why she had been so furious that day. Why she had not only stormed out of the office but had gone on to email other people at the organization to disparage my boss.

I am not a race-ist! stomped its tiny feet across my brain as she spoke, her voice tranquil in my ear once again.

"You don't understand how hard it is to work with her," she told me. "That's why I reacted the way I did."

I had worked with my manager for a long time by then. I knew the excellent colleague and mentor she was to me. "But I don't get why you had to yell like that," I answered.

"It's been a long time coming."

"There's got to be a better way to go about this. There's got to be a way to talk it through with her and come to a resolution."

She huffed on the other end of the receiver. "You're young. Someday you'll see what I mean. You'll see her true colours."

I knew exactly what I wanted to ask next. *Why couldn't you listen to her when she told you that you said something hurtful? Why couldn't you handle her telling you that you used stereotyping language? Do you have a hard time with criticism from the mouth of a Black woman? Does it make you inordinately angry to be told by a Black woman that you might have lots of things to learn and lots of ways to grow? That you might not be as fair-minded a feminist as you think? That you're not infallible? That none of us are infallible?*

"That may be so," I said, instead, "and I know there's stuff between you two I don't know about. But what you're doing isn't the best answer."

I am not a race-ist!

I still think about what happened. I still replay the things I could have said on the phone to her that day.

I thought I was being deft, playing the tiptoeing intermediary. If it had happened now, I tell myself, I would've been more frank. I would have taken the risk to vocalize exactly what I wanted to say and didn't. I would not have minced words and I would not have shrunken back. I would have accepted the woman's likely irritation at my questioning. I would have coped with the discomfort in the confrontation and lived to talk about it.

This is what you do when you're involved in a movement you care about, I tell myself. This is what you do with people you have to believe can be challenged and live up to that challenge, even as they're resisting and arguing with you along the way. This is the way you persist as a racialized feminist who's been at it all this time, wading through the waters of white feminism. This is how you contribute to the efforts of all those racialized feminists who inspire you so much, the ones trying so hard to break the counterfeit bonds that bind whiteness to gender liberation. This is how you demonstrate you believe in something better. This is how you demonstrate your solidarity.

I am not a race-ist! she might have shouted at me.

I would have told her she was behaving like one.

I'd seen others do it. Why couldn't I?

The truth is that I'm still not entirely certain what I would say to that woman now. I can't trust that my temperamental white feminist whisperer wouldn't skip out from behind the corner and prance me off course.

"Horses of a bad disposition or temper, are exceedingly subtle,
and watch their opportunity; they first, as it were, feel for
their rider's firmness of seat, and her resolution, and are sure
to defend themselves upon that point, on which they expect
she will attack them; now, the object of the lady in this

contest must be, to frustrate the horse's intentions, and protect herself from injury in the struggle."
– *The Lady and Her Horse*, T.A. Jenkins (1857)

In *The Melancholy of Race: Psychoanalysis, Assimilation, and Hidden Grief*, Anne Anlin Cheng uncovers melancholy in the white American identity itself. "The racial other is in fact quite 'assimilated' into—or, more accurately, most uneasily digested by—American nationality." Whiteness incorporates the othered into itself and rejects it at the same time, all the while asserting cherished and contradicting values such as freedom and liberty.

Freudian psychoanalysis defines melancholy as a state of endless grief over a lost object. Unlike typical grief that can be remedied, the melancholic person is left consuming their lost object, carrying in them the ghost of it but denying the loss in a cannibalistic cycle.

"Like melancholia," Cheng says, "racism is hardly ever a clear rejection of the other." Racist institutions "do not want to fully expel the racial other; instead, they wish to maintain that other within existing structures." America needs the people it has othered, those it has both lost and feared, to keep its melancholy going. It buries the Black, Indigenous, indentured, and racialized, only to dig them up and resuscitate them as "serviceable ghosts."

If American whiteness is marked by racial melancholia, so must most Western societies be affected by it to some degree, given their own formative liberal ideals, their long-standing hypocrisies of enslavement, thievery, slaughter, and abuse.

So must white feminism swallow the racialized woman and internalize her shadow, denying and excluding her while crowning high-minded principles of gender liberation: intersectionality, inclusion, equity, justice, choice. White feminism, too, must be deeply melancholic, welded to permanent loss and loss-refusal. Dining on the ghost of the other only to gain not one ounce of sustenance.

White feminist whispering only exists because of the melancholia of whiteness. It would serve no purpose otherwise. Without racial melancholia, white feminist whisperers would not need to butler for white-centric feminists, bussing for them as they gorge. You wouldn't spectate this white feminist circus of ghosts ventriloquizing ghosts.

Fleeing the valley of white feminist whispering has been, for me, a journey of stops and starts, not an instant teleportation. But I realized my feet were somehow finding their way that day I stood at the centre of a conference room with about thirty feminists, nearly all white, seated in a circle around me. I presented on digital games as a tool for violence prevention. Why couldn't games help players question ideas about gender and love and control that put so many women at risk of abuse in relationships with men? I asked. Why couldn't people play through difficult emotions and expectations to pattern respectful ways of thinking and acting, even in the charged atmosphere of romance? My eyes skimmed over the narrowed eyes and nodding heads. This topic, it seemed, was of *critical importance*.

Heads stilled and eyes widened when I got to the matter of a video game that was recently released and making news. The game included rewards for players who harmed digital women, and racialized characters were portrayed in stereotyping ways—those notorious soundbites were true. But the developers had constructed their digital world with impressive accuracy and detailed views of city streets and buildings. The best chance for players to eat was found in fast food restaurants and corner stores. The best option for financial services was located in payday loan and pawn shops. The best opportunity for survival was seated in predatory behaviour, the stark choices of hurt or get hurt. I told my audience about racialized educators using the game as a tool to open conversations with racialized young people, helping them recognize economic imbalances embedded in the urban centres where they lived.

"Do you see why this game is so powerful?" I said. "It reflects the realities so many racialized people are living. Imagine if we learned from how educators are using it? Imagine if we understood what the game gets right to make a better game where players can question assumptions and the abuse we confuse with love? Where players get a chance to practise challenging these things?"

One woman's hand rose. She didn't wait for me to nod at her before speaking. "I'm sorry, I would never let my child or any child play that. How could anyone stand behind a video game that says violating women is fun?"

"But here's the thing," I answered. "It's one of the only games that shows how systemic racism is baked into cities. That's why these educators find it useful. I'm not saying the violent play or stereotypes are good; I'm saying we need to learn from it. It's popular for a reason. We can't ignore the opportunity in gaming anymore. Imagine what would happen if we worked with, say, racialized gamers to challenge the high rates of abuse racialized girls have to deal with?"

Cracks broke open; protestations flooded the room. It was, it appeared, *critically important* for everyone to agree that the game in question was irredeemable from a feminist perspective. *Critically important* to disregard racialized educators daring to use it to do something good in their communities. Perhaps they had been misguided in their approach. Perhaps they didn't understand the muck they were frolicking in, the slope they were sliding down. Perhaps, deep down, they didn't care enough about woman abuse.

I refused to concede to the sentiments, my heart beating in my throat, the perspiration pooling at the small of my back. I remember contemplating how easy it would have been to get out of the situation. To iron out the creases of the surly expressions around me. *You're right*, I could have said. *We need to denounce this kind of media, and doing anything with it or learning anything from it means we must be sanctioning it and . . .*

I shook my head again and again, repeating my point, insisting on a complicated, uncomfortable answer. I was battered by waves of sickness and giddiness, upset and thrill, all at once. I realized how conflicted I felt, how badly I wanted to cower and how badly I wanted to assert myself. I realized I had somehow learned how to jostle with the white feminist whisperer inside of me, that I was somehow prevailing over her, even as all those women frowned around me.

I remember sitting down at the end of the presentation, joining the circle. The whole thing had lasted no longer than fifteen minutes, but my body felt weak, as if I had been on my feet for hours. I knew I had failed to convince a single one of my audience members to do or think anything different.

I remember having a hard time listening to the rest of the meeting's proceedings. Having a hard time suppressing the grin on my lips.

For all her faults, I can't despise the white feminist whisperer. I used to be her. I still battle her in me all the time.

Racism is not her doing. She acts as a racial wedge, yes. She accepts perks and proximity to white power that her role affords, but she seems to be in a sorrowful state. Why does she live the whispering lifestyle?

Maybe she feels as I once felt. Maybe she doesn't think she has much of a choice. Maybe she's reeling from fear of the punishments of whisper refusal—and racialized feminists can and do get punished. There are times even now that I worry about the reputational impacts of choosing not to whisper. Perhaps she hopes playing the role will keep her safe. That is not an unreasonable assumption.

Perhaps she isn't conscious of what she's doing in the first place. Maybe her art has been practised too heartily and unquestioningly for too long. Maybe it's become muscle memory for her in a way that never completely happened for me.

Or perhaps the answer is that she herself embodies the pathology of her white feminist environment. Anne Anlin Cheng describes responses of othered people in the melancholic context in which they live as a form of melancholy, too. The racialized is "both melancholic object and melancholic subject, both the one lost and the one losing." They internalize "discipline and rejection—and the installation of a scripted context of perception." Perhaps white feminist whisperers anticipate the consumption, loss, and rejection they suffer from white feminism. Perhaps they scramble to align with it in a hopeless hope of shortcutting the cycle.

It doesn't work. It plays as tragedy any way you look at it.

Cheng says that racial order, as the organizing principle of whiteness, means that gender cannot be upheld as the only or the most important principle to be aware of. She suggests that the artifice of race could be a prerequisite for the meanings of femininity. She upends the typical balance of Freudian psychoanalysis, which from its beginning considered gender identification elemental to the psyche.

It's a concept that disquiets melancholic white feminism, too. If gender discrimination isn't the top factor to address, if overthrowing racism is at least equally important to humanity's well-being and liberty as undoing sexism, then what in the world is white feminism to do?

For white feminist whisperers suspicious of what they're doing—of what is being done to them—the guilt they feel in their whispering might become unbearable. It's what drove me to wonder about the other choices I could make in white feminist circumstances. Dread of a soiled conscience has been an incredible deterrent and gift.

For those in a state of unawareness, ignorance is not necessarily bliss. The unknowing white feminist whisperer may get injured in other ways, missing out on mutual trust and fellowship she could enjoy with other racialized feminists, the ones who likely feel betrayed by her.

And how affirming those relationships can be. Exalted ideals of movements and majorities have a way of obscuring what feminists actually are to each other on a day-to-day, face-to-face basis. We're friends, family, co-workers, kin. We volunteer together. We mentor and endorse each other. We solve problems and make audacious plans. We get mad at each other, say sorry to each other, and forgive. We hang out and joke around and travel and grab a drink. We do bad-feminist things together, binging trashy shows, watching trashy movies, reading trashy books, all the while pretending we're above it. We attend openings and exhibits and concerts and showcases—each other's openings and exhibits and concerts and showcases. We clap and hoot and dance for each other. We date each other. We meet each other's relations, partners, children, parents. We celebrate and dine with each other. We pray and sing and worship with each other.

Sometimes we hold vigil by one another's bedsides. Sometimes we shed tears for each other. Sometimes we mourn with and for each other.

Feminists do the actions of love together.

We're part of a diverse and divergent global community, sure. But I'm convinced our love for each other means more to us than we express out loud. Deluged in viral stereotyping and put-downs—the same boring bra-burning jokes repeated over sixty years—I wonder if our love for one another might be our most delightful secret.

That white feminist whispering is a racialized feminist relationship killer seems to me its worst consequence. I credit racialized feminists, my friends and mentors and chosen family, with saving my life more than once. They gifted me language to voice shared experiences, thrilled me with their arched eyebrows and winks and knowing smiles, and gave me a role to play in the voicing process before I even knew how to do it. They noticed me when other people wouldn't give me the time of day. They believed in me and made me feel valued. They made me feel like one of them, even though they would have been justified in choosing otherwise so many times.

It's the way one of them hired me onto her project even when my white manager told her she didn't believe I could live up to the challenge. *I'm careful about what white women say about young women of colour. I have a feeling you can learn. I have a feeling you're smart.*

It's the way another argued for me when a white woman called her, demanding I be fired for speaking to her out of turn. *What an odd assumption I'd fire you for that. You made a mistake and you won't do it again. It's not the end of the world.*

It's the way a few of them pulled me into a cluster on the front lawn of the church after my mother's funeral, a warm June afternoon, making sure they had a chance to talk to me. *We know you have to get back to your family, but we just wanted to see how you're holding up, for real.*

They sponsored, taught, and invested in me over the years. I can only be thankful to them for this grace. Still, it's the love that made any of it stick. It's the love I've witnessed between and experienced with racialized feminists that has been the most compelling aspect of this movement for me.

I'm like every single person on the planet. All I've ever wanted is love. Love is the one thing that keeps me believing in the promise of feminism.

Many would agree with me that white feminism is not salvageable. But the white feminist whisperer is. What is she to do to rid herself of her melancholia?

She can do what I've done: learn from racialized feminists who have never whispered a day in their lives. She might know some of them personally. She might read their work or watch and listen to their content. She can seek them out, tamp down her reflexes to dismiss them as too brash and baldfaced and not tactical enough. Their frankness, to the ire of white feminism, can be her balm, stinging to the touch and healing in its absorption. She can offer them her highest regard.

The white feminist whisperer can face her emotions, her grief and her rage. These are the reactions to racist abuses white feminism has never stomached in a racialized body, that makes white feminism want to spit the othered right out. She can refuse to mitigate her tone and smooth the lines of her face. She can disagree, rebut, and keep her smiles to herself. She can get passionate. She can embrace her pettier rebellions to build sea legs for the real mutinies.

If she's a model minority, the white feminist whisperer can take the risk and loosen her grip and carry that modelness of hers in open palms. She can begin to treat it with reservation. She can ask who it was actually meant for, all along. She can start to doubt how it serves her. She can ask herself new questions: who and what does this estrange me from? Might it hold me back? Is it what I want? Is it really worth it?

She can attune herself to the go-betweenness of the indentured and presume no permanent landing. She can wonder where she finds her own belonging, constructs her own abode. She can seek a better place for herself, somewhere beyond the quicksand of whiteness.

She can unlearn the art and craft of whispering that she has wasted so much of her energy on. Safe manoeuvre as it seems, whispering only acts as another factor to shrink feminism's capacity to counter the dangers of the world today. There's nothing safe about upholding the dynamics that have alienated those harmed by gender injustices from one another, that cut us off from what we desperately need to achieve in alliance. That cut us off from real love for one another.

But she's not going to manage any of this alone. Those around the white feminist whisperer have to take the project on too, racialized and white alike. We need to enable the white feminist whisperer to heal. We need to stop availing ourselves of her or otherwise detesting and disposing of her. Our self-centredness and self-righteousness serve little good purpose. We can learn better, too. We need to help her find a better path forward, if she's willing to tread it. We need to cheer her along her way so she can, finally and triumphantly, spook the horse.

HOW CAN YOU LOVE THE OPPRESSOR?

"How can you love the oppressor?" a classmate asked.

The shift in the room was tangible. No one was gazing at their binders or picking at their cuticles. Not anymore.

The classmate appeared to be older than me, than many of the other students in the undergraduate Caribbean studies course. Like other humanities classes at the University of Toronto, this one was tucked in the basement of an airless and nondescript building that hadn't been erected recently enough to be state-of-the-art or long ago enough to be archetypal.

I remember the classmate's stylish skirts and square-heeled boots, her hair cropped in curls. I remember her whip-smart clarity, too. "Love can take you by surprise," she continued. "I know it can catch you and do unexpected things. But I don't understand why you would ever do that to yourself. How you would let yourself fall in love with the oppressor. How you could go ahead and marry the oppressor."

The professor was perched on one of the student chairs at the front row of the classroom, one leg crossed over the other. He often wandered away from his podium to sit amongst us like that, angling himself so he could talk to us over his shoulder. His fluffy hair cascaded from his head to blend into a fluffy beard, bright and white against his brown skin. The postcolonial academic books and articles he wrote were fiercely intelligent and critical, intricately argued, and, at times, lyrical to the level of poetry.

But in person, sometimes he kept it simple. "As you said, love can take you." He smiled and passed a hand down the front of his beard. "Stranger things have happened. I can't explain it."

The man knew his Caribbean and Latin American history and politics by heart. For me, a student fresh out of public high school exposed to little more than a smattering of world war geopolitics, the professor's free-form lectures were impossible to follow. He was guided by no outlines I could perceive; he projected nothing to the screen and etched little on the chalkboard to steer us. The instances where he did quote course readings—Édouard Glissant and Frantz Fanon and C.L.R. James—were bubbles in a roiling ocean. They foamed to the surface of his lecture, popped, and fizzled away.

Determined to trace his meandering, I tried scribbling notes. A half hour into the class, I chucked my pen to the page. More than anything, I had to listen to him. Maybe that's why I remember more of his classes than anything else in my first year of university, especially those moments when students broke in with their commentary. It's no wonder that the topic of interracial relationships, specifically unions between Black or brown people and white people, was one of the instances when someone had to speak up. The question of *to love or not to love* was too provoking to stay silent about.

The student pressed her forearms to the lip of her desk and turned her palms up to the ceiling. "The personal is the political.

You can't forget everything like it doesn't matter, like it wouldn't affect your relationship. Life doesn't work like that. That legacy of hatred and exploitation. Why would you do that? I don't understand how you can let yourself love the oppressor."

How can you love the oppressor? I had never pondered the question before. I had speculated about other elements of relationships, what they should be and what I would never abide by in one. But I had no experience with them myself. Love existed in theoretical gives and takes. Mostly takes, the benefits of love with hardly any concessions. Companionship had to be free and clean to be real, I thought, no revolting whiffs of sacrifice. Or worse than sacrifice: settling. Conceding to even the smallest compromise for love seemed archaic and unfair.

"I understand what you mean," the professor said, still smiling. "I see where it's coming from. In spite of all that, though, you see people doing what they do. Loving who they love."

She shook her head. "It's not that simple. It's never that simple."

"You're right about that."

The exchange triggered rustling, cleared throats, and murmurs. Other students seized the opportunity to pipe in.

"My parents taught me and my siblings that you can love anyone," one young woman said. "They taught us you can find a way to come together, if you're both willing to make it work."

"And what about the white people who become allies?" a young man asked the class. "I mean, real allies? Are we saying it wouldn't be okay to get together with them?"

There were moments of heatedness, of joking and incredulousness. What I remember most is how hard it was to unhitch my gaze from the woman who had kicked off the debate in the first place. She was so convinced, arguing and laughing and pressing her point. She was convincing, too.

How can you love the oppressor? She snagged me on that question. I dragged the hook out of the classroom with me when it was over.

She's right, I thought. *I couldn't do it. It would only spell trouble. I couldn't let myself love the oppressor.*

Not even one year later, I began to meet up with the blue-eyed white man I would eventually marry.

Even in the thick of my own concerns, I would discover it wasn't that difficult for a woman like me to be with a man like him. Not from the standpoint of racial judgment. Nobody got upset at us for crossing divides, even after we wed. The most friction we've experienced in public were stray double takes easily written off, a few maître d's who didn't immediately realize that the two people waiting at the podium might want to be seated together. Once, going through customs after a vacation, the border guard sifting through our passports took longer than he should've to make sense of our shared address. He didn't seem to grasp our matrimony even as he waved us through the checkpoint. *You two... live together?* Was it more of an issue of our mismatched last names than our racial configuration?

When we revealed the fact of our romance, there was barely a race-based reaction from our families, friends, co-workers, and acquaintances. On the white side of our relatives, nothing vocalized. On the brown side of our relatives, one or two gentle, predictable comments.

So, you don't want to marry a brown boy, then?

I offered the professor's line. *Love can take you, you know. I can't explain it.*

That tepid response was accepted straight away, to my disappointment.

The whole thing was anticlimactic. I wanted a story to recount about the fight we had to put up for our romance. I wasn't looking to be flattened by a concrete block of opposition, to be clear. I was dramatic; I didn't have a death wish.

Was I wrong to consider it fitting that my man and I have something to chafe against as we committed to interracialness for the rest of our lives? That the reaction to our union should not have been so interchangeable with a monocultural pair? With a white pair? That it would've been more admirable for us to love one another through the parting mists of minor racial heroism?

That's the thing about the immigrant diaspora I'm a part of, that pocket of educated brown-skinned, English-speaking West Indian families I was born into. No one was going to stick a gnarled finger at me and tell me I shouldn't have been marrying a white man. There was little surprise or consternation over my romantic assimilation. In a way, it's what everyone expected. Perhaps it's what they believed needed to happen, in the grand scheme of things. A signal of health and well-being, a forge up the racial ladder, ever closer to making it, ever closer to the goal of whiteness, even if whiteness has a way of vaporizing to the touch.

White people in our lives were not poised to object to our pairing either. That's not what fair-minded cosmopolitan people do in a multicultural milieu. White and brown romance—white and profoundly white-assimilated brown romance—is one of the more acceptable interracial combinations these days. And my particular brand of second-generation immigrant Indo-Caribbean brownness is just about the rightest brown you can find out there, even if you weren't aware it existed before you were introduced to it in the flesh. *English, no triggering accents. Canadian, born and raised. Colonization by the British, three layers deep. Brown skin on the tawny side, not too dark, no Blackness, no kinky hair. Church-going Christian, mainstream Protestant, Hindu and Muslim roots faded into the background. Education, staunchly Western. Sweet and polite young woman in love.*

For all its trappings as a survival mechanism, code switching is also an art and a craft. Some of us are more gifted at it than others. More crucial than our personal talents of the practice, some of us have the base ingredients to sauté and savour its tastier outcomes. Code switching has done wonders for me in the body I've found myself born into, for the mother tongue and upbringing I played no part in choosing, for the time and place in which I couldn't help but enter the earth.

Some of us have discovered it to be an effective matchmaking tool, too. Yes, oppressors would be loved by a woman like me. Yes, oppressors would get married to me, become family to me. Isn't that why the people who came before me worked so hard? For love and acceptance and the promise of kin? Why would anyone want to fight such a thing?

Still, I seemed to prefer the idea of a brawl. I wanted to feel some of my racial transgression reflected back at me, some tangible proof that my brownness, my nagging sensation of otherness, actually meant something in a marriage to a white man.

Stood for something. If it meant that my otherness would have to be an affront, so be it. At least it wouldn't be ignored.

How can I love the oppressor? I imagined saying to my old university classmate. *I will do it without foolish illusions or self-deception. I know exactly what this world does to people like me in love.*

I suppose I wanted to fight to feel alive. Was it wrong for me to not want to be rendered invisible in an interracial marriage? To be embraced by love and, at the same time, not get my brownness swallowed and digested away?

Even in university, I didn't have parental permission to date. I didn't have the chops to introduce myself to anyone on my campus, so even if I wanted to disobey the house rules, my pickings of bachelors, especially the racialized ones, would have been slim. These were the days before digital dating assistance. I prepared myself to wait.

My white blue-eyed man was four years older than me. We had first met at our church. He moved away for college, and I hardly thought of him until, years later, I tracked down his phone number and rang him up to see if he would come back to church to play guitar for the youth choir I was planning to head up. He said yes.

In lieu of falling in love in those days, I'd managed my longings by endlessly talking about them. It was certainly a favourite subject of musing amongst me and my church friends as we sat in our circle every week, Bibles open on our laps. It was during one of these conversations that I bemoaned the fact that no potential suitor I knew of was interested in getting to know me.

Sitting across the circle from me, my white blue-eyed man rolled his eyes. "Kids these days," he huffed for everyone to hear. "They say the darndest things."

Church love can be insular. When a congregation is close-knit, when people feel like *auntie, uncle, cousin,* and *mummy* as much as they've come together as spiritual brother and sister, the plot of romance unfolds in the theatre of community forums, of Sunday school and music practices, of studies and meetings and services. I never had to ask if I could get a witness.

And there are moments when witnesses perceive truths before they dawn on the witnessed. Everyone in the room giggled knowingly, eyes on him, eyes on me.

I was surprised by the heat that rolled over my neck. I could feel the vibrations in my hastily constructed edifices, the rickety structures of who I assumed I could and could not love.

I know what hatred of interracial love between racialized and white people looks like. It's miscegenation and apartheid legislation and counted drops of blood. It's dirty looks and insults and rejection. It's refusals to appear, cold shoulders, withheld invitations. It's roaring preachers and upturned noses, screaming and bobbing signs and thrusted fists. Broken glass, lapping flames, ugly faces on film. *Loving v. Virginia.*

Then again, I don't know what hatred of interracial love looks like, not in the present day. Besides the odd white supremacist tirade, anger and distaste aren't expressed on a mass level, nor are they all that public. Burgeoning interracial partnerships and multiracial families cutting across all lines must mean that mainstream revulsion is trending downward. It probably also means that much of it has burrowed underground and gotten absorbed into the atmosphere. Weighty dark matter, hovering and abundant in theory but difficult to map. That could be why, in the limited studies available on the subject, interracial couples register higher levels of stress, strain, depression, and typecasting than white couples, with variances depending on gender and racial differences.

The picture is complicated in other ways because we now pay more attention to the viewpoints of people who aren't white. One study finds that straight Black women and Asian men express less "warmth" toward interracial pairings, particularly those between Black men and white women for the former and Asian women and white men for the latter. Stereotyping of Black women and Asian men hasn't favoured them as romantic partners. Their representation in popular Western media as objects of empathy, relatability, and desirability is newborn and precarious. It feels as if it could all get abandoned in a heartbeat. When it comes to real testing grounds like dating apps, Black women and Asian men report the worst treatment. In our quick-draw competitions for romance, swipe now or lose out forever, it's no wonder they're not enthused about the ways they get cut off from a chance at love.

And that's a big part of the argument. Is a chance at love, the most worthy, lasting, and good love, even possible in interracial relationships? Naturally, the anti-miscegenists say no.

The debate in my Caribbean studies class focused on that same question, in its own way. "How could you let yourself love the oppressor?" that student asked. *Why cut yourself off from a chance at love with someone who could really and truly understand you and care for you, every part of you, through and through?* she might as well have asked.

Why cut yourself off from a chance at love because you've cast someone in the role of the oppressor? some of my classmates asked in return.

But that student wasn't the one who had positioned white people in the role of the oppressor. Nobody in that lecture hall—every one of us Black and brown—had the capacity to do that. Turn to historical power and politics and capitalism to target your blame.

I couldn't find words for it at the time, but I was unnerved by the way our arguments kept drifting off from the real question, the unspoken one that hung unanswered by the end of the class. The deepest conundrum is not whether you as a racialized person are capable of loving the oppressor or if you should be held culpable for your reckless love. With inescapable forces of stolen land and labour, with bottomless personal and communal investments in racial hierarchies that accompany them, the thornier question is whether the oppressor can ever truly love, know, and value *you*.

If the answer is somehow a yes, go forth and love as you will. If the answer is a no, even "probably not," you get skewered by other questions. Why would you do that to yourself? Why would you put yourself in that position? Racialized lover, don't you love yourself?

Maybe we didn't dwell on the ability of the oppressor to love because it's the trickier variable of the romance equation. Of course the oppressed can love; the oppressed find all kinds of ways to love. We have to.

Maybe we veered away from it because it felt like such a disempowering place to be. As Black and brown people in a basement lecture hall, maybe we sensed we weren't the ones to scramble for the calculus of believable answers to the question of oppressor love. Not us, all on our own.

Early in our relationship, my future blue-eyed white husband and I met up in an underground food court. We both worked nearby.

It was shortly after five o'clock in the afternoon. We chose a two-seater table pressed to a wall and sat with our coffees. The food court was sparsely populated. A man seated a few tables over argued with an invisible companion every so often, shouting and jabbing at him. A crush of people bustled through the corridor beyond the food court, making their way to and from the subway station. The motion of trains rumbled through the floors every few minutes.

"I don't know what this is," he said to me across the table, above the din. "I can't tell what it is that I feel. A strong liking, maybe? Or strong friendship? I don't know what I would call it."

"I know. I'm not sure how I'd explain it either. But it's definitely there."

He nodded at the scratched tabletop. "I think it's too early to call it love or anything like that. It's only been, like, three months."

"Yeah." I swigged the last gulp of coffee in my cup. "But, I don't know. I think it feels like love."

He nodded again.

I felt a lump rise to my throat, tightening it. "I think I love you," I said. "I do love you." I knew it was unwise of me to say it. No one knew we had been talking to each other one-on-one, let alone meeting up. I still wasn't supposed to be dating; I didn't tell my family or friends. On top of that, I was too sensitive a person to be making rash declarations when I didn't know him well enough to know what response they would elicit.

"I love you, too."

I stretched my hand across the table. He set his hand in mine, passed his thumb over mine, again and again. We stayed that way for a while.

Commuters continued to stream behind us. His was the first hand I had ever held and my pulse thrummed. I was thrilled and alarmed, all at once.

Over the years, I've come across a fair amount of advice written for interracial couples consisting of a racialized partner and a white partner. It's concerned with managing less-than-accepting family and friends, answering to stereotypes and off-colour jokes, sharing each other's foods and languages and cultural quirks, hosting uncomfortable conversations with one another on the impacts of prejudice, police brutality and hate crimes, microaggressions in the workplace, and the like.

Very little is geared toward the inner life of the racialized partner themself. I'm interested in that partner more than I'm interested in the complications of their interracial partnerships.

How do we as racialized lovers understand our interracial love? Are we puzzled by it? Or does it feel like the most organic thing in the world? Do we come to our realizations of love perplexed by how we feel? Surprised about who we've offered our hearts to? Do we all anticipate the external oppositions, concerned to receive it and perhaps just as concerned to be spared from it? Do we all slip into the same void, that suspected state of disappearance, when our racially transgressive loves proceed without a hitch?

What convinces us as racialized interracial lovers to take the step to begin to love at all? Do we all have to overcome our skepticism? Our own feelings of discomfort, disquiet, hesitancy?

If we as racialized interracial lovers combat the self-hatred cultivated in us by white supremacy, do we inevitably have to struggle with loving our white partners? Do love and hate, held to self and reflected off of each other, a prism that bounces between lovers and world, always have to battle it out?

These questions may be too individual to answer. Are racialized lovers in racialized–white partnerships a cohort unto themselves? Can we make reference to common denominators in our unique loves?

I can't help but search for what those commonalities might be.

I had a racialized friend who had been married to a white man for years. As I was navigating the first few years of loving my blue-eyed white man, my friend and her husband had long built a family, an entire life, with each other. Theirs was a relationship I wondered if I might be able to squirrel away as a model for my own. "You know how it is when you start out," she told me. "You don't see things being any other way than they are. You don't see yourself as having choices for life to turn out differently. But I think about it now. Would I have given a man who looked like me a chance, if I had met him back then? Would I even have noticed him? Or would all that internalized stuff have been too deep in me to appreciate who he was and who we could have been together?"

Would I have given my heart to a lover who looked like me? The question was like *How can you love the oppressor?* Just about impossible to answer. It floated to the bottom and settled in its place, a pebble under the current inside of me, buffed smooth, nearly frictionless, but always there.

Racialized interracial lover, do you doubt yourself, too? I want you to know it doesn't mean you're neurotic or dysfunctional in your love. It means you are my companion.

I didn't want to get married. On the surface, my reasoning was principled and political: I didn't believe in weddings. I didn't want to peacock around in a pricey patriarchal and colonial ceremony.

I thought it would be fine to date in secret forever, to love casually at arm's length, no long-term commitments craved or required. It seemed the safest and smartest approach, given my family's rules on dating and my own fears and uncertainties about being with my blue-eyed white man.

He seemed to agree with the approach. We got close to each other, in spite of my hesitations in our love. I wrote him a long letter explaining why he meant so much to me. I called him my *amicum*, the Latin word for friend, loved one, ally. He matched it, naming me his *amica*. He printed out his personal diary and slipped it into an envelope, handing the whole thing over for me to read.

We scoured each other's words; we studied each other's deepest thoughts. We basked in the assurance of knowing the other knew our deepest thoughts.

Instead of precious metal and stones, I joked to him one day, I'd prefer the gift of a leather friendship bracelet. A few weeks later, he presented me a brown leather band woven through by dark leather strips. He clipped it around my wrist. He told me that he believed in us as we were, braided as simply as that bracelet. He told me it was a symbol of what we could always be. He didn't expect anything from me but my love.

This is how you love the oppressor, I thought. *You care for him more than anyone in the whole world, but you maintain your barriers. You assure yourself that you've kept a safe distance from the world's foul histories.*

After about five years of clandestine dating, hanging back together after events and stealing time with one another after school and work and lingering next to each other in his car, things changed. He didn't want to be undercover boyfriend and girlfriend for the rest of his life, he said. Suspended in arm's-length stasis, he didn't feel held. We had created a coupled quarantine for ourselves and he couldn't abide by it anymore. He wanted a permanent, public commitment. To him, it meant getting married the old-fashioned way, 'til death do us part.

We broke up. If I had been a consistent individual, I would have been relieved to be released from expectations I didn't think I could live up to. If I had been a mature individual, I would have understood that humans can come to their realizations gradually. That the passage of time is often what changes your mind.

Instead, I felt misled by love. I felt like I had been lied to by my lover. I had conveyed that I wanted to be cherished by him fully and forever without the strings of real obligation. He had answered, sure, why not? To be confronted by a change of heart years later seemed an intentional betrayal, to me.

The agony of our split whittled me down. After a few months, getting back together was pain avoidance, more than anything else. If lost love hurt so excruciatingly, then I would make lost love go away. I would return to my lover, hat in hand, and tell him I wanted to figure out a way to marry now, too. He agreed.

By then, my family had found a way to accept the fact that I was dating. So many changes had rushed over us in the eventuality of my mother's death that this change felt like one of the easier ones to manage. But imminent nuptials didn't mean my concerns about getting married to my blue-eyed white man dissolved entirely. It downgraded to petty rebellion. I took charge of the planning, arranging us to marry as plainly as possible, just a handful of people gathered in a living room and a trip to an all-you-can-eat buffet afterward, no production, no major audience. I told him he could wear a ring, if he so fancied. I myself had no intention of owning one. Of allowing a ring to own me.

We sat in his Chevy, parked in the lot of a mall, wearing our winter jackets and gloves. I thought we would be walking into the department store to purchase a ring for his lone finger.

"I think we're going to have to do this together," he said to me.

"I don't want to feel forced into wearing a ring," I answered. "I told you."

"I don't want to force you. But I don't want to be wearing a ring alone. The point of us getting married is doing it together."

I envisioned a chunky diamond solitaire, rotating and sparkling on a turntable, slightly out of focus. It was a teardrop-cut diamond mounted on a yellow gold band. I heard the crescendo of piano music.

I was not going to be able to get married without getting

married. It was not possible. I was a mere stumble away from becoming a typical woman. A typical wife to a typical husband. A wannabe white lady wife to my blue-eyed white man.

So, this is how you love the oppressor. By denying who you are. By pretending you're someone else entirely. I started to cry. "I don't want to wear a ring. I don't want to resent you for having to wear it."

He stared at the windshield. After a little while, he took my gloved hand in his. He sighed. "This is hard. Neither of us wants to hurt the other. Neither of us wants to make the other person do something they're not comfortable doing."

He bought a ring for himself at the mall that day. A few weeks later, I went to a different mall on my own and found myself a ring, a skinny silver band I could wear along with my other silver rings.

It cost no more than thirty dollars. It was a whole mountain moved.

As a racialized interracial lover, I've always worried about getting lost in my love.

The terms of what it means to get lost change with the passage of time, but I'm surprised by how it persists. It started with the marriage itself, with the expectations of rings and cakes and gowns and other clichéd trappings, heterosexual pomp and circumstance. It shifted to the idea of offspring.

How would my children see me, their racialized mother? How would they relate to me, compared to the way they would relate to their father?

That worry was specific. It sprouted from a rumour I'd heard about a classmate years ago, a boy who supposedly lived with a white father and an Indo-Caribbean mother. I hardly knew him; I can't even remember his name. But a mutual friend relayed to me how he talked about his father all the time, bragging and boasting, while rarely talking about his mother. He barely made reference to her.

"Everyone assumes he's white when they look at him," my friend said. "See how he is? Bullying everyone he doesn't like and stuff? He acts white. His friends are white, too. If they knew about his mom, they'd know the truth about him. I bet he's not happy about that."

It was offhand supposition and I had no place listening to it. But I was instantly convinced that his mother was living a nightmare. I pictured her in a dilapidated kitchen, standing over a stove with the hood light above her, cooking West Indian food in sombre awareness that her son would refuse to eat it. I saw steam billowing from the pot, tears streaming down her cheeks. Roti, dhal, chicken curry, fried rice. It was all for naught. Her son despised her and everything about her. Her husband, too. He mistreated her. In fact, he was the one who had taught her son to hate his mother, to hate the brown part of himself in the first place.

How can you love the oppressor? How can the oppressor truly love you? Why would that man have wanted to marry that woman at all? It must have been some kind of trickery, some kind of blackmail. It must have been abuse.

Would the same thing happen between me and my white-passing children? Would they go to school and never breathe a word about who I was? Worse yet, would they resent me if they emerged from the womb too tanned, too dark-haired and dark-eyed, not white-passing at all? Would they begrudge my dominant genes?

The potency of this tale-spinning and its accompanying neurosis faded over the years the way wallpaper fades in light. But every so often, I became conscious of my anxieties about being consumed by whiteness, a risk I doubt I would've felt so avidly if I weren't in an intimate relationship with a white man.

Fears of subsumption have further softened with the passage of contented married years, and with age. The edges are wispy now. They've airbrushed themselves into nebulous regrets and longings.

Flipping around the channels, catching footage of carnival, of dancing and fêtes and sequinned, tall-feathered costumes. *Why didn't I play mas when I was younger? Why didn't I keep up with playing the steel pan? With chutney music, at least?*

Listening to a new audiobook on the way to work, something about history and politics, read by the author. *I should've majored in Caribbean and Latin American studies when I had the chance. Gone for a master's or Ph.D., even. It's not like the degree I picked instead was rocket science or anything.*

Scrolling through a friend's travel photos. Palm trees and turquoise water, coconuts and mangoes cradled in hand. *I need to book a flight somewhere. Anywhere. It's been too long. I need to go to a place where I can learn. Gain knowledge. Get back to basics.*

Do you muse this way too, racialized interracial lover, at odd times of the day and night? Do you find yourself mourning the very racial respectability you've relied on for too long, your deftness with code switching for love? Do your apprehensions peek out of the bushes once in a while, blink at you, then skitter back to the thicket? Do they disguise themselves as bursts of energy to go somewhere, do something, educate yourself, remember things you fear you may have forgotten?

Are they glaring at times? Red stripes brushed across a white canvas?

When I take stock of what's out there, there really aren't many cultural artifacts, art and movies and books, on the complex and varied perspectives of the racialized interracial lover. The viewpoints of white people in interracial love seem to become overly central to the stories, their swoonworthy declarations of passion against the odds, their soft and transgressive caresses of melanated skin.

Even in the modern proliferation of a diversity of lovers represented in Hallmark movies, I don't think any of it has much bandwidth for the experiences of racialized interracial women lovers in particular. *Bridgerton* is an unabashed interracial fantasy. Its first season contains brief mention of the power of romance to break racial barriers—for the uplift of the leading racialized male heartthrob, of course. Sitcoms like *Bob Hearts Abishola* and the two-season *Mixed-ish* do well in acknowledging uniqueness in the viewpoints of their racialized women lovers, but their format limits their depth. Reality shows like *Love Is Blind* and *Married at First Sight* that revolve around love's physicalities and take pains to neutralize them are just as thin on racialized women's inner conflicts and considerations with white partners in white-dominant contexts. They don't touch on how Black, Indigenous, and Asian women and other women of colour might manage their loves differently based on their particular racializations, so they certainly don't do well at conceptualizing jumbles of ancestral diasporas, twice-removed migrations, or even second- or third-generation immigrant lives.

Why must the racialized interracial woman lover be so nondescript, so formless? She is in love, yes. And sometimes, she fends off ignorant comments and puts up fights to keep her love. But there's so little to illustrate her inner workings, her feelings and doubts and questions in her interracial love, her pondering and uncertainties about the sacrifices she makes for it. The conceptualization of love's real gains and losses, her grappling with the overwhelming legacies of love and hate. Especially when she's in love with a white man.

It's as if the beloved's whiteness is self-explanatory, a thing to underscore and then sweep under the screen. *Of course she loves the oppressor. There's no good reason in the world for her not to.* If the racialized interracial woman's narrative does address these matters from her perspective, it's usually in passing. Plot pivots, deep-seated themes, and character growth don't hinge on them. Her minoritized self carries little weight in the gravity of her love. She herself embodies few stakes.

In other words, the racialized interracial woman lover is too often not entirely human in her story. I don't consider this a passive oversight or naively unasked question. It's a nefarious erasure.

And we're not missing out on her turmoil alone. I'm upset that we don't get to witness more of the racialized interracial woman lover's joys. The elements of love that sustain and hearten her. I'm dismayed that we don't get to experience her growing love and appreciation for her lover, her lover's growing love and appreciation for her, at the same time as we experience her emboldening and solidification in herself. In every part of who she is.

Isn't that what worthy, lasting, and good love does for the lover, in the end? Isn't it something they give that ultimately gets reflected back onto them? Doesn't it help them love their lover more and want to extend love and grace to themselves, too, as the beloved? Isn't that what people mean when they speak of love as a multi-sided jewel, a many-splendoured thing? Isn't that what they should mean?

Maybe the emergence of fresh stories about the mixed and mixed-up longings of the interracial racialized woman lover, such as Celine Song's *Past Lives*, means things are finally going to change. I do hope to see much more of the interracial racialized woman lover portrayed in her fullness and her flaws. Not merely at the dawn of lasting love. All the way through its life, until sunset dapples the sky.

I don't have satisfying answers to questions about loving the oppressor and the oppressor loving you. Whether commentary on the matter comes from racialized or white voices, whether their pronouncements are positive or negative, I can't bring myself to trust anybody driving conclusive nails into the crooked walls of this debate.

I've come to see love as a choice and a compulsion at the same time, existing someplace on the swaying scales of liberation and constraint. No one wants to think of good love as both free and unfree. But we can at least admit that lovers never love each other in vacuum-sealed containers. This could mean that oppressor and oppressed will always have to wrestle with the arms of love and hate in their romances, and to downplay or overstate either element would be silly. Perhaps the more productive question to pose to the lovers is what tools will equip them to grapple with this reality best. They deserve at least that.

How do you love the oppressor? How does the oppressor love you? Maybe the reality is that you have to battle with it every day. Maybe mutual persistence in the battle is the signal of your real love.

I don't believe it too pessimistic to presume that human beings, all human beings, are incapable of loving each other perfectly. As true as love may be, I don't believe pure mortal love can ever exist.

But I feel optimistic about the racialized interracial woman lover herself. I don't want to burden her or carve lines around the loves she's allowed and the loves she's not supposed to access because of the abuses of power and history. My wish for her is to gain more choices, more possibilities and exploration, more chances to thrive wrapped in the care she has always deserved and has been too often denied by everyone, fellow oppressed and oppressor alike. We've all done her some measure of wrong.

Racialized interracial woman lover, I want you to understand that I know where you're coming from. You may feel uncertain in your love. You may want to take your time with it, guard yourself in it, and be bothered by difficult questions, even questions you may not be able to answer straight away. I'm okay with your choices and trust your decisions in love, whatever they may be. And if you don't see your unique, complicated self and your unique, complicated love properly represented or celebrated, I want you to know that you should never doubt their validity.

I see and appreciate you. I think everyone in the world should push to see and appreciate you, too. If pure mortal love doesn't exist, if it's always going to be a work in progress for all of us, this perception is a key aspect of the progress we need to strive for together.

In July 2012, I went to a women's writing retreat for six weeks. Five hours on a plane to Seattle-Tacoma International Airport was followed by a shuttle bus to Possession Sound and a ferry to cross over to Whidbey Island.

I stood at the edge of the deck, gripping the railing and squinting into the wind as I listened to Shad's "Rose Garden" in my earbuds. The sky was overcast. The water was a beaten metal sheet. The shore, growing closer, was a scribble of evergreens.

My eyelids were gritty. I was exhausted, but I had nearly made it to my destination. I was grateful that I had been accepted to the retreat. I also felt a tinge of apprehension. I didn't know what to expect. Would I get along with the other writers? What would living and writing in a handcrafted Amish cottage in the woods be like? What kind of food would I eat there, exactly?

The welcome I received at the retreat centre was open and warm. The other writers were talented women, generous with their company and good advice. The cottages we lived in were cozy; the food they cooked for us, farm fresh and healthy. Gourmet, even.

This rural island setting was idyllic. We could hike through the forested retreat grounds and go on bike rides down picturesque lanes. We could visit a nearby lavender farm, with llamas and horses grazing neighbouring plots. We could journey into town, with its boutiques and coffee shops and bars. We could sit at the shoreline and commiserate about our projects over mint juleps. We could drive down roads padded by towering trees and stop at the bridge that spanned the majestic, swirling Deception Pass strait.

It was a dreamy time. But it was not without its stressors. I wrestled with my second novel in that cottage. Seven years later, *The Lost Sister* would be completed and published, but back then, I didn't know if it would make it. I couldn't get my writing to cohere the way I knew it could, if only I had the aptitude. This manuscript was important. It was based on a life story entrusted to me by a friend about his experiences growing up in an orphanage for Black children in segregated Nova Scotia. He didn't tell me what he went through so I could fail him. I felt like I was failing him.

As the days ticked by, I was certain I had made a mistake in coming to this place. The one constant I could look forward to was walking the path to the farmhouse, catching spotty wifi, and calling my husband in the evening. That became a guidepost. No matter how dejected I was in my writing that day, I told myself I had to get to ten new pages before I could call him.

Every day, I slunk toward that goal. Every day, I rewarded myself by enjoying another dinner with my fellow writers, then slipping off to the back room with an internet connection to talk to him. We made simple conversation, easy catch-ups, like we were in the same home once again. It patched me up after my lack of talent spent all day clobbering me.

When the retreat was over, when I had somehow managed to complete an unruly manuscript, I met my husband in Seattle for a week's vacation. I rose early the day of my departure and said goodbyes. I got into the taxi to drive to the port and cross the sound on the ferry. A sheet of clouds rolled above the shuttle bus going down the highway. I watched the sunbeams begin to pierce through.

I made it to the hotel and dragged my suitcase into the lobby. I spotted my husband leaning against the reception counter, his back toward me. I walked up behind him. "Hey," I said.

He turned, his eyes wide, and fell onto me with a hug. "Oh, hey," he breathed. "It's so wonderful to see you."

The relief in his voice, his exhale, confused me. Over the weeks we had been apart, I hadn't gotten a sense of inordinate missing, of too much distance between us. I hadn't expected to hear such held breath.

How silly I was back then. How slow I am to appreciate the gifts I've been given. More than a decade later, I understand what happened in our reunion. I've come to recognize that I hold my breath when I'm apart from him as much as he does.

You hold your breath when your need for somebody is undeniable. When it's irrefutable how important you have become to each other. You can manage your lives separately, neither of you are hopeless, neither of you are skinless bundles of flesh and nerves. Love has fortified you more than you could have anticipated, and you are thankful for it. But separateness is not normal. It's not the way it should be.

You hold your breath when you're happy but you've been apart too long, when all you can do is hope that you'll get the chance to come together again. To breathe with one another once again. It's never promised to you as a lover, as badly as you wish it to be, but it is always, always longed for.

I get it now. I want to breathe wherever he is.

COOLIE-COOLIE

"You are an artist in need of an image / and your dance is forever / unknown by your roots."
– KHAL TORABULLY, *To a Coolie* (translated from the French by Nancy Naomi Carlson)

~

On summer afternoons growing up, Samira, the girl who lived across the street, would scamper over.

We would situate ourselves on the front yard of my house, two cross-legged and knobby-kneed brown girls in shorts. I wanted to be brash and clever and in charge, a rough-and-tumble tomboy out of the pages of a young adult novel. Samira was a sweet-natured playmate, a tolerant audience for my rambling tall tales. She huffed and puffed with me through long stretches of badminton, frisbee, and bike-riding that would take us right to sunset. We cradled our dolls in our laps as grass tickled our legs. Samira would swap her dolls' outfits, brushing their hair into braids and updos. I would pit my dolls against each other, making them slap and kick until their knotty manes had to be smoothed out.

The sky must have threatened to thunderstorm the afternoon Samira and I decided to play inside. She followed me into my house, unbuckling her sandals and placing them neatly on the shoe mat. She crept behind me with soft feet, peering about the hallway, living room, and dining room with her mouth ajar. She seemed to be memorizing the layout to go home and measure how everything lined up.

We ascended the stairs on the way to my bedroom. Samira stopped to study a plaque on the wall. It was heart-shaped and trimmed with lace. It had been moulded out of what seemed to be coarse, glittering grains of white sand. A poem about love was stamped onto its face in curly red calligraphy.

"I really like this," Samira said. She ran a fingertip over the plaque's prickly surface. "It's pretty. I like all the pretty things your mom has around your house."

"Doesn't your mom have stuff like this, too?" I asked.

"Not really. My house is plain."

Pride flushed me through, head to toe.

"Maybe my mom can come to your house and see how pretty our house can look, too," Samira said.

I nodded, eager at the idea of a tour. "My mom can show her our other plaques and stuff. We have nice ones."

In those preteen days, I loved the clusters of trinkets on our coffee and side tables, the plates with birds and bouquets not meant for eating, the doilies and vases and filigree frames. I cherished them almost as much as my own collections of stickers and erasers, my fat case of novelty pencils and pens. They were the things that made our home special, so enviable to style-naive kids like Samira.

By the time I reached my teenage years, my perspective

curdled. I didn't play with Samira or collect cute things anymore. The delights of my mother's decorations evaporated, drying out to bothersome chachkas. I wasn't compelled to show them off to anyone. I rolled my eyes when friends and study partners came over. *Sorry about all this weird stuff; we're going down to the basement anyway.*

On my own time, I stopped looking at them when I didn't have to. They were old-fashioned and cheap to me, altogether too much to keep dust-free.

The house became a busy place fifteen years later. My mother had died. The first visitors who arrived were close family and friends, some driving in from across town, others driving and flying in from hundreds of miles away. People I'd never met before appeared at the front door to keep company, too. Some were second- or third-removed relatives, more recent arrivals to the country. They had learned of her death through speed-of-light information wormholes of our local Guyanese community. My aunts greeted them as long-lost relations, gasping and hugging them. *Watch you now, it's been years since I last saw you. How you arrive all the sudden? How you find your way to this house?*

I escaped the living room, where new visitors congregated with the old, skittering away from its plates and vases and doilies. I enfolded myself into the kitchen bustle of my closest aunts and cousins as they prepared food and steeped tea and washed up.

I plucked a pot spoon resting on the stove. It was made of cream-coloured plastic. Clusters of flowers stretched over its concave and convex, and vines spiralled up the length of its handle.

"Look at this thing," I said to my mother's sister as she dried dishes next to me. "Why did they have to make this thing so *coolie-coolie*?" I brandished the spoon above my head before plunging it into the stew bubbling on the burner.

My aunt pressed her shoulders to her ears and giggled.

I had to gulp the pang that rose in my throat. Only after she was gone did I realize how many of the little girl gestures of my mother's sisters were also my mother's.

She braced against my forearm. "You know what?" she murmured. "Those new people you met out there, they would love that spoon. They would say it's pretty."

I wrinkled my nose. It made her laugh again.

"It's true. That's the way the old people look at things. They see something fancy and they like it. I don't blame them. Nothing wrong with it."

But we know better, I thought.

Many of the family members closest to me had lived outside of Guyana as long as, or even longer than, they had lived in Guyana by that point. Some were like me, having never resided in the West Indies at all. Our longevity in this environment meant we were not nearly as seduced by gaudy things. We were worldly. We were Westerners. We understood what was too *coolie-coolie* to waste our affections on.

A search of the etymology of the word *coolie* coughs up a furball of results. It might derive from Urdu's *ḳulī* or "slave" and Hindi's *qulī* or "hired labourer" and *kolī*—"weaver" and "low-class." It could be related to Ottoman Turkish's *kul* or "servant," Gujarati's tribe descriptor *koḷī*, Bengali's *kuli* and Tamil's *kūli*, both terms for "daily hire," and Kurdish's *koile* and *quli*, words for "slave" and "servant." It likely influenced the development of Mandarin's *kǔlì* or "hard labour." In the sixteenth century, the Portuguese neologized the term. By the 1800s, the word was used across nations to refer to indentured Asian labourers across many colonies.

Coolie-coolie, the term I use to refer to an aesthetic, is even thornier. I'm certain I'm not the only one who uses *coolie-coolie* to describe a style—or a lack of style—but I can't locate a definition of any authority.

I've posed the question to people I know.

It's red and gold and ugly, one person told me.

It's kitschy, cheap knickknacks, another told me.

It's looking really fresh-off-the-boat, someone else explained, *but from India, not the Caribbean. It's putting on Indian garb and looking like you're truly from the motherland.*

It's copying good taste in a way that isn't actually good taste, but it happens so much by so many people that the look becomes something of its own, a completely different kind of taste people go for on its own terms, another said.

I'm not sure any of them would agree with my specific assessments of what *coolie-coolie* is. We all seem to have our own interpretations. In my struggle to explain myself, I'll have to follow the footsteps of Rax King in *Tacky: Love Letters to the Worst Culture We Have to Offer*. I'll have to appoint myself to the seat of the judge hardly capable of articulating my position but insisting I should be trusted to know it when I see it.

Whether object or style, I see the *coolie-coolie* as garish, fussy, and sentimental. It's not kitsch and it is not memorabilia. It is forgettable, with little chance of becoming quirky or whimsical or an iconic kind of fun with time and nostalgia. It won't find a safe landing in pop culture.

I don't target things from India, China, and other motherlands of the racialized indentured as *coolie-coolie*. It's gaudy Western colonial things that bother me, inauthentic, cheap, try-hard imitations of good Western taste.

My first instinct is to say the *coolie-coolie* aesthetic is aggressively Western European, specifically rococo or baroque. London's Victoria and Albert Museum explains the rococo style of eighteenth-century France as "exceptionally ornamental and theatrical." Baroque, too, is said to be elaborate and dramatic, yanking on the senses and pinching the emotions. I read these descriptors as relevant to the *coolie-coolie* of today, but clicking around the internet to pinpoint distinctions between Western art movements rubs everything into a blur. Doesn't some of the *coolie-coolie* have a Renaissance look? Couldn't it fit into classical or romantic traditions as well? Haven't I been confronted by fashions of the seventies, eighties, and nineties and crowned them *coolie-coolie*, too?

I suppose, then, my *coolie-coolie* is less about particular style traditions and more about the reality that there's hardly a rule-breaking bone in its body. Never mind the fact that, in their early days, many art movements were accused of degeneracy, scandalizing and shirking traditions and provoking the ire of elites. What was once considered rule-breaking gets mass-produced in time, its radical edges sanded down. Perfect for the *coolie-coolie* to gobble it up.

The *coolie-coolie* is stiff and formal. It strives so hard to be high-brow that it stumbles over its own feet and tumbles into the lowbrow, partly because it is not truly antique or vintage. That would run the risk of being too real. If anything, it is a deadly serious factory-made knockoff.

Come to think of it, even if the *coolie-coolie* happens to be one-of-a-kind or expensive on paper, even if it is brand name, bespoke fanciness, it's faceless in execution. That's the problem with the pricey *coolie-coolie*: it's never worth the cost. Custom-chiselled marble, hand-laid gold leaf, pearl detailing slatted by special order. It's blank, blinkless wealth. It means little and says even less.

The *coolie-coolie* has a way of being too girly, with frills and airbrushed pinks and lavenders and peaches. It seems to have no clue about earth tones, muted greys, slates, or blacks. Still, I've come across the masculine brand of *coolie-coolie* in chunky timepieces, square-chained necklaces, and overwrought car detailing. It tries to fool you, but the *coolie-coolie* applies to and encompasses all gendered aesthetics.

The *coolie-coolie* is easy and one-dimensional, thrusting no interpretative demand upon the beholder and confronting them with no perplexity or discomfort. Plainly and assuredly, it is what it is: a glazed, gold-rimmed vase with an English country scene of wildflowers and petticoated women. Indeed, the bouquet-adorned pot spoon on the stove. The crystal punch bowl and cups for parties. The filigree frame for a painting over the couch that depicts glossy grapes and ham hocks and pitchers of wine arranged on a table somewhere in rural Europe. It's the engraved silver cake stand and matching cake server, the porcelain figurines of milky gentlewomen and cherubs, the British tea sets and sauce boats, right along with the embellished china cabinet everything gets locked into for most of the year. It's ordered living rooms where you keep the plastic on. It's embroidered cushions and curtains stiffened by underuse. It's over-polished wood.

The *coolie-coolie* object is domineeringly nice. The *coolie-coolie* attitude is an uncritical attraction to nice things you don't understand why you find nice. It's what you default to until you know better and perhaps can afford better, until you realize you should put your resources into worthier things. More sophisticated things. Cooler things. Modernist things with layers of meaning and straight lines and slick materials, no finicky crests and nooks to dust.

Our aesthetic preferences, whether kitsch or avant-garde, whether widely shared or perspective-shaking, reveal more about our own motivations and vulnerabilities than the art or object in question. In *Status and Culture: How Our Desire for Social Rank Creates Taste, Identity, Art, Fashion, and Constant Change*, W. David Marx unveils the relationship between who we think we are, who we want to be, and how we use style sensibilities to get there. Deny it though we do, we pursue higher status because status determines our quality of life. We adopt and adapt cultural symbols—fashion and art and consumer goods—to solidify our ranking and squeeze our way up to higher tiers, internalizing and rationalizing all the while as if our tastes and notions of ourselves could ever truly be our own.

Far from victims, even the most rebellious and countercultural of us participates in this self-forming and other-appraising. We can't help it. Culture is "a fundamentally communicative activity," Marx says, "and everything we do becomes a symbol of our social position."

My hazy, assumptive, know-it-when-I-see-it definition of the *coolie-coolie* is transparent, easily disrobing my own snobberies and strivings. Why should the supposed tastelessness I label *coolie-coolie* be named *coolie-coolie* per se? Surely many people across many communities are attracted to these aesthetics. It's likely that I despise the *coolie-coolie* as *coolie-coolie* for simple fear of judgment. I worry about what being seen as tasteless leads to for people like me. As Marx explains, so much of our status is based on immutable characteristics and cues. People who are discriminated against in one way or another have to work harder to achieve what would be considered merely normal status.

I suppose I reject what I call the *coolie-coolie* because I can't imagine ancestors of the indentured being afforded room for poor style. We are not a zany grandparent or eccentric neighbour, a weekend artist or offbeat love interest. I'm not sure how many racialized manic pixie dream girls are allowed to live at any one time, period. Harmless and endearing and innately worthy, these so-styleless-they're-stylish personas seem the reserve of white people.

But the truth is that I don't imagine indentured descendants get credit for having good style sensibilities when they indeed have them. How can you be known for great taste when you're hardly known to exist in the first place?

Public figures in the West with indentured ancestries are usually referred to in a manner that skids over that indentureship entirely. Iconic Guyanese actors Anthony Chinn and Shakira Caine are simply known as East and South Asian. Indentured backgrounds of musicians and actors like Nicki Minaj, Melanie Fiona, Foxy Brown, and Tatyana Ali barely register in public. Even V.S. Naipaul, one of the most famous Caribbean writers and 2001 winner of the Nobel Prize in Literature, is often thinly referred to as an Indo-Trinidadian and Anglo-Indian. What his indentured ancestry means to his body of work, pooling around and dripping through his every word as it does, is far less spoken to.

I started writing my first novel when I was twenty-four years old, inspired by a plunge into the works of postcolonial writers like Edwidge Danticat, Chinua Achebe, Shani Mootoo, Austin Clarke, Tessa McWatt, and Dionne Brand. Their flare and lyricality, their wry humour and critical eyes, easily seduced me. Racialized postcolonial writers were the most sophisticated people in the world to me. I wanted to think and write like them. I wanted to be one of them.

I'd never lived in the Caribbean, and I'd hardly written fiction in my life. But I'd take what I'd read in those gorgeous, steel-tongued books, I'd take stories repeated by my family of life in the West Indies, and I'd write my own novel about a duelling sister and brother in a fictionalized, enchanted Guyana.

When I began, rising early to type for an hour or two before commuting to work, I had only the vaguest idea of publishing and half-hearted motivation to pursue a contract. By the time I signed a book deal a few years later, my aspirations had sharpened. I pined to publish a novel with a cover crafted by no one less than Chip Kidd.

I watched documentaries that chronicled Kidd's modernist design for Alfred A. Knopf in New York City. They praised his prolificness, the ways he influenced book covers across the world. Publishers and advertisers everywhere imitated him. Writers itched to work with him.

To me, the man was effortlessly cool. As soon as it was released, I hurried to the store to purchase Chip Kidd's first anthology of book designs. I studied its thick-stock, eye-popping pages. *The Remains of the Day. The Secret History. Barney's Version. My Name Is Red. The Wind-Up Bird Chronicle.* Kidd's savvy combination of visual mystery and piercing clarity was imprinted onto so many of the stories I love.

He reads every book he designs. He never underestimates the reader. He applies best practices of marketing to intrigue potential buyers. He is balanced, never too obvious or too obscure. Celebrity writers express gratitude for the graphic power he paints onto their words. *You get it, Kidd,* they say, *you really and truly get it.*

I couldn't have seriously expected my newbie novel to be graced by a Kidd cover, but I was getting published by the Canadian counterpart of the U.S. company he worked for. I also had the fortune of being introduced to him at a Toronto book event. I had to camouflage my trembling lips as I sipped wine, forcing my eyes to fixate on something other than his signature circle-frame spectacles. He was exactly as I had imagined: an unbothered New Yorker, chatty and witty and unpretentious.

I stood shakily at his elbow, incapable of making small talk. I was so close to his design orbit that it hurt. *You get it, Kidd,* I wanted to quip as if I were one of his lucky American East Coast writers, *you really and truly get it.*

I didn't attempt it. I slunk into the chattering crowd without saying goodbye.

When it was time to design the jacket of my novel, my publisher plunged into a messy internal debate. The team grappled with mockups, too many combinations of palm trees, dirt roads, wistful faces, and cutouts of children and women. They went back and forth about it for weeks.

I was privy to just a snapshot of what was going on. I had my own unvoiced and unvoiceable apprehensions to manage, my own anxieties over a book cover that might turn out too representational, too on the nose, too decorative and curly-fonted. I was worried my jacket might turn out too *coolie-coolie*. I knew I wouldn't survive such a thing.

I had insisted on writing the novel the way I thought an authentic postcolonial writer would, peppering chapters with dialect many readers would not be familiar with and some might find a challenge to follow. I considered myself groundbreaking for pushing it in a story published by a mainstream company.

Still, my righteous literary swagger hit its limit in graphic design.

The jacket of my hardcover wasn't a Kidd, but the publisher did arrive at a purple-blue design that was modern and striking. Not *coolie-coolie*. I sighed with relief when I opened the file. Not *coolie-coolie* in the slightest.

The paperback design that landed in my inbox months later I considered even more Kiddesque than the hardcover had been. It depicted a girl in a sundress pacing a thicket, a plucked bouquet in her hands, her face partly stamped by an embossed circle with the book's title. It, too, was beautiful, save for one problem.

The girl was white. Not a titch too fair-skinned for an equatorial lifestyle. A melaninless organism that couldn't tolerate sun.

Her materialization on my screen pitched me into distress. For a story largely situated in the Caribbean, not a single white character to point to, I didn't know what a reader would do with my cover girl.

They'll call it false advertising. They'll call me a sellout, a poser, a fool.

I called my agent in a panic. She agreed with my assessment and relayed the message to the publisher. The publisher responded by Photoshopping the girl's skin. They placed her in a digital pan, twisted the dial, and roasted her in time for the paperback's release. The publisher said it was the only option at that point. I didn't have the wherewithal or courage to argue with anyone about it.

When I entered a local bookstore a few months later to find my novel on the Summer Reads table, I leaned back and squinted. *To the naked eye, I suppose she looks like she was brown all along.*

White girl, white dress, white flowers, white skin spray-tanned by pixels. I knew the truth. I couldn't put my eye on the cover without zeroing in on the dermis broiled to brownface. Beyond the fact of its publication, the sales were a disappointment.

It is a lovely jacket design; I still believe that. But I avoid looking at my brown-skinned white girl to this day.

Hyper-orientation to the modern aesthetics of Chip Kidd did not save me from publishing troubles. But the experience helped me understand that my knee-jerk avoidance of the *coolie-coolie* is not only haughty and unfair, it's also distracting. I was so caught in it that I didn't properly anticipate the biases of publishing: a history of too-white author lists and tokenization of racialized authors, an underdeveloped audience for works written by and about racialized people, weak marketing investments in racialized writers as worth a read. A recent push by readers and publishers to diversify the makeup and products of the industry, progress that is already shrinking back after a few short years. The publication of more Black, Indigenous, and racialized writers only after the industry has been drained of so much of its legacy prestige, reliable revenue, choices in publishing houses, and hope of offering a living wage. Too many last-minute opportunities in the industry's decline, too many last-ditch efforts. A resulting hesitation to sell summer reads with real brown girls on their covers. A shrivelled appetite for taking real and sustained racial risks.

Running from the *coolie-coolie*, from whatever you worry makes you seem as if you're innately tasteless, is simply not the biggest problem for a racialized writer to get snagged on today.

With its metal and leather, circles and squares and flat facades, the Bauhaus aesthetic seemed the polar opposite of *coolie-coolie* to my early-twenties eyes. I went for the furniture, clothes, and decor that emulated it. I saw it as cosmopolitan, timeless, useful, and refreshingly unfussy. Above reproach.

A key driver of modernist design, the Bauhaus was founded in 1919 as a German school and think-tank to promote new ways of living and learning. It aspired to bring art and design under a unified theory, prioritizing functionality and mass production over aesthetics. The Bauhaus's embrace of the concept of a "universal mankind" scrubbed its products, architecture, and artworks clean, leaving behind the basics: angularity, geometry, primary colours. It claimed nothingness and everything-ness, all at once.

The principles and ambitions of the Bauhaus were so expansive and radical that the Nazis were threatened. They pressured the school into its 1933 closure and prodded its artists and designers into exile. This didn't diminish the movement's prolific spirit. Reinterpretations of the Bauhaus sparked across Britain, the United States, India, Israel, Mexico, and the Soviet Union in the coming decades.

"The Bauhaus's 'universal man' for whom they were designing was the working white man," Elizabeth (Dori) Tunstall says in *Decolonizing Design: A Cultural Justice Guidebook.* On the heels of World War I, the Bauhaus "sought to protect his war-traumatized body and spirit through the economizing of space and the meaningfulness of satisfactory and productive work. Design practices that draw their origin stories from the modernist project thus perpetuate the bias of the supremacy of white bodies and cultural values." The Bauhaus's claim to singular humanity and form took the myth of the Anglo-Saxon and whiteness, maleness, and other kinds of dominance for granted.

Beyond that, admirable aspirations of Bauhaus innovators have been misread, diluted, scrubbed off. Nikil Saval of the *New York Times Style Magazine* says that over the years the movement has weakened into "a way to sell gift-shop-ready objects and promote cultural tourism instead of using design to improve the lives of working-class people." Searching for "authentic Bauhaus lamp" on the internet brings up an array of squat light-pieces priced at hundreds of U.S. dollars each. No wonder dissenting designers, artists, and architects criticize and mourn what they view as an over-reverence for the Bauhaus more than a century after the school was founded.

Five decades back from the beginnings of the Bauhaus, an "indentureship aesthetic" of sorts can be located, crafted not by indentured people or communities themselves but by colonial photographers and printers. At that time, dozens of world fairs across France, the United Kingdom, Australia, Italy, Germany, and more showcased the spoils of empire and the promise of societal advancement. More and more Europeans could afford to buy into a growing tourism industry. And images of racialized people in the colonies were being traded en masse.

Between the late 1800s and World War I, photography-based postcards sold the allure of colonial conquest to everyday Westerners. Producers like Raphael Tuck & Sons of Britain, Purger & Co. of Germany, Neurdein Frères of France, and Curt Teich & Company of the United States printed highly collectible and tradable postcard sets. They became a craze as millions were circulated around Europe and North America every year, partly because they were affordable, partly because postal services were more cost-effective and interconnected than ever. Raphael Tuck & Sons alone printed thousands upon thousands of postcards for the public to exchange. A partial repository of their surviving sets features over 136,000 unique designs.

Examining Dutch-produced postcards of Java, Sophie Junge says that, even as the banality of these images in this so-called golden age of postcards means many historians overlook them, they fulfilled a desire amongst Europeans to know the world and share it with their family and friends. Postcards "established, visualised, and catalysed colonialism through their use of an international visual language."

The Orientalism of British-made picture postcards clasped hands with the public's widespread Egyptomania, fascination with Biblical history, and keenness for foreign antiquities. Raphael Tuck & Sons' "Wide Wide World" postcard series includes hundreds of images of people and locales in Egypt, India, Morocco, South Africa, Australia, and Jamaica. Their "Rise of Our Empire beyond the Seas" series includes pictures captioned "our first footing in Canada," "our first footing in the Bermudas," "British seizure of Jamaica," and "the birth of our Indian Empire."

Postcards of indentured Chinese workers in early-twentieth-century South African gold mines offer idyllic worksite scenes: workers recovering in hospital beds, workers resting in barracks, workers carrying sacks and picks, workers at crisp attention in a police drill. One photo features erect and crouching Black workers in sarongs on the left, erect and crouching Chinese workers in *coolie* garb on the right, and a suited, seated white man at the centre, one leg crossed over the other. "On the Rand," the caption reads: "White, Black and Yellow."

Yet another postcard features a worker in a *coolie* coat. The label reads "John Chinaman," a stock name used to represent Chinese men and populations across the colonies in mainstream literature, news, and cartoons. This man's face is smooth, youthful, and high-cheekboned. He sits at a three-quarter angle, his eyes focused off camera, his mouth unsmiling. His cue is braided and snaked over a shoulder.

Researcher T. Tu Huynh says these postcards portrayed the British as moral and tolerant employers. They affirmed the civility of South Africa's white population as a paternalistic force. They offered "an alternative to abolitionism, positioning the familiar civilizing discourse as part of British imperial identity."

Postcards present Chinese workers in activities meant to suggest fair treatment, especially in contrast to labourers who had been enslaved. They are working diligently and being nursed to health, bathing and cooking and drinking tea, even enjoying local productions of Chinese operas in their barracks. The images evoke benevolent white rule and by nature take issue with critics calling indentureship a form of replacement slavery. At the same time, Huynh says the postcards shaped imaginations of white South Africans and British beholders, assuring them of a new racial order in the colony.

Photography of the Caribbean of the late 1800s was wrapped up with campaigns of colonial administrators, white elites, and American and British hoteliers marketing West Indian colonies for tourism. Their efforts began in Jamaica and the Bahamas and extended to other destinations. They aimed to counter the Western public's fear of the tropics as sites of risk and disease. Their postcards featured fantastical flora and fauna, majestic vistas and waterfalls, colonial buildings erected amongst the palm trees, and "picturesque natives," Africans and Indians posed in ethnic dress or occupied by field, domestic, and army work. Disciplined, orderly, well ruled. Nothing to be anxious about.

To me, the most fascinating images of this golden age are the *coolie* belles of Jamaica, Trinidad, Suriname, and Guyana, captured on film by local studios operated by European men. They photographed indentured Indian women and girls on indoor sets and outside in fields, the cane leaves billowing behind them.

The women and girls are nameless, likely paid for their modelling. Some posed on their own, some hoisted young children on their hips, and some were captured in pairs, clasping one another's hands. Many belles stare directly at the lens. Their forthrightness, combined with bare feet, bare arms, and loose hair spilling from head coverings, contrasts with the demure poses of white women of the same Victorian era.

Most belles dressed in lehenga cholis and donned silver and gold earrings, nose and toe rings, and cuffs, bangles, and necklaces. The jewellery was likely their life's wealth. The photographic aesthetic is reminiscent of that of "nautch girls," adorned Hindu dancers who were considered temptresses by white travellers to India. The complex history of nautch girls dates to pre-colonial India, to at least the seventh century. They were once admired for their dancing, intelligence, and allure. By the colonial era, the figure of the nautch girl had compressed to vice, in no small part due to how British colonists coveted them as mistresses and stereotyped them as sexual threats.

When nautch girls were remade in the lens of whiteness, they lost their social footing. *Coolie* belles were constructed as white men's fantasies, too, frozen as such in film. But theories about the meaning and purpose of these photographs are conflicted. On the one hand, they appear to signify a fabricated story of wealth and well-being amongst indentured women, assurance to Europeans about the rightness of the racialized indentureship model on the whole. They suggest the *coolie* belle's exotic sexual availability as much as they relegate her to a state of forever otherness as an imported labourer.

On the other hand, much of the jewellery *coolie* belles wore in their photoshoots had been smelted from the coins they were paid for their labour. Displaying it might have been a way to show off their financial independence. Instead of, or in addition to, representing eternal otherness, their adornments might have signified racialized indentured women's new brand of Caribbeanness. Working in the colonies, these women had an opportunity to amass their own fortunes, regardless of the risks. Having her own money may have meant the belle could make more of her own choices.

The indentured population transported to the West Indies included fewer women than men, but women are well represented in photography of the era. Their images carried hefty symbolic weight for the region and the empire.

That's hardly a surprise. Women are always loaded by meanings wherever and whenever they live. Their bodies—and what their bodies signify—are sites for individual and social conflict and contestation, accusation and aspiration. I suppose there's rarely a moment when women don't serve as stand-ins for anxieties and passions that have little to do with who they are and what they want themselves. There's rarely a time they have a meaningful say in the process.

The divergent readings *coolie* belle photographs elicit can explain, at least in part, the creative sway they have over their ancestors. In his *Cane Portraiture* series, Andil Gosine's shoots reimagine the belle portraits, amplifying women's agency in negotiating the ways they're represented. Renluka Maharaj embellishes the belles in her *Pelting Mangoes* series. She takes the women and girls framed in the lens of French photographer Félix Morin at his Port of Spain studio in the 1880s and blows them up, adorning them with neon pops of colour, with rhinestones and glitter, foregrounding them over psychedelic patterns. Kelly Sinnapah Mary's paintings reflect a belle quality, sometimes with flora and fauna of the backdrop growing in the skin of the girl in the foreground, sometimes with coral of the crossed ocean protruding right through. In *Reclaimed: Indo-Caribbean HerStories*, Heidi McKenzie transfers belle postcards onto hand-rolled ceramic and fuses them in wooden frames to catch light. Ceramic enables her to magnify and reshape belle jewellery, too. She fashions it into oversized earthy crescents and disks.

Whether in original portrait or artistically refashioned image, the *coolie* belle doesn't stand a chance of striking my impudent eye as too *coolie-coolie,* not in the slightest. The self-possession and defiance etched onto her face precludes any trace of inauthenticity or sentimentality, even when the staging is obvious, even when more than one belle wears the same veil and drapery or the same model is attributed to multiple colonies across different batches of postcard prints.

For me, truth lives in the way the belle glares at the lens, in the blaze of her pupils. Even when her eyes fix someplace beyond the camera, she still punctures the lens. It's the way she seems to refuse to smile, her lips and face flat. She seems so unimpressed by it all.

It's the shape of her smile when she does decide to smile, too. She doesn't seem to do it for me or the photographer. Her lips curl for something or someone unspoken. I can tell she won't waste her time telling me who or what it is. That's her prerogative. I don't deserve to know. I haven't earned her trust.

Coolie belles keep their own secrets, their own memories, their own lives and loves. That aspect of their portraits enchants me. What are they thinking about? What leads them to dress and pose for the camera in the first place? Are they coerced or compelled, or is their experience some muddy mix of the two? Do they screw in the backs of their earrings and feed their wrists through bangles with any satisfaction? Are they delighted by the attention, by the heft of the metal on their collarbones, all that precious currency they worked for? It is their pleasure I wish I could know more about.

Of course the photographs were contrived to stoke fervour, entice travellers, and titillate onlookers in the most predictable white-focused, male-centric ways. But there's an underappreciated panorama to turn to behind our heads in the presence of any work of art, no matter how gauche. Women and girls modelling as *coolie* belles don't appear contrived at all. They don't cower in place, and the narrow prism of white colonists isn't the only scope through which to view them. There's something undeniably and wildly vocal about their portraits.

I'm drawn to the belles for other reasons too. In their expressions, I catch the glimmer of so many women and girls I love, my cousins and aunties, my cousin's nieces, my dear friends and their daughters. They are so familiar, so familial.

As much as I love the belles, as much as I can't help but press close to the screen and inspect every crinkle of fabric, every wavy lock, every ring and bead and bangle, there are also moments I can't handle them. Sometimes I have to look away because of that old pang, that sneaky clench of the belly. I fool myself into thinking I've outgrown it, but I probably never will. I suppose I don't want to when I consider what outgrowing it means.

Well, Mom, watch you now, how you arrive all the sudden? How you find your way to this pretty girl's glinting eye?

I've interrogated and debunked it, dragged it from my unconscious into frigid light, but loathing of the *coolie-coolie* still surges as my visceral reaction. It has absorbed into my skin, seeping into my bones, implanting itself into the marrow. It has fused with me on a molecular level.

"Isn't that just a beautiful pair of pants?" a woman I knew told me the first time I wore wide-legged rayon slacks. The fabric was a lattice of blue, white, and gold flowers.

"Oh," I answered, glancing down at my legs. "Thank you."

"What is it that you people call them again?"

They'd been purchased at a fast fashion store. I'd seen countless women wearing the same trendy, breezy look over the past few months. By the time I'd gotten to it, people were already moving on to the next season's repertoire.

I jerked my leg in a little kick. "I'm not sure what they call them—palazzo, I think? Yes, that's right. Palazzo pants."

She shook her head. "But what do they call them where you come from?"

We had known each other for years. I assumed she knew plenty about me and my family, but she behaved as if we had just met. "I don't think people wear pants like this in Guyana," I said. "I mean, they're not known for it or anything. I got these at the mall."

She crouched and pinched some of the palazzo material between her fingers. She pulled it from my leg as if testing out its stretch. "No, no, you people wear these pants. I see it everywhere. It's part of your culture. You wear them all the time. They're just like this, fancy-dancy, lots of patterns and colours and things."

My ears grew warm. *Oh no, these pants don't look right on me.*

I was immediately slapped by guilt at my own reaction. I wished I could answer her presumptuousness about my clothes and culture with a winsome rebuttal, but I was too preoccupied to try. *She thinks my pants look too* coolie-coolie *on me.*

I don't remember wearing those palazzos again.

Why in the world did I pick this skirt, of all things? came the inner rebuke as I stood at the bus stop in the warm summer breeze. I inhaled the smell of asphalt and gazed at my ankle-brushing wrap, the flutter of its brown and aqua swirls. It's too *coolie-coolie* to wear outside.

My lipstick's too dark, I'd scold myself one day. *My lipstick's too bright*, I'd scold myself the next. *Why do I always do this? Why do I always have to wear makeup that looks so* coolie-coolie *on my face?*

Maybe I shouldn't leave my hair curly today. Or straighten it. Maybe I shouldn't dye it either. Maybe I need to give away this blouse, once and for all. Maybe this purse looks ridiculous on me. Maybe this jacket, too. Maybe none of it is for me. Maybe it's all too coolie-coolie.

This is the consequence of such an unbridled eye for the *coolie-coolie*. It starts out innocently, souring you on little things that don't make much of a dent, maybe a teacup here or soap dish there. But those things multiply, three, four, and five times over, until you've amassed an army of things you can't let yourself like.

Stray objects spiral into ecosystems. You can't turn the tap to cut it off. The loathing expands, doubling and tripling from its original size, sprouting its own sentient and sinister brain, blobbing into an ooze. It takes you over, suffocating everything you might have found lovely or charming, everything you might have derived some small joy from. In the end, anxiety over the *coolie-coolie* stifles you.

Mauritian poet, essayist, film director, and semiologist Khal Torabully coined the notion of "Coolitude." It is a reclamation of a slur, and, more significantly, a framework to voice the under-voiced perspectives, experiences, and self-concepts of indentured peoples. Inspired by Paulette and Jeanne Nardal, Aimé Césaire, and other celebrated francophone theorists and writers of the Négritude movement launched in the 1930s, Torabully defines and explores Coolitude not through stoic prose or academic analysis but through extravagant verse. His 1992 work *Cale d'Étoiles*—in English, *Cargo Hold of Stars*—is a series of stanzas as playful as they are painful, a braiding of Mauritian Creole and Asian and European languages interspersed by swaths of empty space.

Is this poetic Coolitude space supposed to represent lostness and alienation, a woeful distance that can never be closed again? Or is it supposed to serve as room for imagination? A new vista that will not and does not mean to disappear?

Perhaps it's both. The *coolie* as a person and role and status is a dynamic creation of the colonized and colonizer alike. No wonder that the voicing of the *coolie,* in all the ways that voicing can happen, is a creation too. An artistry lived and breathed, just as it is known and forgotten and revived and envisioned again.

Define me please: / what's a Coolie? Torabully asks. But his poetry won't wait for the answer to emerge from somewhere else.

If you recognize me, please
call me proxy slave,
strawman or stand-in,
kapok from fields or ocean vertebrae.
But know that my sabre of blood
has uprooted me to the core.

This question of self-definition is the same one everybody clamours to answer. Agony comes from not having the space to do so ourselves. From not being attended to in that space, even when we do.

I doubt I'm the only one who gets uneasy about the *coolie-coolie* aesthetic. But I can't estimate how common my aversions are. All I can do is keep trying to put a finger on what the *coolie-coolie* means to me. That task is difficult enough.

Maybe sketching the parameters of the *coolie-coolie* isn't a wise project, anyway. I know I'm bothered by my idea of the *coolie-coolie* simply because I'm obsessed with white people, fretful about the way I think they look at me. I assume they can recognize tasteless versions of Western colonial aesthetics more than they recognize the tastelessness of any other tradition. I twitch at the notion that they might see us as behind the times or locked out of contemporary style or uninterested in trends. I cringe at the possibility that we might get dismissed as styleless, as holding no valid point of view about great art, great clothes, and great products to buy. As having no valid point of view about ourselves.

We're more than you think we are, I want them to understand. *We're artists and writers. We're creators and makers and musicians. We have talents and vision. We have the capacity to influence, to change the world, to make our mark. You just refuse to notice.*

It seems I can't stand the thought of white people assuming we don't know what's what. I can't stand the thought that we might not have the cultural sway to be taken seriously when we do tell them what's what.

This is not primarily a matter of materialism. I just don't want to be uncool. That's what all this perturbation is about. I worry that associating myself with the *coolie-coolie* will cause white people to mistake me as guileless. I worry they'll presuppose I can't spar with them on their own terms or stand up to them when it comes to what's good, that they'll politely underestimate and rob me of the chance to prove them wrong. *I'm not fresh-off-the-boat. I know the same cultural references you know. I watched the same movies as you, read the same books as you, listened to the same songs as you. I like the things you like. I was born here too.*

I worry they'll think I'm content to be treated as a foreigner, as a lesser and losing player in the roulette of colonialism and consumption.

This fear is rooted in time and place, my most formative, impressionable years. I remember the times I acted as if I liked sports as a kid. I'd pretend to know things about cars and music and TV shows I didn't; I'd whine for toys and clothes and food that carried little true appeal to me. What a harebrained and worn-out story, my racialized anguish over white people's acceptance and assessments of my worth. How mortifying to drag any of this into adulthood, but here we are.

I do know better than I did back then. I know nothing can shield me from stigma and underestimation and stereotyping. Primping and preening can't gift me the power to render myself visible to anyone who wants to treat me as invisible. But reflexes aren't grounded in logic. I still nurse an emotional affinity for white modern aesthetics. I've brainwashed myself to it, used it to construct a fortification around me, its foundations dug miles deep. Proximity to whiteness and association with refinement and finesse—with the allure of wealth, really—feels prudent, even though I know it's not. As I stand alone in the centre, flanked by bricks and fighting to breathe, it's still what I want.

Perhaps my arrogance toward the *coolie-coolie* is simply that: a longing to collapse into the arms of whiteness. Of course, these arms are deceptive. They are not warm for the racialized, no matter how impeccable your taste may be. Folding yourself into them is not a surety of any sort of safety, let alone the experience of acceptance or visibility or love.

Of my childhood collections, the erasers were my favourite. They looked like food and fruits and flowers, cars and animals, letters and numbers. Some were perfumed, smelling of bubble gum, chocolate, strawberry, watermelon, and grape. I even had a little fast food meal—a hamburger, box of fries, and milkshake I could balance on a tiny plastic tray.

My erasers were icons. To a sheltered kid like me, they represented the delights of the world in miniature, on a clutchable scale. I wanted all the shapes and scents and colours for myself the way I wanted to grow up to have everything I imagined a happy person could have for themselves.

I kept my erasers pristine, never daring to use them as they were intended. I spent hours handling them in a process more forensic, more sensual, than typical play. I turned them about, squeezed and sniffed them, balanced them on my palms to compare their weights. I inspected every ridge and bump with my fingertip. I hugged them to my chest. I sorted them into piles by size, colour, and type. One by one, I gathered them into a box only to dump them back onto the floor and sift through them again.

At times, my mouth would water during my eraser inspection marathons. They seemed to feed some kind of an appetite. They were just so perfect and adorable that they appeared nearly edible. I might have been embarrassed to admit I wanted to consume them, had I been fully conscious of the desire.

Firmly in my forties, I'm gravitating back to this childhood affinity for the cute in the form of polymer clay art, handcrafting micro sushi sets and plates of curry and roti and gourmet desserts, complete with piping, rosettes, icing sugar, and a little bite or cut-out slice. I shape and stack the colours, brush on pastel shading, cover them with liquid clay for sauce and glaze, bake them in my toaster oven, and display the finished products on a stand. More often than making them myself, I watch how-to videos zoomed in on the formation of mini meals and china sets to serve them on, the construction of little kitchens and noodle shops and book nooks and boutiques painted and glued by disembodied hands.

This is no monumental reunion with the *coolie-coolie*. But it's my way of cultivating lost appreciation for darling, unselfconscious things. It's my way of reorienting myself to mouth-watering pleasures. Miniature-making is fun and leads to things that are frou-frou and functionless. It's everything but the Bauhaus, and it is pure gratification.

I imagine many communities have their own *coolie-coolie* aesthetics to disassociate themselves from. For those of us burdened by years of racialization in white-dominant places, I wonder if our versions necessarily include the dread of being cast as uncouth other, as a smileless, silent John Chinaman.

If that is the case, I don't believe otherness in and of itself is the concern. Our issue is that otherness equals voicelessness. And voiceless people are immediately recast as creatures pleased to remain unheard. Voicelessness means people put words in your mouth for the rest of your natural life. How do you manage to get your own words in edgewise?

I don't mean to suggest modern aesthetics are wrong. But I fell for them for the wrong reasons. I wanted to escape my poor othered phantom, a doppelgänger that haunts my mind, even now. She is the rejected woman I imagine I would've been had I allowed the *coolie-coolie* to remain in my life. I thought avoiding her was the smart thing to do, but it had an alienating effect. It twinned and cleaved me, setting me out on the road as a fugitive against myself.

That you can't run away from yourself is a well-worn fact. Much better to let yourself be whole. Much better to rest as one.

I'm not sure I'll ever be able to fully embrace the *coolie-coolie*, and I'm giving myself a break about that. I'm fine with not stamping out my dream of penning a book worthy of a genuine Chip Kidd cover. Maybe the fantasy is more motivating than the reality, anyway. I don't let myself feel like a sellout for admiring an overpriced sack dress with pockets or entertaining a minimalist grey couch for the living room. I just have so many more resources than I've ever had to unmask the delusion that chasing whiteness will rescue me from rejection and shame. I have the poetics of Khal Torabully, all the groundbreaking artists connected to the Coolitude movement, all the artists and thinkers who came before and during and after. I've read more visionary postcolonial writers and watched and listened to more anti-racist filmmakers and musicians around the world who question white supremacy and affirm the art and lives of minoritized people in ways I could never achieve on my own. These brave and beautiful works, every one of them capable of quickening my pulse, I treat as my treasure trove.

And heaven knows I've tried running after whiteness enough, I've failed enough times to understand that grasping at it won't save me from the mortal pain we all carry when we swaddle hearts unknown in our breasts.

More than being seen and listened to, even more than being included and reflected, I believe our hearts badly want to be known. This is why representation seems to matter so much to us. It is a step toward knownness. Too often, it is mistaken for it.

Representation will never be enough. Knownness is what it boils down to in the end, nothing less. A familiar and wrenching human ache.

At least now I have the *coolie* belles. I search them out when I need a reminder, and I still so often need one. They defy me, split open every conceit I harbour with their snarky smiles and narrowed eyes. They glower at my foolishness, perceptive cousin-auntie-friend-ancestors that they are. Astute mothers that they are.

What you want with this Chip Kidd, pickney? they ask, jewellery jingling as they giggle at me and know me for who I am. Compelling me to know them.

COUSIN LOVE

I wake at the sound of my mother's voice. I'm shivering. My lungs feel heavy. The sky beyond the curtains is dark. Sleep tugs at my eyelids and weighs my limbs until I remember why I need to get out of bed.

We are driving from Toronto to the United States today. My mother, father, sister, and I will spend eleven hours in a sedan, interrupted by breaks to refill gas, eat lunch, and go to the bathroom. Excitement sucks the tiredness out of my body. My skin still hot from the blankets, I skip from room to room to change out of pyjamas and into the outfit I laid out last night, check the duffle bag I packed over the last few days, and make last-minute decisions on what travel games and books I want to take with me into the car.

It's summertime. The air warms with the rising sun as we set out on the road. Suburban streets turn into highways. The sky glows, red to yellow to blue, and the sights racing past my window become unfamiliar: tree-carpeted hills and valleys, rivers and bridges and tunnels. My father drives and chews gum. My mother pours cups of tea from a thermos for me and my sister to sip in the back seat.

Each time we make this journey, it feels impossibly long. I'm impatient to see my three cousins and my aunt and uncle at their house in Maryland. We make the drive a few times a year, during summer and March and Christmas holidays. The summer trips are the most memorable. We pack adventures into them, our cousins right alongside us. We go around to the other extended family in the Washington, D.C., area. We visit the Smithsonian museums and Capitol Hill, outlet malls and discount movie theaters. We make day trips to national parks and spend weekends in Ocean City. Our summertime Maryland holidays feel as if they stretch on for weeks and weeks, wrapped in heat and sun. In truth, they last for only one or two at a time.

I look up to my three closest American cousins more than anyone else. Karl is the eldest, nearest to my mother's heart. He is the first-born of her and her siblings' children. Allie is the middle child, the same age as my older sister. The youngest of the five of us is Travis, a precocious little boy eager to tag along. These cousins have cassettes and shoes and toys and clothes I want. They have more daytime television options and their malls have better sales. They have ice cream trucks that crawl down their street every afternoon to sell candies my sister and I can't seem to find where we live: Lemonheads, Red Hots, Push Pops, candy cigarettes. Even the neighbourhood bullies who sometimes catch us off guard while we're playing outside are scowling, foul-mouthed opponents more worthy of our anxieties than the boring bullies at my school.

These are the coolest of my cousins, and they seem to know it. They boast about their classes and friends, the outings they get to go on and know we could never match. But they don't hoard it from us. They regale us with the tale of the Chinese New Year festival they attended, chattering about the food and dancing and fireworks. Travis hoists a blanket over his head and shows us a bobbing Lion Dance. Allie introduces us to the 808-fuelled *Supersonic* by girl hip-hop band J.J. Fad, standing on her mattress with a Miss Piggy puppet over her hand that raps and hair-flips along to the track. Karl shows off the kung-fu moves he learned at his dojo, kicking and striking the air in uniform. *Tiger Claw! Whooping Crane! Earclap!* My American cousins make our summers an exposure.

We reach our twenties. With university and jobs and new relationships and families, our regular trips to the U.S. are over. By then, my mother is too ill to travel. That's when my aunt and uncle make regular trips from Maryland to our home, setting out nearly every Friday to reach us on Saturday, cooking and talking and relieving us of some of our caregiving until Sunday, until their eleven-hour journey back over the Peace Bridge and through New York State and Pennsylvania. My American cousins sometimes accompany them, helping my aunt and uncle drive and manage our house for the weekend.

It's been years since I moved out of my childhood home to take up residence in my own place. Still, I sometimes wake from the haze of a Saturday morning dream with the voices of my American cousins and aunt and uncle mumbling at the edges of my consciousness, as if they were right there, downstairs in the kitchen, boiling tea and frying saltfish and tomatoes for breakfast.

My cousins mean so much to me that I can't envision what I would be without them. I'm confused by the fact that some don't share a passion for cousinhood. I'm disturbed by the reality that some interpret cousin relationships in a different light entirely. A quick internet query demonstrates it: besides technical explanations of firsts and seconds and thirds removed to endless degrees, much of the search results about cousins are preoccupied with marriage and procreation.

I suppose it's a reminder that kissing cousins were once normal everywhere, including in the U.S., Canada, and Europe. For ruling families, stockpiling wealth and power has meant long traditions of insular marriage, including unions between cousins and between other relatives. The reigning House of Windsor, known for consanguinity as much as other royal families, is head of state for fifteen countries and several dependencies and territories. They have amassed untold billions' worth of land, real estate, art, and valuables, and they will continue to do so as they're favoured by lawmakers and largely tax-exempt. Cousin romance has been an arrow in their financial planning quiver over the years.

Marriage between cousins only started falling out of favour in the West in the latter half of the nineteenth century, as eugenic concerns mingled with political and economic reorganization, changing norms, and new methods of finding non-related spouses, such as railways to whisk suitors from other regions to you. By the mid-twentieth century, cousin marriages were considered a practice of the world's "primitive peoples" and mostly irrelevant to the Western world. Marriages between second cousins or closer relatives are rare in the West now, but consanguineous marriages represent up to one third of marriages across North Africa, the Middle East, and West Asia.

Pakistan has the highest rate of consanguinity, with half the population marrying a first or second cousin, strengthening inter-family and group ties and better ensuring compatibility, security, and familiarity.

The moral consensus about romancing your cousin is a near-universal positive: cousin marriages are permitted or prescribed across most religious and faith groups. These days, science won't beg to differ. Genetic risks for children born of first cousins are only slightly higher than those of non-cousin offspring. It seems hardly worth the hassle of testing, and any public policy angst over it would be overblown. Medical journals seem to have taken a harm reduction turn about it, treating consanguinity not unlike substance use or smoking or sexually transmitted infections. Cousin–cousin conception is something to be *managed*. It's all about non-judgmental conversations, healthy alternatives, and informed consent.

Religious and scientific alignment is probably why U.S. states, even those engrossed in sexual and reproductive controversies, don't appear to be in a rush to adjust their cousin marriage laws. Some allow it, some don't, but there'll probably be no breaking news or heated protests over it in the near future. Canada, too, isn't fussed about its cousin unions, nor is it questioning lawful marriage between a nephew or niece and an aunt or uncle, for that matter.

Legalities and legacies aside, the suggestion of any kind of consanguineous amour unsettles me. I understand the logical reasons as to why cousin marriage happens and why it isn't genetically or culturally troublesome, but that doesn't mean I'm not scandalized by it. I'm certain I'm like many in this regard. Our reaction is a modern peculiarity.

In the *Am I Normal?* podcast's "Is it really that bad to marry my cousin?" episode, Mona Chalabi says part of the contemporary Western "ick" over cousin marriage is the fact that it's now practised mostly by racialized cultures. "Doesn't matter that cousin marriage is good enough for the Queen of England," she says. "If Arabs and North Africans and South Asians are doing it too, then some people are going to think it's gross."

In addition to having a supremely selective memory, white-dominant thinking is indeed suffused with beleaguered disgust for practices presumed to be racialized. How this tends to manifest in any one person is as a propensity for identifying *ick* everywhere. This is why racism is not only dangerous and debilitating to the fate of humanity, it is also irritating. The overwrought nose-wrinkling fatigues me.

Still, as much as I've tried to temper my own aversions to cousin courtship, browsing an article entitled "15 Signs Your Cousin Is Sexually Attracted to You" on a website for "dating enthusiasts" is not an experience I'd care to repeat.

If global traditions, astute wealth planning, and biological consequences won't assist me, my only defensible argument against turning your cousin into your lover is what you end up losing in the process. Romance and courtship steal essential cousinness away from cousins. This is what we haven't appreciated enough: how special cousins can be to one another as cousins, if only we'd get off their case and allow them to remain that way.

The cousin as a power consolidator or kin adhesive or tradition carrier or object of eros—the cousin as anything or anyone but the cousin—gets in the way of true cousin love. For me, that's the real problem with cousin romance.

Cachet and Marcia, the daughters of one of my mother's sisters, and my sister and I were all born within a four-year span. Save for a brief immigration separation between our parents we're too young to recall, these cousins have always lived a short drive from our house. I can't count the number of Saturdays and Sundays I've begged my parents to take us to visit them, if they aren't already planning a visit to our house instead.

"Why are we out on the road?" my father says at the wheel of the car on the afternoon we get caught in traffic as soon as we loop over the ramp onto the highway. "Because we always do what Andrea tells us. We always got to go see Cach and Marce."

Cach and Marce. Marce and Cach. This is the duo my sister and I grow up closest to. We chase one another across back yards and meet at barbecues in parks. At times, we set out with our four parents on road trips to our shared Maryland cousins or else venture to new destinations entirely: Martha's Vineyard, Lake Placid, New York City, Philadelphia, Connecticut.

It's the winter our parents drive us to Ottawa that Cach and Marce and my sister and I claim a double hotel suite for ourselves, leaving the adults in the room next door. At about one or two in the morning, a fire alarm peels through the hallways. We are jolted awake.

"What's that?" one of us says in the dark. "Is it real?"

"It's not real," another answers. "Wait a few minutes. They'll turn it off."

They don't turn it off. We groan and slide out from under the covers, reluctant to take action beyond peering out of the window. One of us pads over to the door to answer the knock.

My mother pokes her sleep-mussed head into our room. "Get going," she says, her voice groggy and low. Her head ducks back out and the door closes.

We trail our parents down the fire escape and out onto the street, coats slung over our pyjamas. We shiver in a clump on the sidewalk with the other hotel patrons, watching breath billow out of our mouths.

Get going, the four of us say to each other again and again to fits of laughter. *Get going,* we order the fire truck approaching our hotel, flashing and wailing its way down the street.

There are all kinds of birthday parties and Christmas and Thanksgiving and Easter celebrations amongst the four of us over the years. They can certainly happen in the company of other cousins and aunts and uncles, other great-uncles and great-aunts and friends and extended family, but they never happen without *Cach and Marce. Marce and Cach.* Something too great is missed otherwise.

Decades later, we make a point of getting together when our birthdays roll around, usually taking the opportunity to visit trendy restaurants we've heard about and save for each other. We strategize our orders, making sure we can sample and sip from one another, making sure we can all get our money's worth from the experience. We babble and joke as we always have, still only four years between the four of us, still living within an hour or two's drive from one another.

Get going, I sometimes say under my breath, impatient for a streetcar or subway train to lumber up and unfurl its doors for me.

Cousins are a dying breed. Demographic analysis predicts that they, along with nieces, nephews, and grandchildren, will decline around the world in the coming decades, at the same time that the number of grandparents and great-grandparents will increase. Sprawling family trees are shrivelling into beanstalks.

The Max Planck Institute for Demographic Research says that in 1950s North America and Europe, the average sixty-five-year-old woman had twenty-five living relatives. By 2095, that number will fall to sixteen. Drops will be all the more pronounced across Asia, Africa, and the Caribbean, where families have traditionally trended larger.

Shrinking families translates into shrinking care for all sorts of people at all stages of life. For regions without affordable support services to tap into, it is poised to become a crisis. It could mean that women and girls will be weighed by care and housekeeping pressures more than they already are, given the lion's share of unpaid and underpaid responsibilities they carry for children, elders, and other dependants.

What does the decline in living relatives and, more specifically, the associated cousin decline mean beyond gendered caregiving conundrums? How else can it hurt us?

It's parenting and motherhood articles that readily count the blessings of cousins, especially for the sake of young children. They feature idealized photos of adolescent cousins clustered on couches and cluttered around tables, cousins climbing jungle gyms and romping over grass and across seashores. Childhood cousins are like siblings that "don't annoy you as much," reads one article. They'll "always have each other's backs—forever." Even if they grow up and grow apart, the author is assured that her children and their cousins "would do anything for one another."

Are cousins truly unconditional relations as they grow up? People do feel more altruistic toward their kin, especially in relationships where genetic relatedness pairs with a sense of emotional closeness. Friendship altruism, on the other hand, tends to hinge on relationship quality alone. That can make friendships more breakable when camaraderie and connectedness get shaken.

This may be part of the reason cousinhood can be so special. Cousins may be more likely than other family relationships to get sealed by multiple bonds at once. Perhaps cousins are more likely to become real friends with each other, alongside their marked benefit of the kinship premium.

In her article "The Great Cousin Decline," Faith Hill says "cousins occupy a weird place." As different as their personalities and rearing may be, they know what it's like to exist in the same extended family. They dwell in a "strange gray area between closeness and distance." Unlike other family relationships an individual carries with them into adulthood—siblings, parents, grandparents—Hill says you have to opt into your cousin relationships. Adult cousinhood is only and exactly what you make of it. The "low stakes" of the relationship can turn cousins into perfect familial allies, quicker than anyone to respond with that magnetic blend of empathy and compromise and forgiveness, "but the potential for detachment also means you have to work for it."

This insight must be tempered by the reality that cousins mean different things to different people. In cultures and contexts that bend toward individualistic living, cousins might not feel as essential as they do in cultures and contexts where communality is highly valued.

And communality tends to come into sharpest relief in the light of shared struggle. For Black communities across global diasporas, for example, an expansive understanding of kin that includes cousins and other relatives, friends, neighbours, and faith community members can serve as a buffer and respite in the face of structural racism. Such wide biological and fictive kinship networks stretch beyond the purposes of resistance alone. They serve a collective vision of joy, too.

"The enduring beauty of Black family, both chosen and biological, is its versatility and unconditional presence," writes Elete Nelson-Fearon in "The Joy of Being Black and Having an Extended Family." Cousins, both blood-related and adopted in as play cousins, are right in the thick of multi-household networks where "any occasion—birthdays, anniversaries, losses—necessitates an inter-household gathering," where houses combine to become shared locations of solace and Sunday dinners alike.

Familial allies, partners in resistance, partakers of joy. This is the experiential blend that describes what deep cousinhood means to me. It is with my indentured ancestor cousins, both those adopted and those who are biological, that I find this triangulated congruence I can find nowhere else.

My cousins see things about me others simply cannot. *Indian? Immigrant? From where? English speaker? Hindu or Muslim or Christian background?* From the outside looking in, there are all kinds of confusions and unspoken questions and assumptions about who I might be. But my cousins are on the inside looking in. We share hidden histories, the poorly recalled migrations of our foreparents. We know what it's like to be once, twice, three times removed from homeland and lineage, cobbling meaning somewhere in the shifting middle. We experience our legacy of indentureship as something more than what it can get simplified down to, this forever forgottenness and forever foreignness. We know it's not all split allegiances and suspicion and insularity and camouflage, not all under-acknowledged pains and political upheavals and non-belonging. We know it can be a treasure.

To me, there are so many ways in which racialized indentureship feels like a secret and precious legacy shared by those of us who live and know and get it. All day long I roll it like tiny, smooth gems over my palms. Sharing these gems with others who share the same secret, passing stones hand to hand with hardly anyone else aware that we're doing it, can be sheer pleasure.

It has been with my closest indentured-ancestor cousins and their loved ones that I've most relished these clandestine gems. Our particular and peculiar family memories, our contradictory Asianness and Caribbeanness and Westernness, our backing and forthing, sometimes sensing belonging and sometimes feeling cast out. Occasional sadness about it and more common incapability of caring less. This cousinhood is affirming to receive and give back, even as the complexities of being a child of the indentured constantly eludes and befuddles those around us, if they bother to notice at all.

When my closest cousins are around, I don't need to be understood by anybody else. There is a peace and settledness, what I can only describe as a sensation of *cousin satisfaction*. I felt it as a preteen when my cousins and I strolled to a park and a boy sauntered up, trying to sweet talk the oldest and cutest of us in Spanish. *I don't understand a word you're saying,* my cousin kept insisting over the boy's persistence and our giggles, *I'm not your kind of brown.* I felt it at an Indian restaurant when my cousins and I ordered butter chicken and naan for dinner, disappointing the waiter. *The curry we go for is different, okay?* I felt it all those times I told my cousins about name mispronunciations I've experienced, all those times people reacted to the unfamiliarity of my surname and debated themselves about where in India my family could have possibly originated. I feel it every time my cousins remind me of their mispronunciations, every time we repeat them to each other as terms of endearment. *Nobody knew how to read and no one bothered to spell properly back then—of course we're all Rajpaulroopsinghs over here. Let someone else figure it out.*

Cousin satisfaction has been a delight to me since I was a child. It's the reason why, as an adult, I continue to choose cousinhood, even as my general cousin status is a given by virtue of my family's cultural value of closeness.

I have to be a cousin; I have no choice in that. But I don't necessarily have to live like a cousin, not by any means. I adopt cousinhood every day because I want to. The paradoxes are compelling, this underseen legacy of indentureship only cousins can understand, this chosen-unchosen brand of Indo-Caribbean cousinality. They've intermingled in a way that has become most valuable to me. I wouldn't ask for it to be any other way.

It's everything but low stakes. No wonder I feel so guilty about being a flunky cousin all the time. In my mind, full and true cousin bliss is associated with competencies I don't naturally own: entertaining, cooking, and hospitality; hosting huge, happy family gatherings. The very notion of cousinhood evokes delicious aromas and sounds of banter and boisterous laughter, the tropical swelter of a cramped, bustling living room and basement, no matter the location of the gathering or the real temperature outside. This self-stoked, particularly womanly brand of cousinality is a standard I know I don't actually have to achieve to live as a good cousin. It's emotionally potent to me, nonetheless.

The truth is that I know I haven't been the cousin I want to be in the greater sense of the term. I've let myself grow apart and away from the cousinhood of my childhood. I've let myself get too busy, too absorbed in my own pursuits, too oriented toward my career, too overwhelmed by hurdles I'd need to overcome to get back to the cousinality I wish I had maintained all along. My cousin absenteeism is shortsighted, I know that, and I am overtaken by guilt about the quality of cousin my cousins deserve in me and don't receive. But there's still an inertia here. There's still a gormless taking for granted.

There's a sense in which writing about the power of cousinhood feels like utter hypocrisy on my part. I battle cousin regret every day. I live in constant cousin shame.

In a 2020 article in *The Atlantic*, David Brooks provocatively declares the American nuclear family a mistake. This paradigm for marriage and parenting has been "crumbling in slow motion for decades," he says, "and many of our other problems—with education, mental health, addiction, the quality of the labor force—stem from that crumbling." The nuclear structure affords only the most privileged men freedom and assistance to fulfill their dreams. In transitioning from rambling extended families to atomized nuclear families, economically vulnerable people have been set up to fail.

No wonder the dream of nuclearness is fading in America, Brooks says. We've been burned by it. We hunger "to live in extended and forged families, in ways that are new and ancient at the same time."

Some beg to differ with his framing. They point to societal and economic pressures that have set the nuclear family on a path to disintegration. They say our problems aren't so much about family formats but about how we've failed to create the conditions for health and wellness, no matter the constitutions and sizes of our families. Some assert the advantages and staying power of nuclearness in Western societies, even as we contend with our isolation, our fear of being in it alone.

In this flutter over the rights and wrongs of modern families, how they've thrived and been abandoned to fail, hardly anyone has anything specific to say about the decline of the cousin, whether demographic or symbolic or both. They reference a shiny ideal of wide-armed kinship without acknowledging the reality that cousinhood, both biological and gifted, has to be a major element of it.

The conceptual gap perplexes me. Are we only supposed to be siblings and parents and aunts and uncles to each other? It's a missed mark in our imaginings of what family means to us now and could mean to us in future, if only we would name and nurture it. It presents us with all sorts of untapped opportunities, too.

In the vacuum of substantive research about cousinhood, I turned to literature and media to explore what it means to be a cousin, what it might feel like beyond my finite frame of reference. I wondered if others speak to that mix of cousin satisfactions and regrets as I do.

"With so much true merit and true love, and no want of fortune and friends, the happiness of the married cousins must appear as secure as earthly happiness can be," reads Jane Austen's *Mansfield Park*, referencing the story-wrapping matrimony between Fanny and Edmund somewhere in early-nineteenth-century Britain. Their cousinhood is barely important to who they are as people. Same for du Maurier's *My Cousin Rachel*, Balzac's *La Cousine Bette* and *Le Cousin Pons*, Gaskell's *Cousin Phillis*, and Fitzgerald's *The Great Gatsby*. These kissing, sparring, and misbehaving cousins of classic Western novels don't give me much to go on.

Cousin Oliver on *The Brady Bunch* and Cousin Balki on *Perfect Strangers*. Bill and Vinny of *My Cousin Vinny*. Cousins of the 1975 French film *Cousin Cousine* and its 1989 American remake, *Cousins*. George Michael and Maeby of *Arrested Development*, Jessa and Shoshanna of *Girls*, bumbling first-cousin-once-removed Greg of *Succession*. Contemporary television and film featuring white cousins similarly don't contain elements I can draw out or particularly relate to when it comes to deep cousinhood.

It begs the question posed by Damon Young, author of *What Doesn't Kill You Makes You Blacker: A Memoir in Essays*. "Do white people have cousins?" Literal answers aside, he wonders about the truths of "cousin culture," where cousins factor into how you navigate the world but degrees of cousins don't, where non-blood cousins are full cousins to you because they were always around and "you didn't even know they weren't technically related to you until you were, like, 25."

It is this kind of cousin culture I've located in works by racialized artists focused on racialized stories in the Western media landscape. I remember my prickling eardrums the first time I heard Spice 1's 1992 "Welcome to the Ghetto." The song must have come to me through my avid teenage Upstate New York radio listenership and my viewership of MuchMusic's *RapCity*. They were amongst the handful of broadcasts that allowed kids in Canada to enjoy American hip-hop. In one swift line, Spice 1 refers to a cousin who died, a cousin he still mourns after a year. The lyric was sampled in the album version of Tupac's 1994 "Pour Out a Little Liquor." The video edit of the song features a sparse chorus over footage of libations offered at burial grounds. It's the unaltered audio version of "Pour Out a Little Liquor" where Spice 1's cousin lyric plays as a hook for the chorus, a haunt that echoes through over and over again.

The line lodged in my brain. As a fourteen-year-old who could hardly handle the notion of death, I found it torture to ponder what it would feel like to lose one of my close cousins. I knew of no other song that acknowledged the cruelty of the experience. I understood that only the most observant artists would mine words for cousin grief. No one else seemed to notice enough to talk about it.

And it's still under-acknowledged. Many workplace bereavement programs and leaves, for example, don't apply to passed cousins. It's not expected that our cousins would matter enough to interrupt our paid employment.

Other underspoken realities of cousin culture shimmer through Donald Glover's *Atlanta*. As eccentric and Afro-surrealist as the series gets, Earn and Alfred's cousinhood is the grounding factor. Before Alfred is known as rapper Paper Boi, he plays the role of school trendsetter, protecting Earn from bullies mocking his off-brand clothing. In adulthood, Earn becomes Alfred's manager. Their business incompatibilities stoke tensions, but their cousin's care for one another is tenderly reaffirmed.

Pass it over to Earn, Alfred communicates with a nod and finger point, noticed only by the mutual friend holding the blunt and the viewer themselves. *He's having a hard day.*

These cousins will not re-enact the severed trust of their family's older generation. In one scene, Alfred and Earn escape an argument between their parents and aunts and uncles, slinking off side-by-side through a recording studio's enchanted back door. They are warned like Lot and his wife not to look back, lest they be sucked back into the family drama by their warring aunt. In one of the last scenes of the series, Alfred breaks his quiet contentment over mastering the rustic peril of his new "safe farm" to call Earn and crack jokes. He reclines on his porch and laughs with his cousin. The two of them are one another's true safe place.

Briar Grace-Smith and Ainsley Gardiner's *Cousins*, a movie based on the Patricia Grace novel of the same name, explores visceral affection between three Māori cousins. When Mata is granted short leave from the institution where she lives to stay on ancestral land with her whānau, her extended family, she meets Makareta and Missy for the first time. Their lives plait into each other, pasts and presents pulled apart and woven together again. They are separated for years, but their bond lasts, rooted in land and conveyed in lived memories. Sun flaring in the margin between leaves. Streams tinkling between rocks. Breeze undulating tendrils of hair. The tip of a feather swept over a cheek. Theirs is a vivid, embodied cousinhood, a feast of nature for the senses that placed a lump in my throat.

Not every cousin relationship can be so nurturing. Lee Sung Jin's *Beef* pokes at the ill-intended cousin who leverages the business-blood-friendship triad of immigrant familyhood for his own gain. He presumes his scammery is disguised in his clownery. He presumes his cousins would never nurse a grudge. In this series, the cousin plays the role of trickster antagonist, not unlike the Anansi, the West African spider figure known by many names. He is cunning and in charge. He is a lesson and a fool. It is his close cousinhood that makes him such a formidable foil to his cousins.

Rebecca Zlotowski's *An Easy Girl* addresses cousin role modelling by chronicling a dreamy summer shared by a pair of working-class Algerian cousins in rich white Cannes. The younger is captivated by her older, more worldly cousin, perceiving the vulnerability, kindness, and grief in her no one else can see. In the end, the younger does not follow in the footsteps of the older, but she understands what her cousin has done for her. She has offered a pathway for the younger's clarity about her own future and understanding of her worth. The younger only wishes for her older cousin's happiness when the older disappears to London without saying goodbye.

Mindy Kaling and Lang Fisher's *Never Have I Ever* allows the older cousin to transform from rival into protector and mentor of the younger. In the last episode of the series, cousins Devi and Kamala's choreographed dance at their paati's wedding paints new dimensions onto the romantic Bollywood hit *Saami Saami*. They move in sync, darlings to one another as much as they and other women characters have become darlings to their lovers.

The most resonant of the racialized cousin portrayals I've seen is Sterlin Harjo and Taika Waititi's *Reservation Dogs*. In the small Muscogee Nation town where most episodes take place, familial and community lines are beautifully blurred. It is the death of Willie Jack's cousin Daniel that launches the story forward in the first place, motivating her and their three best friends to make their way to the shores of California. Having pushed through their journey's hilarities and missteps, through their upsets and annoyances with one another, they stand in the Pacific Ocean, holding each other in a circle. Sunbeams stream on their heads; waves crash at their backs. Daniel appears with them, holding them, too. It is one of the series's many scenes where spirit and earth merge, both profound and a matter of course.

Spirit and earth, all at once, just as these five are simultaneous cousins, friends, allies, troublemakers, and beloved children. Community and ancestral and kin relations are presented with no limiting boundaries. So, too, are life and death. Grief over a lost cousin is amplified and soothed, all at once.

It's *Reservation Dogs* that made me consider the underspoken relationships undermined, unformed, and entirely snatched away in the crosshairs of colonial abuses: enslavement, genocide, displacement, compelled and forced migrations. Stolen parents and children and lovers and siblings are the ones we tend to remember first. The loss of cousins is hardly recounted. Still, back then and now, the opportunity to have and know and hold on to our cousins is a privilege. All sorts of brutalities and misfortunes have taken them from us.

Losing our cousinhood is one of the underseen tragedies of our histories. It has been one of many tactics to disintegrate family and community and remake them into a disempowered labour force, an endgame of colonial violence. Perhaps affirming our cousinhood has to be part of our future if we're going to find a way to break our vicious cycles. Perhaps collective mourning over the cousins we've lost can lead us to a new kind of cousinness with one another.

In 2024, our car pulls up to the side of Santa Bárbara de Nexe's parochial church in the southern Algarve region of Portugal. A series of mishaps amongst our group of family travellers from the U.S. and Canada—a missed shuttle bus and more than one set of heels and soles cracked by cobblestone—have made us late.

Sunlight gleams on the church's white facade and surrounding walls. The sky above is clear, a brilliant springtime blue. The church was constructed in this hilly town on the site of an ancient chapel in the fifteenth century, when Portuguese navigators like Vasco da Gama and Duarte Pacheco Pereira sailed for commerce and conquest, for some kind of future away from the calamity of plague. The building is modest and charming, its bell tower edged by brown brick.

The day is windy and warm. My uncle, aunt, cousin, husband, and I climb the front steps of the church in time to watch the bride and her father, another cousin and uncle, step through the main entryway in white dress and black suit. The double doors close behind them.

We giggle at the comedy of our morning. We are pointed through the church's side entrance. We skulk into the sanctuary as the priest leads the ceremony in careful English. My cousin Alana and I creep past the knees of seated attendees, all the way to the other end of the church. We sit on a small pew against the left-hand wall, the only two guests seated there.

Only now do I realize I haven't been to a real Catholic wedding before today. The bride and groom sit on stools beside each other at the filigreed gold altar. A lone violinist bows, situated at the opposite wall of the sanctuary. My eyes keep sliding to the life-sized Christ statue crucified in a recessed arch above my shoulder. His forehead is slumped to his arm and his eyes are closed. His mouth relaxes open. His wounds weep red; both knees are skinned. Below his nailed feet, a bird of paradise bouquet fans its audacious orange-purple petals. It is perched on a glass-sided coffin where another Christ statue is laid, his pale arms and legs bruised and slashed up and down by wounds.

He is twinned next to me, deity dying above and buried below.

Alana's mother passed before my mother passed. Both have been absent for over two decades. They were the first of us closest first cousins' mothers to go. Since then, more of our parents have died across North America and the Caribbean and Latin America. I imagine my mother and other missing aunts and uncles in their fancy dresses and suits, nestled along with the people in these pews. I'm only able to picture them as they were when my cousins and I were little. They teased their hair in curls and wore shoulder pads and business suits, pink blush and dangling earrings.

They sprayed colognes and perfumes on their wrists and necks that made my nostrils itch. I can still smell them.

Our parents were the same age my cousins and I are now. They, too, probably had a hard time envisioning the day we wouldn't all be here. An ache pierces me. I don't want to be surprised by these inescapable losses. They are our fate, no matter what we do. I want to live so I don't need to carry them as welts of remorse inside of me like this.

"We ask you to remember our family and friends who have departed this life," a woman reads at the podium, "and for all dearly departed of those here today. Lord, hear us."

Lord, graciously hear us.

The priest raises his hands to the attendees and tells us to speak peace to our neighbours.

Everyone rustles to their feet. Mumbles echo across the stone walls of the sanctuary. I turn to Alana and we embrace.

"I am so glad you're here," I say into her hair. It smells sweet.

We hold each other for a while. When we pull away, we keep our grip on each other's arms. Our eyes are clouded by tears.

Humour writer and digital storyteller Evelyn Ngugi, known as Evelyn From The Internets, names everyone who enjoys her content her "internet cousin." Her food review videos are my favourite. She narrates her sampling of unfamiliar snacks and sodas from around the world and assigns them ratings. She reads the colourful product descriptions, fumbles into packages and snaps open tabs; she sniffs and peers in, frowns and raises her eyebrows and tilts her head. She sips, she chews, she giggles and muses.

I try not to spiral into parasocial relationships, but Ngugi's commentary and spot-on descriptions of tastes and textures, her silliness and infectious enthusiasm, really do make me feel as if I'm watching my cousin onscreen. In spite of myself, she offers me a sense of internet cousinness.

Whether digital or adopted or based in blood, cousinhood can become more expansive to us than we might realize.

Research suggests that non-related people with faces so similar they can be considered doppelgängers may truly share genes and lifestyle traits. "In a growing population," reads one article, "there's bound to be some genetic overlap just by happenstance."

But it's not a coincidence. Every human being is related to one another, a declaration that seems obvious on paper but is prone to leaking out of our minds the moment we attempt to take stock of it. Our genetic makeup is 99.9 per cent identical. The genetic isopoint, the point in history where the world's current family trees converge and distill to the same human seedlings, might have taken place as recently as between 5300 and 2200 BCE.

In the spacious timescape of the globe, this is a single breath. We humans are a vibrant collection of adolescent cousins. In the unfathomable scale of every species, of countless stars and planets and galaxies and atoms and particles and the strings of vibrating energy that comprise them all, we cousins are a microscopic family.

There is no real reason we couldn't be close to each other. In *It's All Relative: Adventures Up and Down the World's Family Tree*, A.J. Jacobs mines the dream of a tight humanity of blood cousins. In part reacting to the fact that we don't behave as kin to each other, the book chronicles Jacobs's ambition to throw a record-breaking, multi-country Global Family Reunion. He describes his designs to hijack the biases we have for our own families and offer a prism to view every stranger as a relative. *I am a cousin*, read the signs held up by a sea of smiling attendees in one of the Global Family Reunion's group shots.

We are all a cousin. In this sense, it's the most prevalent relation on the planet. If we are the only survivor left of our specific kin and kind, we are still a cousin. Perhaps that's why we tend to forget about it. Cousinality is ubiquitous. It won't mean much to us if we don't make it into much. For first cousins as much as for seventieth cousins, simply being a cousin is not the same as living like a cousin.

It is, again, a chosen and unchosen state. "We have kin everywhere," Naomi Klein writes. "Some of them look like us, lots of them look nothing like us and yet are still connected to us. Some aren't even human. Some are coral. Some are whales. And they are there to connect with, if we can get out of our own way for long enough."

Doppelganger: A Trip into the Mirror World starts with Klein's personal problem with mistaken identity and sweeps into an analysis of our human fantasies and denialism, looming authoritarianism and climate disaster. Wrestling truth from misinformation seems harder than ever. We miscast the dangers we face, too easily dismissing them or else devising faulty solutions, too glibly scratching lines between those in the right and those in the wrong, those who have and those who have not.

We are our own trickster antagonists. Cunning and in charge. A lesson, and fools. Klein makes an urgent case for unifying action, for a clear-eyed reality where we live with "no sacrificial people and places." She calls for the birth of an active, uncompromising sense of interconnection.

What if we were to choose cousinhood as our model to start this connectedness from, expanding our embedded kinship premium to live as if everybody in the world were our family? What if we made the effort to bring cousin culture from the margins to the centre, bolstering it as a schema for our interrelatedness? What if we were to consciously develop what Jean-Luc Nancy calls "being singular plural," where "being cannot be anything but being-with-one-another, circulating in the with and as the with of this singularly plural coexistence," as cousins?

I imagine we would open space for new forms of inclusion. For extending those classic liberalist ideals of inalienable human rights and citizenship, personhood and suffrage, liberty and freedom. Limited in execution, they are expansive in soul. We can win them. We can redeem and recreate them.

Efforts to define healthy digital citizenship would indeed be built on the scaffolding of internet cousinhood. Learnings and benefits of Black fictive kin networks and play cousin relations would be woven into our social service, medical, and helping profession approaches and standards. Educational bodies would explore cousinesque mentorship models such as Vancouver Island University's Community Cousins and the University of British Columbia's Medicine Cousins. Both bring together new and existing Indigenous students with shared heritages and study interests, helping new students ease into the campus atmosphere and make connections. That they are framed as cousin communities by and for Indigenous students, and not as fraternities or sororities, seems telling. The imposition of Greek life, with all its secrecy, elitism, and competitiveness, would not be strong or relevant enough to spark real belonging.

Cousinhood, not coercion, compliance, or clienthood, would become our organizing principle. Our mutual resistance and celebration as caring cousins would root and bloom.

Many more of us would be graced by the sublime pleasures of passing secret, precious gems of understanding from hand to hand. Cousinhood would become our daily lived experience. We would see each other as far and close at the same time, as people we must make the choice to maintain true connectedness with.

We would accept that our cousinhood requires our intention. It doesn't happen by virtue of genetics or proximity or affinity alone. Those things in and of them themselves have their restrictions, and our chosen-unchosen human cousinhood is a bond unlike any other. An essential one, bigger than family or friendship, a connectedness that could enable our beset species to survive through this difficult era. A time when we must make the choice to hold one another and this planet as our closest allies.

Human siblinghood? We've heard about that. We've tried to sing that song.

Human cousinhood? It awaits us now, brand new.

PEPPERPOT

When I think of Guyanese pepperpot, a cherished Christmastime dish, I think of the remnants of my family's seasons past. Gold-edged ribbons folded into bows, velvety on one side, slick to the touch on the other. Fat multicoloured light bulbs. Staticky tinsel tossed on the needles of a plastic evergreen. Carols belted in basements, backed by uncles on the keyboard and harmonica and guitars.

Pepperpot's smell, earthy and charred and marked by leafy sweetness, is wholly nostalgic. As decadently spiced and aromatic as all the other Guyanese dishes my mother used to make were, no dish smelled quite like it.

I remember its components on the cutting board: pink cubes of beef, gristly nubs of oxtail. I remember the jar of Guyanese cassareep sauce on the counter, the black, viscous, staining liquid inside. My mother would simmer the meat with the cassareep on the stove for hours. Steam accumulated on the underside of the lid and dripped back into the pot, over and over.

My parents said pepperpot was a dish worth waiting for, always better the next day. But I don't recall waiting for the night to pass when the cooking was done, when the house was fragrant with my mother's efforts. My family and I hunched over our bowls to breathe it as soon as we could, the cinnamon and cloves perfuming each inhale. We ripped chunks of egg bread and pressed them to the bottom of the bowl around the beef, catching as much of the thinned cassareep sauce as the bread would absorb.

My bowl was always more sauce than meat. When I was a child, cassareep sauce seemed like a secret only my family knew about, along with a handful of other families like mine. I preferred we keep it to ourselves. Turkey and stuffing and mashed potatoes and brown gravy—none of the foods other families relished during the season could handle our cassareep anyway. It was too potent for the holiday dinners of sitcoms and movies. Cassareep would blotch the meat and blacken the cream, splash the treats and smear the plate. It was far too unabashed for a white Christmas.

Even Guyanese pepperpot itself seemed barely capable of handling its cassareep. Meat and sauce with the vehicle of bread to transport it to the stomach: that was all the dish was in my home. My mother added no extraneous vegetables, no potatoes or rice or sprigs of garnish.

Cassareep sauce was the glory of pepperpot. Later on, I would learn the true scope of its fame.

Exploring the facts of Guyanese pepperpot whisks you to the Amazon's nearly seven million square kilometres of forest, savannas, and rivers. Pepperpot is grounded in the innovations of Indigenous communities there. Amazonia is dissected into Brazil, Bolivia, Peru, Ecuador, Colombia, Venezuela, Guyana,

Suriname, and French Guiana. Indigenous populations constitute about 9 per cent of the region's total population, or one and a half million people. In pre-colonial times, many more Indigenous people called Amazonia home, up to ten million people, speaking hundreds of languages. They include the First Peoples of Guyana on the land today: Akawaio, Arawak, Arecuna, Carib, Makushi, Patamona, Wai Wai, Wapixana, and Warao communities.

Everything in the world seems to have been subject to racialization. Even dirt. Abundant ruddy clay sand in Amazonia was christened *terra mulata* or "mulatto earth" by Portuguese colonists. Though it boasts vast canopies, four tiers of foliage, and looming trees, Amazonian land is flushed of nutrients by constant rainfall. Indigenous people honed a legacy of expertise with deluged soil, mixing it with char and fertilizer and organic matter and even broken pottery to sustain crops. Portuguese colonists called this dirt *terra preta do índio*. "Black soil of the Indian."

The Indigenous Amazonian legacy of cultivating cassava in these soils stretches back long before any colonizer knew of the place or its people. *Manihot esculenta* or cassava plants, also called yuca, manioc, and mandioca plants, are well adapted to paradoxical dirt and taxing conditions. They thrive where other plants cannot.

Cassava plants spread as short trees with starred leaves, similar to hemp leaves but without the serrations. People around the world cook and eat these leaves as a vegetable and add them to stews and sauces. Cassava's roots are shallow-lying tubers with fibrous skin and fluffy white innards. People cook and eat the tubers or else turn them into flour and tapioca and liquor. It is from these tubers that Indigenous people in Amazonia extract juice and boil, spice, and pepper it into cassareep.

Something about yuca tubers looks human to me in a way other root vegetables, potatoes and turnips and yams, do not. Maybe it's their formation. They expand outward like hands, splaying like fingers stacked over each other. Or perhaps their thick-to-thin length seems to me like thighs, like lounging brown-skinned people with legs outstretched to catch sun.

If the root of the cassava plant is the body, then cassareep is its lifeblood.

Eating other people's food is a form of intercultural exchange. It's so available to us now that it has become invisible. Swapping clothes, language, music, art, ways of living and thinking and being is much harder than tapping a screen and purchasing a meal.

I'm romanced by the notion of fostering a diverse and adventurous palate. Amongst the people I know, I'm most attracted to the broad-minded diners, at least at mealtimes. They're just more fun to be around. The ones with no interest in sampling different kinds of dishes, not because of health or faith practices but the result of palates oriented to a narrow assemblage of cuisines, frankly concern me.

It's a bit juvenile, isn't it? I think before slapping my inner wrist for my rudeness. This judgment I battle in myself about other people's culinary preferences—it too easily and unfairly washes over their whole existence. *To be so close-minded, to never step out of your comfort zone. It's no way to live.*

Consider the panoply of restaurants in cities like Washington, D.C., New York City, London, Toronto, and Montreal. The ones that can boast about their authentic multicultural dining options seem to have so much going for them. From kibbeh to asado to biryani to jerk chicken, goulash to sushi to fufu to pad Thai. Vast choice in cuisines is a major element of what it means to exist as a cosmopolitan centre. Unicultural dining doesn't help any destination make it onto our bucket lists.

You might be hesitant about flying to a foreign land, but chances are you'd be willing to try that land's cuisine. Even the most xenophobic amongst us can rally the gumption for dish sampling. Even white nationalists can't help but love tacos.

How odd is this sunny open-mindedness when it comes to sharing food across divides? How is it that we can participate so easily and enthusiastically when there are so many other things we can't seem to do for and with each other? It's as if ingesting a meal, salivating and swallowing and absorbing it into our membranes and bloodstreams and cells, trusting it to elate and satiate, is not an intimate process. Digestion spans hours. The body is vulnerable to its whims the whole way through. Other intercultural exchanges don't last nearly as long. Most aren't nearly as immersive. They don't merge with the flesh, fusing into it, right down to the molecule.

Of course, our multicultural food fetish masks sordid intercultural legacies. Break dishes down to their parts: millions of acres robbed, millions of souls exploited for spices, cocoa, sugar, rice. Economies constructed and blown apart, governments overthrown for bananas and coffee and tea. Environmental and climate disaster courted for meats and milks. Ingredients emerge from a pressure cooker of want and need and greed, of tensions and wars and tenuous alliances.

The cliché is that our neglect of history places us at risk of repeating it. I can't help but wonder if the risk haunts us no matter what we do. I can't help but wonder if food fights have become human nature.

We've lived the reality of food gathering us together. We forget that it's not always in fellowship.

As tasty as my mother's pepperpot was, the best pepperpot I ever ate was in Guyana itself, in 2004. That trip was the first and only time I visited the country of my parents' birth. I was twenty-six years old, suspended in the surreal months between my mother's funeral and my wedding day. My family and I flew down mid-September, the hottest time of the year. The air was humid and the breezes were sluggish. I remember local family members and their neighbours there, most of whom I was being introduced to for the first time, complaining about relentless heat.

We stayed at my grandmother's house near the mouth of the silty Demerara River in a village named Vreed en Hoop. "Peace and hope." That's what Dutch colonists decided to name the sugar plantation they established there, largely worked by enslaved and indentured people. It became the future village's namesake. When plantation owner Jonas Fileen died in 1822, his will made a point of declaring Brandina, one of the women he enslaved, free, adding two thousand guilders to her name.

Ever since I read about her, I've wondered about Brandina: what her life was like, who Jonas was to her, who she was to the others on the plantation with her. What were her dreams? Did they include Jonas? I wonder about the other enslaved and indentured workers who toiled on *peace and hope* with her. They're harder to track, but at least some of their memories live on in the village's oral histories and family genealogies.

To me, people in Vreed en Hoop seemed like family right away. My grandmother's caregiver treated us like kin, making pepperpot for us even though it wasn't close to Christmastime. She was welcoming us to a homeland we barely knew with a familiar dish. Perhaps she made it because of me, more than anyone else in my entourage. I'm certain I wouldn't have been able to hide my enthusiasm for the dish or steer her toward a less intensive meal when she asked what my favourite things to eat were.

She spooned the stew into bowls in the kitchen on the ground floor of my grandmother's house. Her pepperpot's scent was more sumptuous than anything I had ever breathed. I imagined it was what I would've been eating had my parents not left the country of their birth before I was born. Like my mother's recipe, this pepperpot consisted of meat and sauce with no vegetables. But the ingredients had a natural edge: cassareep that did not need to be shipped over waters, cow heel and oxtail from a local butcher, accompanying bread, knotted and spongy, purchased at a nearby bakery.

That pepperpot was a delight to my tongue and tummy. When we had finished savouring it and sipped the last of our sodas at the table, my grandmother's caregiver covered the serving dish with plastic wrap and placed it on the kitchen counter. The dish stayed there until the next day, when she reboiled and served it again, and the day after that, when she did it all over again.

It's not that my grandmother's house did not have a refrigerator. They say you don't need to refrigerate Guyanese pepperpot. Indigenous communities designed the stew in an era before refrigeration. Their "pepper pots" were communal vessels on an everlasting fire, embracing meat and vegetables and bones and spice and pepper and anything else they added. They added and ate, added and ate, for days, months, years.

Even in the sweltering tropics, the humidity of a Vreed en Hoop September, they say mould and bacteria can't survive a pepperpot's cassareep. Recipes repeat the mantra: so long as you boil before serving, so long as you add more cassareep to blanket the contents, you can leave pepperpot out. Yuca's preservative power is more effective than salting. Cassareep is more capable of ensuring human well-being than any electric appliance.

People like me insist on refrigerating our pepperpot anyway. My skepticism of folk knowledge, my hypervigilance about food-borne illness and sickness in general, make it impossible to entrust myself to such claims.

When I was in Guyana, unrefrigerated beef on a counter to be boiled and reboiled should've terrified me. I should've made excuses to weasel out of eating it alongside my family. But it didn't frighten me. I found myself trusting those who seemed to know better about it, about so much else in life, than I did. I found myself assured of the properties of cassava blood in the place of its origin. In its very veins.

Perhaps the person I am, who I might've been all along, is different on that land. This was a place I'd been raised to revere and hearken back to, a place my parents and their siblings loved best, but one I had not personally known. Still, it was a source. There's something sacred about returning to a source, as removed from it as you may be, as unbelonging to it as you may feel. It still somehow quiets anxieties and objections. Renders them oddly irrelevant.

⁂

Pepperpot requires real cassareep. Blasphemous counterfeits, bottles labelled *Authentic Pomeroon Style* but produced nowhere near Guyana's Pomeroon-Supenaam region and its bending river, will not do. Those duped by the knockoffs say they taste like they're concocted from soy sauce and burnt sugar and molasses, packaged and priced to look like the real thing in a jar. It's only in the cooking that the ugliness is unmasked.

You can find videos of women describing how they make cassareep in the traditional Amazonian method. They cup yuca roots in their palms and drive wide-bladed knives into them, cleaving off the tubers' ends and shaving their tough skin with the nonchalance of daily practice. They dice and grate the innards into a pulp that they stuff into a woven tube, a matapi or matapee. They hang the matapi, taut with cassava, from one looped end and slap its sides, triggering the ooze of cloudy juices. They insert a branch into the bottom loop of the matapi and leverage body weight to pull it down, squeezing the tube. Extracted liquid is caught in a container. Women turn the pulp into cassava flour for bread, cakes, and wafers. They use the liquid for liquor, sauces, and cassareep.

It's an arduous undertaking, this coaxing of cassava's juice from its flesh. It takes the whole body, the labour of deft hands. Women boil and churn the liquid over a fire until its sugars caramelize and its volume reduces by half. The juice refines, thickening from chalky water to rich black syrup.

The products of milked almonds and rice and soybeans aren't nearly as dramatic as that of milked yuca. Those wrung liquids turn out similar to how they start. The same goes for most saps refined into syrups. They end close to where they begin. It's the process of turning the root of the cassava into cassareep that demands nothing less than a transfiguration. It is a revelation. An unveiling of power.

I've always been intrigued by what articulate European travellers penned about the land and people claimed as colonial property in the zenith of expansion. I read simultaneous repulsion and obsession in their words. I take it as insight into the psyche and lexicon of domination. You must count the ways you hate what you love and love what you hate to empower yourself to dominate it. There is no such thing as domination without fascination. There is no other way.

A handful of these travellers wrote about cassareep. Sailing to Guyana to manage his uncle's plantation, Charles Waterton documented his Amazonian expeditions in *Wanderings in South America*, the first edition of which was published in 1825. The book was influential and said to have inspired men like Charles Darwin. Its 1885 edition's "Explanatory Index" was written by Reverend John George Wood and speaks of local cassareep production. Wood carried the now-passé priestly rank of parson-naturalist and embarked on nature tours as part of his clerical duties. Amongst *Wanderings in South America*'s portfolio of over one hundred fine drawings are Wood's illustrations of a cassava bowl and a matapi, referred to as a "cassava press."

I'm particularly interested in what European travellers chose to record about the women they met in the colonies. German botanist

Moritz Richard Schomburgk detailed his visit to a Warao community in the mid-1800s, where he observed local women making "cassarip." He narrates their bodies in garish ethnographic form, declaring women's "bloom of life" entirely spent by age twenty.

Colonial travelogues are to be taken with caution. This one is a nasty read. Still, I'm impressed that the wizardry of cassareep and pepperpot shines through. Schomburgk references Dutch colonists who raved to him about the dish. He highlights a Dutch housewife who maintained her own pepperpot with fresh cassareep for thirty years, presuming it a "real gem."

Three whole decades of pepperpot for the sheer pleasure of it. Fantastical pepperpot stories enter the contemporary realm, too. Betty Kent Mascoll, a British World War II veteran who lived in Grenada, entertaining Ronald Reagan and cooking for his troops during their 1983 invasion of the island, blamed the destruction of her hundred-year-old pepperpot on the communists. On his website, an American prepper praises the antiseptic wonders of cassareep, offering his own tips on preventing bacteria from infecting a pepperpot. He warns novices not to consume the "super root" it is made from raw or attempt to extract its juice on their own.

He doesn't name the root cassava until the very end of his article.

Perhaps he wrote the piece wrestling with an impulse to keep cassareep a secret, the same impulse I had once tussled with as a child. Maybe pepperpot is the hidden marvel that will keep us fed in disaster, fallout, apocalypse, Armageddon. Maybe cassareep will preserve the human race from oblivion.

For years, I was reliant on my aunts for pepperpot, on their chance invitations to dine on that particular meal. When stay-at-home restrictions of the COVID-19 pandemic rendered that impossible, I decided to try to make pepperpot myself.

My mother was praised for the savoury dishes and desserts she used to prepare for family parties when I was young. She used to regale me with elaborate dreams she had about Guyanese markets, the meat and fruits and fish she used to buy whenever she wanted before immigration to the northern hemisphere evaporated them into nighttime visions. *Breadfruit, star apple, mangoes, saltfish*, she would tell me. *You wouldn't believe what I saw when I closed my eyes.*

I am not the passionate chef she was, dreaming about food. I am not versed in West Indian cooking techniques or embedded in the Guyanese culinary heritage, an unparalleled blend of diasporic African and Indian traditions mixed with Indigenous Amazonian and Chinese and European traditions. My pepperpot would have to be simplified. I would cook it the fast way, in an Instant Pot pressure cooker, not on the stovetop. I would replace Guyanese wiri wiri peppers with more sourceable Scotch bonnet peppers. I would skip boiling cow heel as some recipes recommend—the notion intimidated me. Most importantly, I would enlist my husband in the effort, as I was like a novice doomsday prepper enticed by raw cassava. I could not be trusted to handle it on my own.

I would draw the line at compromising on cassareep. I would not skimp on that.

The first store we entered in search of cassareep was not a West Indian grocery but a Middle Eastern and northern African one. I'm not sure why I imagined it might have what we needed. I suppose I hoped that the immigrant-heavy suburban neighbourhood it was located in, populated by people from around the world, so many communities and cultures jumbled together, might compel the owner to expand offerings on the shelves. But the stock on display was unfamiliar. The meld of spices in the air was alien to me.

The young man braced against the counter asked me to show him a picture of what I was searching for. He glanced at my phone's screen and offered a giggle, a little shake of his head, to confirm they didn't carry it.

I searched on my phone. I pinpointed a West Indian grocery store just a few streets over. It's the shop we should have visited in the first place. It did carry cassareep, along with bottles of sorrel, bags of plantain chips, and small plaques depicting Vishnu and Lakshmi and Ganesha. It smelled of the spices I was acquainted with, right alongside freezer-burned fish and meat. It smelled the way all the import Caribbean stores I grew up visiting with my parents smelled.

"You guys need help?" the clerk asked as we browsed the shelves. He seemed concerned for us, his voice softened by a Guyanese accent. The sound of it made me shy. But I realized we couldn't have been the first pair to enter his establishment in search of goods the regular grocery stores didn't stock, perplexed and trailing in only second- and third-hand experiences.

We bought one bottle of cassareep, 250 millilitres, for fourteen dollars. We used it that very evening upon study of an instructional video shared online by a Guyanese chef in America. We seasoned cubed stewing beef with pepper, salt, onion powder, and garlic powder. We browned and locked the beef in the Instant Pot for an hour, opening it to add a cheesecloth bundle of cloves and cinnamon sticks, along with the Scotch bonnet, some water, and a sticky-sweet cup of cassareep.

Waiting on the pressure cooker to work for another hour, I was bothered by how easy it had been. The recipe's motions were too dumbed down, stripped of their alchemy. We had robbed the dish of its cow heel and Amazonian peppers; we had no plans to simmer it on the stove for hours then let it rest for a day to boil and reboil before eating.

I felt naive for expecting authentic pepperpot from the experience. I sank into disenchantment.

The smell that seeped through the apartment, burnt and sweet and intensifying by the minute, was what rescued me. It reminded me that pepperpot, more than anything else, is cassareep. In this initial attempt, we didn't have the wherewithal for all of pepperpot's mechanics, but we had enough.

Cassareep is ancient. Thousands of years mightier than my incapacities.

Cassareep begins with the cassava plant domesticated in prehistory, up to ten thousand years ago, in the lower flank of Amazonia. The world only recently learned that ancient Maya used to grow it. Joya de Cerén, the Salvadoran lost city, was smothered and preserved by volcanic ash, earning it the nickname "Pompeii of the Americas." Archaeologists excavated ridged planting beds tunnelled by irrigation channels, what they would expect in any yuca plot. More proof came from pouring plaster into the hollows of the hardened ash, a technique archaeologists used to unearth Pompeiian dwellers who perished in the eruption of Mount Vesuvius. In Joya de Cerén, cavities assumed the shape of yuca stocks, with their distinctive spiralled leaf nubs.

The discovery explains how the Maya population managed to balloon to millions. Cassava is rich in starch, calories, carbohydrates, and vitamins. Maize and beans alone could not have nourished all those urbanites.

Prehistory's cassava diversified into hundreds of varieties. Winds of colonialism introduced it to Africa, Asia, and Southeast Asia. Today, the African continent cultivates over half the cassava in the world. Yuca tubers and leaves feed close to one billion people.

Cassava succeeds in diverse conditions: high and low altitudes, moderate and hot temperatures, moist and sandy soils. Plants are born not only of seed but also of cut stems that spring out of any plane. Much of the world, especially the Global South, relies on yuca's resilience to enable its own, both for food and for revenue.

Spanish colonists who encountered cassava in the fifteenth and sixteenth centuries did not appreciate any of this. They found it insubstantial compared to the oil and wheat and wine they craved from their homeland. Spanish seamen with no choice but to stock their holds with cassava bread complained of gastrointestinal discomfort. They would not have expected yuca to ascend as a staple of our species, "the bread of the tropics," as requisite as corn and wheat and rice are to us now.

I doubt most Westerners understand the full extent of the gift to humanity cassava is. Many of us haven't had enough exposure to this drought- and pest-resistant shapeshifter of a root, as transmutable to beer, bread, cake, chips, and syrup as it is.

And most of us don't know the sense in which it's a blight, too. Biting into raw yuca tubers triggers a cracking open of cells walled off from each other. Cyanogenic glycoside collides with enzymes to produce cyanide. Just how much capacity cassava has to poison insects, animals, and human beings depends on its type. All varieties can be prepared for consumption, but sweet varieties are safer and easier to tame.

In some sub-Saharan African communities, including those in Angola, the Democratic Republic of the Congo, and Zambia, a condition called konzo, or "tied legs," is known to strike children and women. It comes on after exertion, creating muscle tremors, weakness, and stiffness, followed by cramping, numbness, and the sensation of electrical sparks in the calves. It can stabilize after a few days, but aftershocks are a risk. Those most impacted are left with fused ankles and pointed toes.

Konzo is associated with an overreliance on bitter cassava, a result of poverty and famine conditions, in likely combination with genetic factors. But a simple flip to sweet cassava in affected communities isn't realistic. It's bitter cassava that flourishes in their soils.

Bitter cassava preys on other regions of the world, too. During Venezuelan food shortages, people died after eating the bitter cassava they had acquired on the black market. In the Philippines, dozens of children died and were hospitalized after eating caramelized cassava treats during recess. Complaining of a bitter taste, some children had only consumed a few bites.

A Chinese bulker departing Thailand with a crew of twenty-one men was attacked by food poisoning. More than half of the crew died, in the end. The investigation hasn't come to a published conclusion I can locate, but the bulker's cargo was cassava.

It may be critical to our survival, but yuca can resist us. At times, it can lash out.

For our second attempt at pepperpot, my husband and I purchased a roast, hoping it would tenderize well in the Instant Pot. As we had done the first time, we bought a loaf of challah bread to soak up the sauce. We dutifully acquired more Scotch bonnet peppers and cinnamon sticks.

How my heart fell when I unscrewed the lid and realized we didn't have enough cassareep to coat a second batch of pepperpot. As my husband sautéed the beef over the stove, I pinched an eighth-inch teaspoon between my fingers to scrape as much of the dregs of the cassareep as I could into a measuring cup. By the time my knuckles were sticky with syrup and I could salvage no more, I had collected less than half a cup.

I searched online. There was no West Indian store within a reasonable distance of my apartment. I almost convinced myself that one of the nearby convenience stores would carry cassareep, but I knew I'd waste time trying to find it there.

The beef sizzled with the oil and onion and garlic powder, quickly browning. I was frantic. *Cassareep substitute*, I typed into the search bar, and the internet offered a pepperpot recipe from a women's magazine. It said I should order cassareep online or find it at a well-stocked Caribbean market. But if I couldn't get it where I lived, it assured me I could substitute a homemade replica of molasses, soy sauce, and Worcestershire sauce.

This was a delinquent stroll down a back alley. I'd already been warned about cassareep knockoffs. But I calculated the measurements and combined the mishmash of sauces with the cassareep to make my own imitation anyway.

The thing about cassareep is that, to the untrained eye, it seems uniformly thick and black in a sealed jar. But it pours with a surprisingly fluid give. Its edge, lined against the side of a bowl, reveals a reddish-brown tinge. Its coating in an emptying bottle produces the dimples and rivulets of stained glass. Cassareep's colour and texture, like its taste, contain dimensions.

Even when blended with the real thing, the women's magazine hybrid was too black and thick. Its scent was evocative but too sharp in the nostrils. I had not made a valid alternative. I had sired Frankenstein fluid. We wrinkled our noses and slathered it over the beef.

A curious scent intensified during the hour and a half of pressure cooking, infiltrating the apartment. The closets were closed, but I worried about fumes weaselling into my clothes, my jacket and scarves. I couldn't say the odour was terrible, exactly, but I couldn't say it was pepperpot, either.

Chewing silently, slowly, my husband and I consumed the stew we had spawned. I frowned into my bowl. The beef was blackened; the sauce was oil-speckled as it should have been. But molasses had made the dish too sweet and strangled the bitterness and acid. Cinnamon overpowered everything, snuffing the Scotch bonnets.

Leftovers of our apocryphal pepperpot lasted too long. We had to eat it for a whole week and a half. After a few days, I abandoned the sauce, scooping the meat and tipping the spoon to drain the liquid back into the container. I toasted Wonder Bread and moodily ate molasses-saturated beef in a sandwich.

I didn't see the point of honouring what we had made. It was a poor approximation of something West Indian, Amazonian, and inherent to ancient land, the way I'd often felt myself. Too many times removed.

The Makushi community in southern Guyana are expert horticulturalists. Embedded in that ecosystem of vast animal and vegetative diversity, they grow all kinds of crops and plants. Bitter cassava is their speciality. They cultivate hundreds of varieties. Sweet cassava isn't as important to them—they don't consider it real cassava.

Far from farming to survive, Makushi people are gardening people. Plants are woven into their lives, an inextricable element of their culture and cosmology and senses of self. They understand plants to have personhood. They understand that humans and plants live with one another in multispecies family relations. In working their plots, in weeding and caring for their crops, Makushi farmers communicate with their plants through poetry and song. Plants communicate back through sways and rustles in wind, through dreams and visions where vegetal spirits morph into speaking beings.

Makushi people refer to their cassava plants as children. They treat them as beloveds. At the same time, cassava is a unified spirit, a mother named Cassava Mama. She is dynamic, embodying the yuca plants and guarding them as they develop. She is to be afforded respect by humans, gifted songs and spells and tobacco and beer.

Cassava plots are not to be approached by a human when they're sick or in a weakened state. Cassava Mama may ambush that individual with spiritual fever. She may capture their soul and take it out of their body, leaving them susceptible to death.

Cassava Mama is a giver of life. She is a claimer of it, too. Just as bitter cassava is not to be dealt with lightly, just as it is toxic and integral all at once, the spirit of cassava who embodies and protects and fosters is not to be trifled with. She is not to be taken for granted.

Our third attempt at pepperpot was a lark. I noticed my grocery store had begun stocking Pepperpot Cooking Sauce marketed by a major food brand. The liquid in the jar was a beefy-brown colour. *Authentic Guyanese recipe,* read whimsical script at the top of the label. *Prepared in Canada,* read authoritative block print across the bottom.

On the back of the bottle, "beef broth" was listed as the first ingredient. "Sugars" was listed as the second. In parentheses that followed, "cassava root syrup" could be found, a concoction including blackstrap molasses and soy.

I searched the product description online. It promised that Scotch bonnet infused during manufacture had been simmered to harmlessness. It suggested pairing the cooked dish with a baguette.

I expected an interesting flavour from this experiment. I hadn't expected the smell of the pressure-cooking stew to be so reminiscent of cooking with real cassareep, at least in the beginning.

By the midway point, that had dissipated. The meal we scooped out of the pot was a respectable beef stew that worked well with bread, yes. But it was not pepperpot, not close. Still, I was stunned at how the cassava root syrup's aroma had coiled through obscurations of the molasses and soy and beef broth.

I thought of the association Makushi people make between cassava and snakes. They compare the plant stem to a slithering serpent and liken the tuber's sap to venom. I remembered a Makushi cassava origin story I'd read. Some varieties of the plant are believed to have grown from a snake that had been dissected and buried in the Amazonian soil. The snake was murdered by vengeful brothers in retaliation for charming and impregnating their sister.

Cassareep, as weakened as it was in this Canadian sauce, could still break through. It could still, at some level, drop from a tree and seduce the senses.

Jamaica Kincaid's "Girl" was published in the fiction pages of *The New Yorker* the year I was born. It's a 685-word run-on sentence, instructions from an Antiguan mother on how her daughter should behave and dress and interpret the world and do her chores. The mother is interrupted only twice, once by a protest, once by a question presumably from the girl herself, which the mother barely pauses to answer. Her diatribe sucks the girl's sentences into itself, envelops them in italics and semicolons, and keeps whirling along.

The story seared me when I first read it over two decades ago in a Caribbean literature class. The mother's admonitions poked hot into my chest: ". . . be sure to wash every day, even if it is with your own spit; don't squat down to play marbles—you are not a boy, you know . . ."

I envisioned the mother as dour and berating, even menacing in places. She would harm her daughter to prove her point, I had no question about that: ". . . this is how to hem a dress when you see the hem coming down and so to prevent yourself from looking like the slut I know you are so bent on becoming . . ."

I never learned to cook myself, Guyanese-style or otherwise. Lack of motivation when I was young and should've developed my skills was partially an absence of talent, partially an absence of necessity. As excellent a cook as she was, as pleased as I'm sure she would've been to teach me, and as often as I saw her rolling and slapping roti and stirring curries and folding pine tarts, I don't remember my mother pressuring me to accept her tutelage.

Maybe she sensed the other aspect of what bothered me about learning how to cook: I didn't want to be saddled by what seemed a woman's lonely burden. Maybe my mother, though savvy in the kitchen, didn't want to encumber me either. Maybe that's why she didn't beg or cajole me the way my friends' mothers begged and cajoled their daughters.

I regret my reticence with the art and craft of Guyanese cooking. I should've learned it from my mother when I had the chance, if only because it is so distinctive, the convergence and compression of far-flung time and space and people. Every dish bears its wounds of conflict, its markers of hard-won camaraderie. On top of that, in my adulthood, I swoon with admiration and envy when I sample the eats of home chefs I know, when I binge-watch popular chefs I wish I knew. Making good food and sharing it is sheer joy.

But I empathize with my little girl self, with how averse she was to the way women are treated. She saw women disrespected and dismissed for loving food, left unthanked when they cooked for the ones they loved. Especially women who cooked ethnic food: stinky stews, funny seasonings, freakish animal parts. They were the most unfortunate, the most hated for loving and making the wrong dishes. Eschewing it all, the loving and the making alike, seemed the only protection a girl could rake over herself.

". . . this is how to make pepper pot," the mother in Kincaid's "Girl" says near the end of her oration, "this is how to make a good medicine for a cold; this is how to make a good medicine to throw away a child before it even becomes a child; this is how to catch a fish; this is how to throw back a fish you don't like, and that way something bad won't fall on you; this is how to bully a man; this is how a man bullies you; this is how to love a man, and if this doesn't work there are other ways, and if they don't work don't feel too bad about giving up; this is how to spit up in the air if you feel like it, and this is how to move quick so that it doesn't fall on you . . ."

The story reads differently to me now. I hear pleading in the mother's words to her daughter, a trace of protection, subversion, and playfulness laced under the scold. She's not an infallible mother; she's not a flawless mother. I doubt she's a particularly safe mother. But she does seem to understand the bind of girlhood, its troubles and joys, even if her memory is smudged by womanly hardship. I'm hopeful a bud of camaraderie can erupt between mother and daughter in all of that. Maybe a spirit of communion can be nurtured between them, too.

From cooking to speaking hard-to-speak things to facing what pains me to fighting for relationships with people nothing like me. I'm finally ready to let myself appreciate the things I once worried would restrict and recast and ruin me. I'm ready to let myself love them. Not because those things can never hurt me. Simply because, in working so hard to protect myself from them, I've pushed their promise away from the place they can root and bloom in my life. I don't want to cut myself off from the hope of their beauty forever. It's no way to live.

It's possible that everything beautiful carries within it an element of danger. I suppose the only way you can manage the threat of toxicity is to approach it with humility and reverence, never taking it for granted.

In December 2022, we decided to make pepperpot for Christmas Day the traditional way, primarily cooked over the stove. I had to muster the bravery to try the cow heel version, no shrinking back, so I told family and friends about it in advance. I can't blame some of them for interpreting it as a cry for help.

My father offered a bottle of cassareep he had purchased from a store he had visited in Guyana. My aunt sent over sprigs of fresh thyme to contribute to our pot. Sensing my uncertainty about where to locate the cow heel, my friend rang up a halal butcher.

"I'll take you to them," she told me. "I need lamb and you'll probably have questions. I can talk to them in Farsi for you."

Meat was butchered at the back of the store behind shelves of rice, tea, sauces, honey, sweets, nuts. The man behind the counter that evening was perfectly fluent in English. "Cow foot, over there." He pointed a gloved finger to chest freezers on the other end of the store, lined up against the wall.

My friend and I peered into the freezers of mysterious livestock parts. We decided that a frosty bag of four peaked hooves was what we were searching for. I held it up for the butcher to see.

He shook his head. "Goat." He lifted the counter flap and came toward us. "Imagine a cow standing on those things."

He showed me what I really needed: a bag with one large frozen hoof, cloven pink at the bottom and white at the top. The butcher power-sawed the foot into smaller chunks. He gestured toward a pile of cubed bone-in stewing beef on display.

I cradled my open Guyanese cookbook in front of me. I had bought it years ago from an independent bookstore that specializes in works from the Caribbean and African diaspora and Global South, but this was the first time I was actually using one of the book's recipes. "I think I need four pounds," I told him, "half stewing, half oxtail."

"No oxtail left," he answered. "And make it five pounds. I charge you four."

The cow heel and meat was knotted in four layers of plastic, weighty in my hand when we walked it back to my friend's car. "You didn't buy anything," I told her. "Where's your lamb?"

"They didn't have the kind I wanted."

"I made you chauffeur me to cow foot? I should've been able to do that on my own."

"I wanted to help," she answered. "It was fun."

I had just purchased thirty-five dollars' worth of cattle, over six pounds of it. Earlier in the week, I had visited a high-priced supermarket to buy cassava flour, paying fourteen dollars for a 567-gram bag. The silky off-white powder was pristine in its package, too uniform to have been grated or strained by hand. But I knew I wouldn't be able to reproduce the cassava bread of the videos I had watched anyway, women palming pulped yuca into a disk over a hot metal plate and leaving it to dry in equatorial sun. I would bake some other kind of cassava bun or loaf, alongside yeasty Guyanese plait bread.

My husband seasoned the cow foot and beef, letting them ease up to room temperature in bowls. They released an almost gamey aroma. Then he pressure cooked the cow foot for forty-five minutes and browned the beef in a stock pot, squinting and stirring, elbow cocked. He added dollops of cassareep along with thyme and brown sugar. He fished the jiggling nubs of cow foot from the pressure cooker with a straining spoon and added them to the stock pot.

We debated the cassareep. I had more beef than I had meant to buy; we would likely need more cassareep than what recipes called for. But each brand of cassareep is spiced differently and each pepperpot is unique to its chef. Every video we had watched stressed the point: every family has their own version of the dish, bespoke measurements and passed-down steps to honour. More than allowed, plurality is encouraged. Use the meats you want, they said. Spice to your taste, add cassareep to achieve your desired colour. Home chefs stated it so emphatically that I wondered if they might've been reacting to some kind of pepperpot controversy, a dogmatic cook who had boasted of a singular pepperpot truth. There are few musts and no judgment in the hallowed realm of Guyanese pepperpot. Cassareep might be its only universal doctrine.

Cooking our stovetop pepperpot spanned five hours. Add proofing and baking to the count and we pushed past eight. Were our homemade pepperpot and breads, made the authentic Guyanese way, perfect? In all honesty, no. Our skills are in their infancy. One jar of cassareep simply didn't contain enough flavour for the amount of beef I had bought. The cow heel we combined with stewing beef turned out too fatty and gelatinous. The cassava bread baked too densely. The plait bread hadn't quite risen enough either.

Still, I loved what we created. I insisted we eat it on Christmas morning as if it had come out the way we had hoped it would. This pepperpot was our pepperpot. All of ours. Friends and family had helped us find our way, nudging us along. Home video makers and cookbook writers had coached us from over their stoves, miles and years away. Cassava and cassareep had made the whole thing possible in the first place, immemorial Amazonian wisdom that it is. I was too grateful for the soil and land and ancestors and mentors far and wide to do anything but treat the pepperpot as a grand feast.

CODA: ON SELECTIVE COLLECTIVE MEMORY

For years I've bustled past the Chinese Railway Workers Memorial in downtown Toronto without even noticing it. The structure is dwarfed by behemoths, the CN Tower and sports stadiums and glass-walled condominiums. It's situated between a small street and the railway lines that trace Lake Ontario for three hundred kilometres until the water siphons into the St. Lawrence River and escapes into the North Atlantic. In the other direction, the tracks curve southward, branching into the United States, and westward, over the other Great Lakes and through the prairies and mountains of Turtle Island, surging all the way to the Pacific Ocean.

Designed by multidisciplinary artist Eldon Garnet to evoke a traditional paifang, at first glance the memorial could be mistaken for a utilitarian archway. Its legs are concrete. Steel beams criss-cross to climb up and over and meet at the top. Emotive details are discernable upon closer examination: the figure of a Chinese worker balancing in a wide stance above. He holds the end of a rope that threads into a pulley. A worker at the base of the memorial arcs his back, bracing and clutching the joist behind him with one hand. His other hand reaches toward a dangling beam.

Neither man is protected by a hard hat or harness. They are precarious. A few feet out from the main memorial, large rocks are planted into the walkway. They are chunks of mountain, blasted off of the Rockies themselves.

Like this structure, the Iron Road Pioneers statue in San Luis Obispo, California, features two men. Their cues and jackets swing out as they co-operate to lever a rail with sticks. The railway worker of Vancouver's Downtown Eastside Chinatown monument strides into the wind, coat flapping behind him like a cape, shovel hoisted over his shoulder. The Chinese railway workers of the memorial in Sacramento, California, look even more like superheroes with Adonis physiques. They yell and glare and dominate their labour. One poses bare-chested, muscles rippling as he drives a sledgehammer into rock.

The Chinese railway workers' monument in Salt Lake City, Utah, in contrast, includes no people. It is a solemn cubist formation of the hardware of the *coolie* labour: bronze, steel, granite, sandstone. The memorial site east of Boise, Idaho, yards away from an active track and the twisting Snake River, is designated by a tombstone for a worker who died. The original marker had been battered by weather and vandals, even a derailed train. It's now a fresh block chiselled with Chinese and English words, but the deceased worker's name has been lost.

There's something different about the memorial in Toronto. It isn't exactly a veneration of its subjects or a glorification of their achievements, but it isn't mournful or head-shaking, either. In my reading, it conveys a layered tale. Its workers are tentative.

They are the two diminutive elements of the structure. Daunted as they are, they try at their tasks anyway. The impact of their labour is undeniable. The evidence of what they've made possible is metres away, those train lines traced every day for cargo and commute. But crawling over that archway, just the two of them, there is a futility to the danger the men face. The danger that underlies their grimaces.

They are not mythic. Wind doesn't billow their clothes and hair. They are not an intrepid duo. They're men. Recognizable, isolated, breakable. Caught in a go-between much wider than their existence.

I started at a loss for words to articulate my own go-betweenness. That loss was grounded in memories that waned long before I was born. Between my childhood and adulthood, gradually gaining the language to speak this complicated history of our globe, I remember my high school teacher telling the class how the rail lines spanning Canada and the United States transformed both countries. He praised the Chinese immigrants for their commitment in constructing the most perilous stretches of the tracks. Free consent was assumed in the way he referred to what they did. I don't remember him saying anything about these immigrants being indentured and coerced labourers. If he had breathed a word, I would have made the connection to my ancestors, however tentative. I don't recall him saying anything about the terms or conditions that framed their lives and so many of their deaths, let alone the crises and ambitions that might have driven them out of their homelands in the first place.

He applauded their *contributions*. Racialized contributions are readily memorialized, one manic skip away from *excellence*.

Contributions are dignified, ringing out a single note. It is easy to loiter in this realm for racialized ancestors. Contributions straighten the unmannered edges of what happened to them. It soft-focuses their underheard stories, sorts them neatly into the past and zooms them away from where we have landed today.

It's the flipside of contributions, the cultivation and fruits of racial exploitation—the profiteering that plants it—that remains perpetually difficult for everyone involved. It is painful, embarrassing, and distasteful all around. Exploitation is intentional and organized, but truly reckless. Decreed and legislated, yet deeply anarchic. No wonder so many of us are eager to deny and underplay it, pricked with offence at its mere mention. No wonder the ways humans get set up and knocked down, treated as one and the same as their labour, blur in no time.

One by One the Walkers Vanish, reads the plaque on one of the mountain boulders of the Toronto Chinese Railway Workers Memorial. If we don't insist on remembrance, we will forget. We will make sure we forget.

The overseer, the enslaved, the Indigenous, the indentured and coerced. What can we do to sharpen our hesitant perceptions of them together in a way we rarely have? How do we repair our own potholed memories?

We won't get far by attempting it on our own. More than the endeavour of an individual brain, memory is the project of many brains. Whole families and communities and peoples. Psychological research on collective memory shows that just as we selectively remember and forget on our own, we participate in group remembering and forgetting. In simple terms, we're motivated to disregard and recall selected shared experiences when we feel highly aligned to one another, speaking to each other about our preferred memories to bask in and solidify our connection.

Interestingly, when we believe our group identity is under fire, our collective memory gets less selective. It gets nuanced. We become more attuned to the complexities of our shared lives in order to douse the threat. We become more capable of perceiving the multitudes of the reasonings, justifications, and choices we embody as individuals in a group.

We give our own selves and our own groups room to be messy, imperfect, and complicated, and we like to talk about it with our own.

In the very last line of *Inglorious Empire: What the British Did to India*, Shashi Tharoor concludes that "sometimes the best crystal ball is a rearview mirror." If hardy recall is essential to our ability and willingness to break the patterns we've locked ourselves into, a critical step toward changing our world for the good of more people, we have to take our collective memory and our tendencies toward partial collective memories seriously.

And if selective collective memory is at least part of the reason we have such a hard time recalling our full pasts to conceive of our interlinked futures, we have to make a point of growing our sense of shared identity, both in sheer number and in kind of those remembering. We have to work hard at sewing our little tents together so more and more hearts and minds and souls and brains get covered under the one expanding patchwork quilt. So more and more of us on this planet get into the fold of who exactly recalls and forgets together.

The way selective collective memory works means we have to do whatever we can to blow out the scope of our shared sense of self. We have to battle the forces that box it in and squeeze it tight. They are legion, they are tenacious, they are convincing. Many times, they are well intentioned. Just about all the time, they believe themselves to be in the right.

We need to believe they're wrong. We need to fight them so when threats to our identity inevitably confront us, we have muscles to flex for a wider, wiser recall of the intricacies of our shared life on earth, one that is more helpful to more of us. Ultimately more valuable to us.

We are going to feel threatened. That much is a given. We need to figure out how to feel threatened together. Dedicate our resources and capabilities to it. More and more of us need to get in on the project of saying yes to alignment with one another, to gift ourselves the capacity to feel the same fire and better collectively remember and forget together.

I'm making a case for greater belonging. But not only the sunny or sweet kind. I'm making allowance for begrudging intergroup belonging. For wearied-eye partnerships where we pull one another in not only with happy hugs but also with urgent yanks. In the midst of mounting oligarchy and authoritarianism, the fighting and war that go along with them, with our destinies orchestrated by a handful of perversely powerful individuals and the economic, human rights, and climate disasters to match, we might not have another choice.

You are your labour. It's entirely possible this logic that launched ships centuries ago, underpinning so much unfree labour and our work and worth today, will become more potent for more people than it has ever been. It's entirely possible this logic is going to set us up to knock us down anew.

Perhaps, then, what I mean to do is reformulate the lessons of racialized indentured labour exploitation and make a case for a shared sense of go-betweenness. Perhaps we all need to grow our understanding of being liminal people together, unsettling our taken-for-granted ideas of ourselves. In our split-apart groupings, we spend a lot of time convinced of who we are and what it means to live a good life. We think we know what's in our own interests. We think we know what we need. Maybe we need to force ourselves out of the assumption that we know ourselves. That our pasts and presents are all that distinct from one another. Kick ourselves off the shore and wade in the murky waters together.

Maybe basking in liminality is our opportunity. And maybe we have a real chance of agreeing to such a collective shakeup because whenever we sit with whoever we think we are, we become aware that liminality is the essence of what we are on this earth. Breathing in the sliver between life and death alongside one another.

We are impermanent creatures here. We each understand this when we slow down, steal away, and peek over the fences of our delicate, splintered selves. We each understand this when we push ourselves to perceive the simple truth of our mortality.

We have to perceive our mortality together. Get stubborn about conceding to it, arm linked in arm, as traumatic as it can be. We need to pay attention to the memorials of life and death that have become part of our landscape, and heed what they tell us.

Perhaps the shared truth of our impermanence can humble us. Harden the foundation for our insistent, stronger, and more inclusive collective memory. Our insistent and stronger and more inclusive collective future, given the short time that remains.

ACKNOWLEDGEMENTS

A reader is a gift to a book. Reading is an act of grace to a writer. Thank you, reader, for gifting this book your time and gracing me with your attention. I appreciate you.

My sincere thanks to Haley Cullingham, Stephanie Sinclair, and the McClelland & Stewart team. I couldn't have asked for a more excellent and supportive publishing experience.

My deep gratitude to Suzanne Brandreth of CookeMcDermid. For your writing advice and great taste, for your kindness over many years.

Many early readers reviewed this manuscript in part or in full and offered encouragement, feedback, and wisdom. Thank you for sharing your smarts and savvy. Thank you for your sweetness, too. It's entirely heartening to me.

In particular, I am grateful for the unparalleled talent and friendship of Shoilee Khan and Allison LaSorda of Bluegate Collective. We have something wonderful. Thank you for having me.

Thank you to the Toronto Arts Council, Ontario Arts Council, and Writers' Union of Canada, who have generously supported my literary education and practice through their grantmaking programs.

This book stands on the works of writers and researchers listed in the bibliography, and it is influenced by many others not listed. My favourites include Gaiutra Bahadur's *Coolie Woman: The Odyssey of Indenture*; Ulbe Bosma's *The World of Sugar: How the Sweet Stuff Transformed Our Politics, Health, and Environment Over 2,000 Years*; Anne Anlin Cheng's *The Melancholy of Race: Psychoanalysis, Assimilation, and Hidden Grief*; Cathy Park Hong's *Minor Feelings: An Asian American Reckoning*; and Lisa Lowe's *The Intimacies of Four Continents*. I savoured each one. They were the most delightful element of the writing process. I encourage you to explore them yourself.

Finally, always, in Christ.

Produced with the support of the City of Toronto through Toronto Arts Council.

FUNDED BY
THE CITY OF TORONTO
TORONTO
ARTS_COUNCIL

BIBLIOGRAPHY

Aapravasi Ghat World Heritage Site Brief history. (n.d.). Government Online Centre. https://aapravasi.govmu.org/aapravasi/wp-content/uploads/2020/09/Brief-History-of-the-Aapravasi-Ghat-World-Heritage-Site.pdf

Aapravasi Ghat. (n.d.). UNESCO World Heritage Centre. https://whc.unesco.org/en/list/1227/

About Us. (n.d.). TheDream.US. https://www.thedream.us/about/

About: Indigenous peoples in Guyana. (n.d.). DBpedia. https://dbpedia.org/page/Indigenous_peoples_in_Guyana

Adjin-Tettey, E., Calder, G., Cameron, A., Deckha, M., Johnson, R., Lessard, H., Maloney, M., & Young, M. (2008). Postcard from the Edge (of Empire). Social & Legal Studies, 17(1), 5-38. https://doi.org/10.1177/0964663907086454

Ali, G. A. (2020). Liminal Spaces: Migration and women of the Guyanese diaspora. https://library.oapen.org/bitstream/20.500.12657/42450/1/9781783749898.pdf

Allan, D. (1998, January 9). Spice world. The Herald. https://www.heraldscotland.com/news/12283226.spice-world/

Allen, R. B. (2012). Re-conceptualizing the "new system of slavery". Man in India, 92(2), 225-245. https://www.researchgate.net/publication/289661924_Re-conceptualizing_the_new_system_of_slavery

Allen, R. B. (2017). Asian indentured labor in the 19th and early 20th century colonial plantation world. Oxford Research Encyclopedia of Asian History. https://doi.org/10.1093/acrefore/9780190277727.013.33

The Arrival of the Portuguese in British Guiana. (2018, January 2).

Guyana Chronicle. https://guyanachronicle.com/2012/05/05/the-arrival-of-the-portuguese-in-british-guiana/

Al-Solaylee, K. (2016). Brown: What Being Brown in the World Today Means (to Everyone). HarperCollins.

Anderson, C. (2009). Convicts and Coolies: Rethinking Indentured Labour in the Nineteenth Century. Slavery & Abolition, 30(1), 93-109. https://doi.org/10.1080/01440390802673856

The Arrival of the Portuguese in British Guiana. (2018, January 2). Guyana Chronicle. https://guyanachronicle.com/2012/05/05/the-arrival-of-the-portuguese-in-british-guiana/

Arroyo-Kalin, M., & Riris, P. (2020). Did pre-Columbian populations of the Amazonian biome reach carrying capacity during the Late Holocene? Philosophical Transactions of the Royal Society B Biological Sciences, 376(1816). https://doi.org/10.1098/rstb.2019.0715

Auerbach, S. (2022). Of Rights and Riots: Indenture and (Mis)Rule in the Late Nineteenth-Century British Caribbean. The English Historical Review, 137(589), 1662-1692. https://doi.org/10.1093/ehr/cead002

Austen, J. (1994). Mansfield Park. [eBook edition]. The Project Gutenberg. https://www.gutenberg.org/cache/epub/141/pg141-images.html (Original work published 1814)

Bahadur, G. (2014). Coolie Woman: The Odyssey of Indenture. University of Chicago Press.

Bahadur, G. (2015). Postcards from Empire. Dissent Magazine. https://www.dissentmagazine.org/article/postcards-from-empire/

Bahl, A. (2021, December 16). The Startling Postcolonial Poetics of "Coolitude". The Nation. https://www.thenation.com/article/culture/cargo-hold-coolitude/

Balan, S. & Mahalingam, R. (2015). "Good Asian Moms": Engendering the model minority myth among Indian immigrant working women. In O. M. Espín & A. L. Dottolo (Eds.), *Gendered journeys: Women, migration and feminist psychology* (pp. 104–122). Palgrave Macmillan/Springer Nature. https://doi.org/10.1057/9781137521477.0012

The Baroque style. (n.d.). Victoria and Albert Museum. https://www.vam.ac.uk/articles/the-baroque-style

Bartlett, J. T. (2019, August 26). The Iron Road Pioneers. Atlas Obscura. https://www.atlasobscura.com/places/the-iron-road-pioneers

Bates, C. (2017). Some Thoughts on the Representation and Misrepresentation of the Colonial South Asian Labour Diaspora.

South Asian Studies, 33(1), 7-22. https://doi.org/10.1080/02666030.2017.1300372

Bates, C. (2024). Introduction. In C. Bates (Ed.), Beyond Indenture: Agency and Resistance in the Colonial South Asian Diaspora (1-16). Cambridge University Press.

Bazelon, C., Vargas, A., Janakiraman, R., & Olson, M. (2023). Quantification of Reparations for Transatlantic Chattel Slavery. The Brattle Group. https://www.brattle.com/wp-content/uploads/2023/07/Quantification-of-Reparations-for-Transatlantic-Chattel-Slavery.pdf

Beach, B. (2013). Riding and Driving for Women. [eBook edition]. The Project Gutenberg. https://gutenberg.org/cache/epub/42229/pg42229-images.html (Original work published 1912)

Benedict, R., & Weltfish, G. (1946). The Races of Mankind. Public Affairs Committee Inc.

Benton, G. (2022). Chinese Indentured Labour in the Dutch East Indies, 1880–1942. Springer Nature.

Between unfreedoms: How caste was a major determining factor in deciding return migration of indentured workers. (2021, July 16). University of Reading. https://research.reading.ac.uk/global-development/between-unfreedoms-how-caste-was-a-major-determining-factor-in-deciding-return-migration-of-indentured-workers/

Beyond this Day–29 January 1838: Indian Indentured Trade and "The First Crossing". (2020, January 29). Royal Historical Society. https://blog.royalhistsoc.org/2020/01/29/beyond-this-day-29-january-1838-indian-indentured-trade-and-the-first-crossing/

Bittles, A. H. (2012). Consanguinity in Context. Cambridge University Press. https://doi.org/10.1017/cbo9781139015844

Black, E. (2013, July 28). Farming Utopia: The Promised Lands of the Peace Mission and Peoples Temple. Alternative Considerations of Jonestown & Peoples Temple. https://jonestown.sdsu.edu/?page_id=34228

Blame, Bullying and Disrespect: Chinese Canadians Reveal Their Experiences with Racism During COVID-19. (2020, June 22). Angus Reid Institute. https://angusreid.org/racism-chinese-canadians-covid19/

Boer, N. (2019, May 13). Indenture. Global South Studies. https://www.globalsouthstudies.org/keyword-essay/indenture/

Bosma, U. (2023). The World of Sugar: How the Sweet Stuff Transformed Our Politics, Health, and Environment Over 2,000 Years. Harvard University Press.

Brand, D. (2023). A Map to the Door of No Return: Notes to Belonging. Vintage Canada.

Brooks, D. (2020, March 15). The Nuclear Family Was a Mistake. The Atlantic. https://www.theatlantic.com/magazine/archive/2020/03/the-nuclear-family-was-a-mistake/605536/

Buckingham, J. (2024). Disabling labour: race, disability and Indian indentured labour on Fijian sugar plantations, 1879–1920. Postcolonial Studies, 27(1), 83-98. https://doi.org/10.1080/13688790.2024.2320088

Buijs, G. (1999). Migration and the Disappearance of Caste among Indian South Africans. Alternation, 6(2), 180-192. https://hdl.handle.net/10520/AJA10231757_161

Building the Railway. (2017, January 19). Government of British Columbia. https://www2.gov.bc.ca/gov/content/governments/multiculturalism-anti-racism/chinese-legacy-bc/history/building-the-railway

Burgemeester, A. (2022, September 2). 15 Signs Your Cousin Is Sexually Attracted To You. Romantified. https://romantified.com/signs-your-cousin-is-sexually-attracted-to-you/

Cahn, L. (2025, April 22). 10 Royals Who Married Their Relatives. Reader's Digest. https://www.rd.com/list/royals-who-married-their-relatives/

Calderon, P. S. P., Wong, J. D., & Hodgdon, B. T. (2022). A scoping review of the physical health and psychological well-being of individuals in interracial romantic relationships. Family Relations, 71(5), 2011-2029. https://doi.org/10.1111/fare.12765

Cassareep. (n.d.). In Wikiwand. https://www.wikiwand.com/en/Cassareep

Chalabi, M. (Host). (2021, November 29). Is it really that bad to marry my cousin? [Audio podcast episode]. In Am I Normal? https://www.ted.com/podcasts/am-i-normal-is-it-really-that-bad-to-marry-my-cousin-transcript

Chang, K. (2015). Coolie. In C. J. Schlund-Vials, L. Trinh Võ, & K. Scott Wong (Eds.), Keywords for Asian American Studies. New York University Press. https://keywords.nyupress.org/asian-american-studies/essay/coolie/

Cheng, A. A. (2000). The Melancholy of Race: Psychoanalysis, Assimilation, and Hidden Grief. Oxford University Press.

Chinatown Memorial Monument. (2023, January 17). Veterans Affairs Canada, Government of Canada. https://www.veterans.gc.ca/en/remembrance/memorials/national-inventory-canadian-memorials/details/7699

Chinese Railroad Workers Memorial. (2021, September 22). Ontario Association of Architects. https://oaa.on.ca/whats-on/bloaag/bloaag-detail/Chinese-Railroad-Workers-Memorial

Chinese Railway Workers Memorial, Part 1. (2024). City of Toronto. https://www.artworxto.ca/on-demand/chinese-railway-workers-memorial-part-1

Chinese Railway Workers Memorial, Part 2. (2024). City of Toronto. https://www.artworxto.ca/on-demand/chinese-railroad-workers-memorial-part-2

Choenni, C. (2020). Indentured Hindustani Women in Suriname. In F. Gounder, K. Hiralal, A. Pande, & M. S. Hassankhan (Eds.), Women, Gender and the Legacy of Slavery and Indenture (pp. 73-97). Routledge. https://doi.org/10.4324/9781003132219-4

Chuang, R., Wilkins, C., Tan, M., & Mead, C. (2021). Racial minorities' attitudes toward interracial couples: An intersection of race and gender. Group Processes & Intergroup Relations, 24(3), 453-467. https://doi.org/10.1177/1368430219899482

Claveyrolas, M. (2015). The "Land of the Vaish"? Caste Structure and Ideology in Mauritius. South Asia Multidisciplinary Academic Journal. https://doi.org/10.4000/samaj.3886

Clement, C. R., Denevan, W. M., Heckenberger, M. J., Junqueira, A. B., Neves, E. G., Teixeira, W. G., & Woods, W. I. (2015). The domestication of Amazonia before European conquest. Proceedings of the Royal Society B Biological Sciences, 282(1812). https://doi.org/10.1098/rspb.2015.0813

Community Cousins. (n.d.). Vancouver Island University. https://indigenous.viu.ca/community-cousins

Conrad, J. (1995). Heart of Darkness. [eBook edition]. The Project Gutenberg. https://www.gutenberg.org/files/219/219-h/219-h.htm (Original work published 1899)

Conrad, J. (2006). Typhoon. [eBook edition]. The Project Gutenberg.

https://www.gutenberg.org/files/1142/1142-h/1142-h.htm#link2H_4_0001 (Original work published 1902)

Coolie. (2005, February 19). In Wiktionary. https://en.wiktionary.org/wiki/coolie

Coolies: How Britain Reinvented Slavery. (2002). [Film]. BBC Four Corners Documentary.

Curry, O., Roberts, S. G. B., & Dunbar, R. I. M. (2012). Altruism in social networks: Evidence for a "kinship premium." British Journal of Psychology, 104(2), 283-295. https://doi.org/10.1111/j.2044-8295.2012.02119.x

Curt Teich Co. records. (n.d.). The Newberry Library. https://archives.newberry.org/repositories/2/resources/1282

Daly, L. (2021). Cassava Spirit and the Seed of History: On Garden Cosmology in Northern Amazonia. Anthropological Forum, 31(4), 377-395. https://doi.org/10.1080/00664677.2021.1994918

Daly, L. (2016). Cassava Spirit and the Seed of History: The Biocultural History of a Staple Crop in Amazonian Guyana. Commodities of Empire. https://commoditiesofempire.org.uk/research/research-journeys/cassava-spirit-and-the-seed-of-history/

Damir-Geilsdorf, S., Lindner, U., Muller, G., Zeuske, M., & Tappe, O. (2016). Bonded Labour: Global and Comparative Perspectives (18th-21st Century). Transcript Verlag.

Darby, S. (2021). Sisters in Hate: American Women and White Extremism. Back Bay Books.

Davidoff, L. (2011). The Rise and Fall of Close Marriage. In L. Davidoff, Thicker than Water: Siblings and their Relations, 1780-1920 (pp. 225-249). Oxford University Press eBooks. https://doi.org/10.1093/acprof:oso/9780199546480.003.0010

Davis, C. (2015, July 20). This Super Root Preserves Meat Indefinitely! Ask a Prepper. https://www.askaprepper.com/this-super-root-preserves-meat-indefinitely/

de Leon, K. (2022, October 2). Portland is still the whitest big city in America. The Seattle Times. https://www.seattletimes.com/seattle-news/portland-is-still-the-whitest-big-city-in-america/

de Souza, J. G., Schaan, D. P., Robinson, M., Barbosa, A. D., Aragão, L. E. O. C., Marimon, B. H., Marimon, B. S., da Silva, I. B., Khan, S. S., Nakahara, F. R., & Iriarte, J. (2018). Pre-Columbian earth-builders settled along the entire southern rim of the Amazon. Nature Communications, 9(1). https://doi.org/10.1038/s41467-018-03510-7

Deguzman, K. (2023, September 10). Romanticism in Art—Definition, Examples & Traits. StudioBinder. https://www.studiobinder.com/blog/what-is-romanticism-art-definition/

Deolall, I. (2021, December 23). Savouring history in a pepperpot. Stabroek News. https://www.stabroeknews.com/2021/12/23/features/first-person-singular/savouring-history-in-a-pepperpot/

Dharani, B. (2021). Migrant labour in Singapore: Indentured servitude by another name. Routed Magazine. https://www.routedmagazine.com/omc21-1miglabour-singapore

Ding, L. (Director). (1997). Coolies, Sailors, and Settlers: Voyage to the New World. Ancestors in Americas. [Film]. The Center for Educational Telecommunications.

Dirks, G. (2024). Immigration Policy in Canada. In The Canadian Encyclopedia. https://www.thecanadianencyclopedia.ca/en/article/immigration-policy

Dow, L. (2021, May 25). Indentured Indian Workers and Anti-Colonial Resistance in the British Empire. The Gale Review. https://review.gale.com/2021/05/25/indentured-workers-and-anti-colonial-resistance-in-the-british-empire/

Dowlah, C. (2021). Cross-Border Labor Mobility: Historical and Contemporary Perspectives. Palgrave Macmillan.

Dowlah, C. (2021). Foundations of Modern Slavery: Profiles of Unfree and Coerced Labor through the Ages (1st ed.). Routledge. https://doi.org/10.4324/9781003160182

Duong, G. (2022, May 30). You're called a "model minority" as an Asian American—until they decide you aren't. NPR. https://www.npr.org/2022/05/30/1101790205/as-an-asian-american-youre-called-a-model-minority-until-they-decide-you-arent

Eddo-Lodge, R. (2022). Why I'm No Longer Talking to White People About Race. Bloomsbury Publishing.

Elsie, R. (n.d.). The Purger Postcard Collection. http://www.albanianphotography.net/purger/

Emerson, R. W. (1975). The Journals and Miscellaneous Notebooks of Ralph Waldo Emerson: 1848–1851. Harvard University Press.

Equal Justice Initiative. (2022). The Transatlantic Slave Trade. https://eji.org/report/transatlantic-slave-trade

Ette, O. (2016). From the Transarchipélique Antilles: The Coolitude of Khal Torabully. The Ameena Gafoor Institute for the Study of

Indentureship and its Legacies. https://ameenagafoorinstitute.org/from-the-transarchiplique-antilles-the-coolitude-of-khal-torabully

Explore a Future in Medicine. (n.d.). University of British Columbia Faculty of Medicine. https://med-fom-ugrad.sites.olt.ubc.ca/files/2021/06/md-indigenous-students-brochure-pss-v5.pdf

Families Will Change Dramatically in the Years to Come. (2024, January 8). Max Planck Institute for Demographic Research. https://www.demogr.mpg.de/en/news_events_6123/news_press_releases_4630/press/families_will_change_dramatically_in_the_years_to_come_12790

Farrington, K. (n.d.). Pepper Pot: The Allegorical Dish of Caribbean Culture. http://di.salemstate.edu/provisions/exhibits/show/pepper-pot--the-allegorical-di

Fatehi, K., Priestley, J. L., & Taasoobshirazi, G. (2020). The expanded view of individualism and collectivism: One, two, or four dimensions? International Journal of Cross Cultural Management, 20(1), 7-24. https://doi.org/10.1177/1470595820913077

Félix Morin photographs of East Indians in Trinidad. (n.d.). ArchiveGrid. https://researchworks.oclc.org/archivegrid/collection/data/1201199405

Fok, W. (2022, September 13). The Rise and Fall of Chinese Indentured Labour. The Gale Review. https://review.gale.com/2022/09/13/the-rise-and-fall-of-chinese-indentured-labour/

Fong, T. W., & Tsuang, J. (2007). Asian-Americans, Addictions, and Barriers to Treatment. Psychiatry (Edgmont), 4(11), 51-9.

Foo, S. (2023). What My Bones Know: A Memoir of Healing from Complex Trauma. Ballantine Books.

Forbes, N., Yang, L. C., & Lim, S. (2023). Intersectional discrimination and its impact on Asian American women's mental health: A mixed-methods scoping review. Frontiers in Public Health, 11. https://doi.org/10.3389/fpubh.2023.993396

Forcinito, A. (2016). Testimonio: The Witness, the Truth, and the Inaudible. In Y. Martínez-San Miguel, B. Sifuentes-Jáuregui, & M. Belausteguigoitia (Eds.), Critical Terms in Caribbean and Latin American Thought (pp. 239-251). New Directions in Latino American Cultures. Palgrave Macmillan. https://doi.org/10.1057/9781137547903_22

Francis, Angelyn. (2021, March 27). The "model minority" myth explained. What you need to know about how it has propped up anti-Asian racism in Canada. Toronto Star. https://www.thestar.com/news/canada/the-model-minority-myth-explained-what-you-need-to-know-about-how-it-has-propped/article_5fbe02da-7084-52e6-a529-9b89660ff4ce.html

Frazier, N. (2013, July 28). The "Other" Jim Jones: Rabbi David Hill, House of Israel, and Black American Religion in the Age of Peoples Temple. Alternative Considerations of Jonestown & Peoples Temple. https://jonestown.sdsu.edu/?page_id=34259

Frediansyah, A. (Ed.). (2021). Cassava: Biology, Production, and Use. IntechOpen eBooks. http://doi.org/10.5772/intechopen.87488

Frew, R. (n.d.). St. Vincent, the Forgotten Saint. Algarve Daily News. https://algarvedailynews.com/history/7717-st-vincent-the-forgotten-saint

From India to Guadeloupe. (2021, December 15). Foyer. https://readfoyer.com/article/india-guadeloupe

Fukuyama, F. (2022). Liberalism and Its Discontents. Farrar, Straus and Giroux.

Gandhi, L. (2013, November 25). A history of indentured labor gives "Coolie" its sting. NPR. https://www.npr.org/sections/codeswitch/2013/11/25/247166284/a-history-of-indentured-labor-gives-coolie-its-sting

Gao, Z. (2021). Sinophobia during the Covid-19 Pandemic: Identity, Belonging, and International Politics. Integrative Psychological and Behavioral Science, 56(2), 472-490. https://doi.org/10.1007/s12124-021-09659-z

Gardner, S. (2023, June 16). What Women Have Gained From Affirmative Action. Politico. https://www.politico.com/newsletters/women-rule/2023/06/16/what-women-have-gained-from-affirmative-action-00102397

Genetics vs. Genomics Fact Sheet. (n.d.). National Human Genome Research Institute. https://www.genome.gov/about-genomics/fact-sheets/Genetics-vs-Genomics

Gilroy, P. (1993). The Black Atlantic: Modernity and Double Consciousness. Harvard University Press.

Gosine, A. (2016). My Mother's Baby: Wrecking Work After Indentureship. In G. J. Hosein & L. Outar (Eds.), Indo-Caribbean Feminist Thought: Genealogies, Theories, Enactments (pp. 49-60). Palgrave Macmillan.

Gosine, A. (2017). Visual Art after Indenture: Authoethnographic Reflections. South Asian Studies, 33(1), 105–112. https://doi.org/10.1080/02666030.2017.1299308

Goodkind, D. (2019). The Chinese Diaspora: Historical Legacies and Contemporary Trends. United States Census Bureau. https://www.census.gov/content/dam/Census/library/working-papers/2019/demo/Chinese_Diaspora.pdf

Goucher, C. L. (2014). Congotay! Congotay! A Global History of Caribbean Food. Taylor and Francis.

Graeber, D. (2011). Debt: The First 5,000 Years. Melville House.

Groeneveld, E. (2017, May 15). Early Human Migration. World History Encyclopedia. https://www.worldhistory.org/article/1070/early-human-migration/

Guinn, J. (2018). The Road to Jonestown: Jim Jones and Peoples Temple. Simon & Schuster.

Gupta, P. (2024). They Called Us Exceptional: And Other Lies That Raised Us. Random House.

Hackett, A. (2023, June 29). July 1 marks the 100-year anniversary of the Chinese Exclusion Act. Concordia News. https://www.concordia.ca/cunews/main/stories/2023/06/29/july-1-marks-the-100-year-anniversary-of-the-chinese-exclusion-act.html

Hamamy, H. (2011). Consanguineous Marriages. Journal of Community Genetics, 3(3), 185-192. https://doi.org/10.1007/s12687-011-0072-y

Harkup, K. (2017, June 22). Cassava crisis: the deadly food that doubles as a vital Venezuelan crop. The Guardian. https://www.theguardian.com/science/blog/2017/jun/22/cassava-deadly-food-venezuela

Hayes, A. M. (2008). The Horsewoman: A Practical Guide to Side-Saddle Riding, 2nd ed. [eBook edition]. The Project Gutenberg. https://gutenberg.org/cache/epub/26318/pg26318-images.html (Original work published 1903)

Hershberger, S. (2020, October 5). Humans Are All More Closely Related Than We Commonly Think. Scientific American. https://www.scientificamerican.com/article/humans-are-all-more-closely-related-than-we-commonly-think/

Hill, F. (2023, December 19). The Great Cousin Decline. The Atlantic. https://www.theatlantic.com/family/archive/2023/12/cousin-relationships-fertility-rate/676892/

Hirst, K. K. (2019, January 20). The History and Domestication of Cassava. ThoughtCo. https://www.thoughtco.com/cassava-manioc-domestication-170321

Hirst, K. K. (2018, September 24). The Lost Village of Cerén in El Salvador: The North American Pompeii. ThoughtCo. https://www.thoughtco.com/ceren-lost-village-of-el-salvador-170770

Hirst, W. & Coman, A. (2018). Building a collective memory: the case for collective forgetting. Current Opinion in Psychology, 23(C), 88-92. https://doi.org/10.1016/j.copsyc.2018.02.002

History. (n.d.). Promontório de Sagres. https://promontoriodesagres.pt/en/about-the-promontory/history/

Hollup, O. (1994). The Disintegration of Caste and Changing Concepts of Indian Ethnic Identity in Mauritius. Ethnology, 33(4), 297-316. https://doi.org/10.2307/3773901

Park Hong, C. (2021). Minor Feelings: An Asian American Reckoning. One World.

Hosein, G. J. (2022). Post-Indentureship Caribbean Feminist Thought, Transoceanic Feminisms, and the Convergence of Asymmetries. The Scholar & Feminist Online, 16(1). https://sfonline.barnard.edu/post-indentureship-caribbean-feminist-thought-transoceanic-feminisms-and-the-convergence-of-asymmetries/

Hossain, P. (2021). "A Matter of Doubt and Uncertainty": John Gladstone and the Post-Slavery Framework of Labour in the British Empire. The Journal of Imperial and Commonwealth History, 1-29. https://doi.org/10.1080/03086534.2021.1985335

Hossain, P. (2022, September 8). 'More Akin to the Monkey than the Man': Race and labour in the Indian indenture trade. Economic History Society. https://ehs.org.uk/race-and-labour-in-the-indian-indenture-trade/

Hunter, T. (2019, April 16). When Slaveowners Got Reparations. The New York Times. https://www.nytimes.com/2019/04/16/opinion/when-slaveowners-got-reparations.html

Huynh, T. T. (2008). Loathing and Love: Postcard Representations of Indentured Chinese Laborers in South Africa's Reconstruction, 1904–10. Safundi, 9(4), 395-425. https://doi.org/10.1080/17533170802349523

Huynh, T. T. (2024). From South Africa to the World: The Political and Legal Legacies of Chinese Indenture in the Transvaal. Slavery

& Abolition, 45(3), 461-480. https://doi.org/10.1080/0144039X.2024.2344389

Hyman, L. (2018). Temp: How American Work, American Business, and the American Dream Became Temporary. Penguin Random House.

Hymowitz, K. (2020, February 11). Yes, David Brooks, the Nuclear Family is the Worst Family Form—Except for All Others. Institute for Family Studies. https://ifstudies.org/blog/yes-david-brooks-the-nuclear-family-is-the-worst-family-form-except-for-all-others

Immerwahr, D. (2008, April). On B. R. Ambedkar and Black–Dalit Connections. University of California, Berkeley. https://faculty.wcas.northwestern.edu/daniel-immerwahr/Ambedkar.pdf

Indian women became the faces of Victorian-era postcards, well over a century later Prof Andil Gosine reimagined the postcards in his photo series "Cane Portraiture." (2021, January 19). York University. https://euc.yorku.ca/news-story/indian-women-became-the-faces-of-victorian-era-postcards-well-over-a-century-later-prof-andil-gosine-reimagined-the-postcards-in-his-photo-series-cane-portraiture/

Iqbal, S., Zakar, R., Fischer, F., & Zakar, M. Z. (2022). Consanguineous marriages and their association with women's reproductive health and fertility behavior in Pakistan: Secondary data analysis from Demographic and Health Surveys, 1990–2018. BMC Women's Health, 22(1), 118. https://doi.org/10.1186/s12905-022-01704-2

Isen, T. (2024, August 19). The Hidden Racism of Book Cover Design. The Walrus. https://thewalrus.ca/the-hidden-racism-of-book-cover-design/

Isen, T. (2022). Some of My Best Friends: Essays on Lip Service. Doubleday Canada.

Islam, N. (2022, July 28). Reclaiming the "Coolie Belle": On Renluka Maharaj's Pelting Mangoes. ASAP | art. https://www.asapconnect.in/post/447/singlealbums/reclaiming-the-coolie-belle

Jacobs, A. J. (2018). It's All Relative: Adventures Up and Down the World's Family Tree. Simon and Schuster.

Jayawardena, C. (1980). Culture and Ethnicity in Guyana and Fiji. Man, 15(3), 430-450. https://doi.org/10.2307/2801343

Jenkins, T. A. (2011). The Lady and Her Horse. [eBook edition]. The Project Gutenberg. https://gutenberg.org/cache/epub/37445/pg37445-images.html (Original work published 1857)

Jin, C. H. (2021, May 25). 6 Charts That Dismantle The Trope Of Asian Americans As A Model Minority. NPR. https://www.npr.org/2021/05/25/999874296/6-charts-that-dismantle-the-trope-of-asian-americans-as-a-model-minority

John Chinaman John Confucius. (2015, February 23). Thomas Nast's Cartoons of Chinese Americans. https://thomasnastcartoons.com/john-chinaman-john-confucius/

John Chinaman on the Rand by An English Eyewitness. (2019). [eBook edition]. The Project Gutenberg. https://www.gutenberg.org/files/60959/60959-h/60959-h.htm (Original work published 1905)

Johnston, P. (1995). BC's "Island of death" marked a sad chapter in Canada's medical history. Canadian Medical Association Journal, 152(6), 951-952. https://www.cmaj.ca/content/152/6/951

Jonestown Memorial. (2018). https://www.jonestownmemorial.com/40th-anniversary

Jonestown Research. (2013, January 5). Alternative Considerations of Jonestown & Peoples Temple. https://jonestown.sdsu.edu/?page_id=47

Joshi, R. S., Rigau, M., García-Prieto, C. A., Castro de Moura, M., Piñeyro, D., Moran, S., Davalos, V., Carrión, P., Ferrando-Bernal, M., Olalde, I., Lalueza-Fox, C., Navarro, A., Fernández-Tena, C., Aspandi, D., Sukno, F. M., Binefa, X., Valencia, A., & Esteller, M. (2022). Look-alike humans identified by facial recognition algorithms show genetic similarities. Cell Reports, 40(8), 111257. https://doi.org/10.1016/j.celrep.2022.111257

Junge, S. (2018). Groet uit Java: Picture Postcards and the Transnational Making of the Colony around 1900. History of Photography, 42(2), 168-184. https://doi.org/10.1080/03087298.2018.1500742

Junn, J. (2007). From Coolie to Model Minority: U.S. Immigration Policy and the Construction of Racial Identity. Du Bois Review, 4(2), 355-373. https://doi.org/10.1017/s1742058x07070208

Jurjević, A. (2021, October 16). Friendly Dockings: On Khal Torabully's "Cargo Hold of Stars: Coolitude". Los Angeles Review of Books. https://lareviewofbooks.org/article/friendly-dockings-on-khal-torabullys-cargo-hold-of-stars-coolitude/

Kabir, A. J. (2020). Beyond Créolité and Coolitude, the Indian on the Plantation Re-creolization in the Transoceanic Frame. Middle Atlantic Review of Latin American Studies, 4(2), 174–193. https://doi.org/10.23870/marlas.304

Kashala-Abotnes, E., Okitundu, D., Mumba, D., Boivin, M. J., Tylleskär, T., & Tshala-Katumbay, D. (2019). Konzo: a distinct neurological disease associated with food (cassava) cyanogenic poisoning. Brain Research Bulletin, 145, 87-91. https://doi.org/10.1016/j.brainresbull.2018.07.001

Keltie, J. S. (1903). India, the Colonies, Protectorates, and Dependencies of the British Empire. In J. S. Keltie (Ed.), The Statesman's Year-Book (pp. 108-374). Palgrave Macmillan. https://doi.org/10.1057/9780230270329_2

Kempadoo, K. (2017). "Bound Coolies" and Other Indentured Workers in the Caribbean: Implications for debates about human trafficking and modern slavery. Anti-Trafficking Review, 9, 48-63. https://doi.org/10.14197/atr.20121794

Kendall, M. (2021). Hood Feminism: Notes From the Women That a Movement Forgot. Penguin Books.

Kenny, K. (2023). The Antislavery Origins of Immigration Policy. In K. Kenny (Ed.), The Problem of Immigration in a Slaveholding Republic: Policing Mobility in the Nineteenth-Century United States (pp. 141-162). Oxford University Press eBooks. https://doi.org/10.1093/oso/9780197580080.003.0006

Khader, S. (2024). Faux Feminism: Why We Fall for White Feminism and How We Can Stop. Beacon Press.

Kidd, C. (2005). Chip Kidd: Book One: Work: 1986-2006. Rizzoli International Publications.

Kim, D. S. (n.d.). The Seduction of Comparisons: Untouchability beyond Caste in Africa, Asia, and the Middle East. Project on Middle East Political Science. https://pomeps.org/the-seduction-of-comparisons-untouchability-beyond-caste-in-africa-asia-and-the-middle-east

Kincaid, J. (1978, June 26). Girl. The New Yorker. https://www.newyorker.com/magazine/1978/06/26/girl

King, R. (2021). Tacky: Love Letters to the Worst Culture We Have to Offer. Vintage Books.

Klein, N. (2023). Doppelganger: A Trip Into the Mirror World. Penguin Books.

Kraff, H., & Jernsand, E. M. (2022). Multicultural Food Events—Opportunities for Intercultural Exchange and Risks of Stereotypification. Tourism Recreation Research, 48(6), 1-12. https://doi.org/10.1080/02508281.2022.2126922

Kumar, A. (2024). Alternative history of indenture: view from margins. South Asian Diaspora, 1-18. https://doi-org.myaccess.library.utoronto.ca/10.1080/19438192.2024.2420536

Kumar, M. (2013). Malaria and Mortality Among Indentured Indians: A Study of Housing, Sanitation, and Health in British Guyana (1900–1939). Proceedings of the Indian History Congress, 74, 746-757. http://www.jstor.org/stable/44158878

Kumar, V. (2004). Understanding Dalit Diaspora. Economic and Political Weekly, 39(1), 114-116. http://www.jstor.org/stable/4414473

Kuta, S. (2022, August 24). Doppelgängers Don't Just Look Alike—They Also Share DNA. Smithsonian Magazine. https://www.smithsonianmag.com/smart-news/doppelgangers-dont-just-look-alike-they-also-share-dna-180980635/

Laing, O. (2021). Everybody: A Book about Freedom. W. W. Norton & Company.

Lal, B. V. (2021). Indian indenture: History and historiography in a nutshell. Journal of Indentureship and Its Legacies, 1(1). https://doi.org/10.13169/jofstudindentleg.1.1.0001

Lal, B. V. (1998). Understanding the Indian indenture experience. South Asia: Journal of South Asian Studies, 21(sup001), 215-237. https://doi.org/10.1080/00856409808723356

Lal, B. V., & Shineberg, B. (1991). The story of the haunted line: Totaram Sanadhya recalls the labour lines in Fiji. Journal of Pacific History, 26(1), 107-112. https://doi.org/10.1080/00223349108572653

Lee, C. (2000). A Gesture Life. Riverhead Books.

Lee, J. S. (2023). Superfan: How Pop Culture Broke My Heart. McClelland & Stewart.

A Lesson to John Chinaman. (1857, August 9). [Illustration]. Punch. https://babel.hathitrust.org/cgi/pt?id=hvd.hnv1wk;view=2up;seq=206

Lewis, S. (2025). Enemy Feminisms: TERFs, Policewomen, and Girlbosses Against Liberation. Haymarket Books.

Li Baksh, A. (2024, Spring). Bitter Roots: Guyana's festive national dish is a marvel of Indigenous knowledge and heritage. Maisonneuve, 91, 19-25. https://maisonneuve.org/article/2024/04/12/bitter-roots/

Li, Y., & Nicholson, H. L. (2021). When "model minorities" become "yellow peril"—Othering and the racialization of Asian Americans in the COVID-19 pandemic. Sociology Compass, 15(2). https://doi.org/10.1111/soc4.12849

Liber Peristephanon, Poem V. (2015, November 17). University of Oxford. https://portal.sds.ox.ac.uk/articles/online_resource/E00858_Latin_poem_on_Vincent_deacon_and_martyr_of_Saragossa_and_Valencia_S00290_composed_by_Prudentius_writing_c_400_in_Calahorra_northern_Spain_The_poem_part_of_his_Crowns_of_the_Martyrs_Peristephanon_gives_details_about_Vincent_s_sufferin/13801748/1

Lim, I. (2021). The Chinese Protectorate. National Library Board Singapore. https://www.nlb.gov.sg/main/article-detail?cmsuuid=04d3f708-c117-457a-9ea0-9717f9f03971

Lloyd, C. M., Alvira-Hammond, M., Carlson, J., & Logan, D. (2021, March 5). Family, Economic, and Geographic Characteristics of Black Families with Children. Child Trends. https://www.childtrends.org/publications/family-economic-and-geographic-characteristics-of-black-families-with-children#_ftn15

Lowe, L. (2015). The Intimacies of Four Continents. Duke University Press. https://doi.org/10.1215/9780822375647

Madhwi. (2015). Recruiting Indentured Labour for Overseas Colonies, circa 1834–1910. Social Scientist, 43(9/10), 53-68. https://www.jstor.org/stable/24642373

Mahabir, J. (2013). Alternative Texts: Indo-Caribbean Women's Jewelry. Caribbean Vistas Journal, 1(1). https://caribbeanvistas.wordpress.com/mahabiralternativejewelry1/

Mahoney, M. (2021, January 26). "The Great Experiment": Explaining the advent of indenture to the West Indies. The National Archives. https://blog.nationalarchives.gov.uk/the-great-experiment-explaining-the-advent-of-indenture-to-the-west-indies/

Mahoney, M. (2020, December 3). A "new system of slavery"? The British West Indies and the origins of Indian indenture. The National Archives. https://blog.nationalarchives.gov.uk/a-new-system-of-slavery-the-british-west-indies-and-the-origins-of-indian-indenture/

Major, A. (2017). "Hill Coolies": Indian Indentured Labour and the Colonial Imagination, 1836–38. South Asian Studies, 33(1), 23-36. https://doi.org/10.1080/02666030.2017.1300374

Malhotra, A. (2018, September 13). A teenager traces her Indian great-great grandmother's life as an indentured labourer in Fiji. Scroll.in. https://scroll.in/magazine/886645/a-teenager-traces-her-indian-great-great-grandmothers-life-as-an-indentured-labourer-in-fiji

Malone, K. (2016, July 31). Winnipeg presentation to tell the little-known story of Canada's British Home Children. CBC News. https://www.cbc.ca/news/canada/manitoba/winnipeg-presentation-to-tell-the-little-known-story-of-canada-s-british-home-children-1.3702576

Manic Pixie Dream Girls Aren't Black. (2023, November 28). American Music Theatre Project at Northwestern University. https://amtp.northwestern.edu/manic-pixie-dream-girls-arent-black/

Manjapra, K. (2018, March 29). When will Britain face up to its crimes against humanity? The Guardian. https://www.theguardian.com/news/2018/mar/29/slavery-abolition-compensation-when-will-britain-face-up-to-its-crimes-against-humanity

Marsh, J. (2017). The "Other" Last Spike. In The Canadian Encyclopedia. https://www.thecanadianencyclopedia.ca/en/article/the-other-last-spike-feature

Martínez, J. T. (2024). Retaining Chinese Indentured Labour in Interwar British and French Pacific colonies. Slavery & Abolition, 45(3), 521–540. https://doi.org/10.1080/0144039X.2024.2344392

Martínez, J. T., & Lowrie, C. (2024). Introduction: Historicizing the Abolition of Chinese Indentured Labour. Slavery & Abolition, 45(3), 432–441. https://doi.org/10.1080/0144039X.2024.2344387

Marx, W. D. (2022). Status and Culture: How Our Desire for Social Rank Creates Taste, Identity, Art, Fashion, and Constant Change. Viking.

Maslow, A. H. (1943). A theory of human motivation. Psychological Review, 50(4), 370-396. https://doi.org/10.1037/h0054346

Matthias, M. (2021, March 25). Why Have So Many World Leaders Married Their Cousins? Encyclopedia Britannica. https://www.britannica.com/story/why-have-so-many-world-leaders-married-their-cousins

McAlmont, C. (2013, August 1). African immigrants: They arrived too. Stabroek News. https://www.stabroeknews.com/2013/08/01/news/guyana/african-immigrants-they-arrived-too/

McClenaghan, M., Evans, R., Dyer, H., Hunter-Green, Z., & Kalanaki, M. (2023, November 23). Revealed: King Charles secretly profiting from the assets of dead citizens. The Guardian. https://www.theguardian.com/uk-news/2023/nov/23/revealed-king-charles-secretly-profiting-from-the-assets-of-dead-citizens

McKenzie, H. (2023, June 21). Reclaimed: Indo-Caribbean HerStories. https://www.heidimckenzie.ca/career-blog/2023/6/21/reclaimed-indo-caribbean-herstories

Mead, T. H. (2013). Horsemanship for Women. [eBook edition]. The Project Gutenberg. https://gutenberg.org/cache/epub/42938/pg42938-images.html (Original work published 1887)

Meadows-Fernandez, A. R. (2024, January 15). The Unapologetically Black Tradition of Expanding the Definition of Family. Parents. https://www.parents.com/kindred/the-unapologetically-black-tradition-of-expanding-the-definition-of-family/

Merten, M. (2019). Keeping it in the family: consanguineous marriage and genetic disorders, from Islamabad to Bradford. BMJ (Clinical research ed.), 365, l1851. https://doi.org/10.1136/bmj.l1851

Mintz, S. (n.d.). Historical Context: Facts About the Slave Trade and Slavery. The Gilder Lehrman Institute of American History. https://www.gilderlehrman.org/history-resources/teacher-resources/historical-context-facts-about-slave-trade-and-slavery

Misganaw, C. D., & Bayou, W. D. (2020). Tuber Yield and Yield Component Performance of Cassava (Manihot esculenta) Varieties in Fafen District, Ethiopia. International Journal of Agronomy, 2020, 5836452. https://doi.org/10.1155/2020/5836452

Mishra, A. K. (2022). Mobilise to Immobilise: Recruitment of Indian Indentured Labourers for British Sugar Plantations in Mauritius. South Asian History, Culture and Archaeology, 2(1), 9-23.

Mishra, V. (2017). Writing Indenture History Through Testimonios and Oral Narratives. In R. S. Hegde & A. K. Sahoo (Eds.), Routledge Handbook of the Indian Diaspora (pp. 29-50). Taylor and Francis.

Misrahi-Barak, J. (2017). Indentureship, Caste and the Crossing of the Kala Pani. Studies in Humanities and Social Sciences, 14(2), 18-36. https://hal.science/hal-03067915

Montell, A. (2021). Cultish: The Language of Fanaticism. HarperCollins Publishers.

Morrison, T. (2019). The Source of Self-Regard: Selected Essays, Speeches, and Meditations. Vintage.

Murakami, H. (1998). The Wind-Up Bird Chronicle. Vintage.

Nadeem, S. (2015). Indian Arrivistes and Cyber Coolies: Reflections on Global Outsourcing and the Middle Class. Sociology Compass, 9(4), 289–298. https://doi.org/10.1111/soc4.12255

Naipaul, V. S. (1961). A House for Mr. Biswas. André Deutsch.

Nancy, J.-L. (2000). Being Singular Plural. Stanford University Press.

Nelson-Fearon, E. (2020, November 29). The Joy of Being Black and

Having an Extended Family. Vice. https://www.vice.com/en/article/xgz893/the-joy-of-being-black-and-having-an-extended-family

Neurdein Frères. (n.d.). McCord Stewart Museum. https://collections.musee-mccord-stewart.ca/en/people/12853/neurdein-freres

Nguyen, S. A., & Quang-Dang, U. (2022). The Model Minority Myth and Medicine: Racism, Sexism, and Mental Health. Psychiatric Times, 39(8), 16-17. https://www.psychiatrictimes.com/view/the-model-minority-myth-and-medicine-racism-sexism-and-mental-health

Notting Hill Carnival. (n.d.). The Origins of Steel Pan. Google Arts and Culture. https://artsandculture.google.com/story/the-origins-of-steel-pan-notting-hill-carnival/AAWBxQd4TKb21w?hl=en

Nwoko, H. (2023, November 2). Play Cousins Boost Black Kids' Social-Emotional Development—And More. Parents. https://www.parents.com/play-cousins-help-black-kids-social-emotional-learning-8386620

Nwulia, M. D. E. (1978). The "Apprenticeship" System in Mauritius: Its Character and Its Impact on Race Relations in the Immediate Post-Emancipation Period, 1839–1879. African Studies Review, 21(1), 89-101. https://doi.org/10.1017/s0002020600019090

O'Donoghue, P. (2012). Ladies on Horseback Learning, Park-Riding, and Hunting, with Hints upon Costume, and Numerous Anecdotes. [eBook edition]. The Project Gutenberg. https://www.gutenberg.org/files/39501/39501-h/39501-h.htm. (Original work published 1881)

Oelze, S. (2019, January 8). Myths and misunderstandings. Deutsche Welle. https://www.dw.com/en/100-years-of-bauhaus-myths-and-misunderstandings/a-45087876

Oluo, I. (2021). Mediocre: The Dangerous Legacy of White Male America. Seal Press.

Oppenheim, N. (2021, July 13). Hazel Daniels: Pepperpot Philosophising. British Library. https://blogs.bl.uk/americas/2021/07/hazel-daniels-pepperpot-philosopy-.html

Ortlieb, S. A., & Carbon, C. (2019). A Functional Model of Kitsch and Art: Linking Aesthetic Appreciation to the Dynamics of Social Motivation. Frontiers in Psychology, 9. https://doi.org/10.3389/fpsyg.2018.02437

Painter, N. I. (2011). The History of White People. W. W. Norton & Company.

Paul, D. B., & Spencer, H. G. (2008). "It's Ok, We're Not Cousins by Blood": The Cousin Marriage Controversy in Historical Perspective. PLoS Biology, 6(12). https://doi.org/10.1371/journal.pbio.0060320

PC Pepperpot Cooking Sauce. (n.d.). President's Choice. https://www.presidentschoice.ca/product/pc-pepperpot-cooking-sauce-/21427725_EA

Peakman, J. (2019). Licentious Worlds: Sex and Exploitation in Global Empires. Reaktion Books.

Persaud, A. (2019). Escaping Local Risk by Entering Indentureship: Evidence from Nineteenth-Century Indian Migration. The Journal of Economic History, 79(2), 447–476. https://doi.org/10.1017/S002205071900007X

Pillai, R. (2019). A Question of Voice: Indo-Caribbean American Feminism through Music in New York City. WSQ: Women's Studies Quarterly, 47(1-2), 65-82. https://doi.org/10.1353/wsq.2019.0024

Pillay, E. (2019, July 20). Dalit History in Indentured Labour Movements. https://izlandkuli.wixsite.com/cooliereturns?pgid=k4sg21a2-167236a4-5adb-44d2-8ac6-be8dff1e4a71

Pitre, J. (2022, November 1). The Eerie Comfort of Liminal Spaces. The Atlantic. https://www.theatlantic.com/culture/archive/2022/11/liminal-space-internet-aesthetic/671945/

Pittman, P. S., Kamp Dush, C., Pratt, K. J., & Wong, J. D. (2024). Interracial Couples at Risk: Discrimination, Well-Being, and Health. Journal of Family Issues, 45(2), 303-325. https://doi.org/10.1177/0192513X221150994

Porter, E. (2011). The Price of Everything: Solving the Mystery of Why We Pay What We Do. Portfolio Penguin.

The Portuguese Exploration. (n.d.). Sutori. https://www.sutori.com/en /story/the-portuguese-exploration--DLcWQ2sVRZADQ1JvcHWEgvuE

Pothecary, S. (2005). When was the Geography written? Strabo the Geographer. https://www.strabo.ca/when.html

Prashad, V. (2001). The Karma of Brown Folk. University of Minnesota Press.

Provost, R. (2022, September 4). Bauhaus—Art Movement, Style & History Explained. StudioBinder. https://www.studiobinder.com/blog/what-is-bauhaus-art-movement/

Quick Facts: Oregon. (n.d.). United States Census. https://www.census.gov/quickfacts/fact/table/OR/PST045222

Rabe, S. G. (2006). U.S. Intervention in British Guiana: A Cold War Story. University of North Carolina Press.

Rahim, G. (2017, December 24). Our Pepperpot: A Guyanese Christmas tradition. Guyana Chronicle. https://guyanachronicle.com/2017/12/24/our-pepperpot/

The Rail, from Sea to Sea. (n.d.). Canadian Museum of History. https://www.historymuseum.ca/history-hall/the-rail-from-sea-to-sea/

Ramchand, K. (2018, August 12). VS Naipaul obituary. The Guardian. https://www.theguardian.com/books/2018/aug/12/vs-naipaul-obituary

Rao, A. (2020, September 1). The Work of Analogy: On Isabel Wilkerson's "Caste: The Origins of Our Discontents". Los Angeles Review of Books. https://lareviewofbooks.org/article/the-work-of-analogy-on-isabel-wilkersons-caste-the-origins-of-our-discontents/

Raphael Tuck & Sons. (n.d.). The British Museum. https://www.britishmuseum.org/collection/term/BIOG77171

Read, J. H. (2009, September 3-6). "The Limits of Self-Reliance: Emerson, Slavery, and Abolition." Presented at the Annual Meeting of the American Political Science Association, Toronto, Ontario. http://ssrn.com/abstract=1451487

Reddi, S. (2017, July 28). The End of Indentureship in Mauritius: A Preliminary Investigation. Mauritius Times. http://www.mauritiustimes.com/mt/the-end-of-indentureship-in-mauritius-a-preliminary-investigation/

Regional Labor Experiences: Sugar and Tobacco. (n.d.). Lowcountry Digital History Initiative. https://ldhi.library.cofc.edu/exhibits/show/africanpassageslowcountryadapt/sectionii_introduction/sugar_and_tobacco

Repeal laws banning cousins from marrying: geneticists. (2008, December 23). CBC. https://www.cbc.ca/news/science/repeal-laws-banning-cousins-from-marrying-geneticists-1.752965

Rivera, T. (2022). Model Minority Masochism: Performing the Cultural Politics of Asian American Masculinity. Oxford University Press.

The Rococo style—an introduction. (n.d.). Victoria and Albert Museum. https://www.vam.ac.uk/articles/the-rococo-style-an-introduction

Roopnarine, L. (2006). Indo-Caribbean Social Identity. Caribbean Quarterly, 52(1), 1-11. http://www.jstor.org/stable/40654531

Rosato, J. (2019, June 7). A Look at the New Monument to Honor Chinese Railroad Workers. NBC Bay Area. https://www.nbcbayarea.com/news/local/a-look-at-the-new-monument-to-honor-chinese-railroad-workers/188278/

Sagres. (n.d.). Portugal Online. https://portugalonline.com/portugal/portugal-cities-towns/sagres

Sailing the British Empire: The Voyages of the Clarence, 1858–73. (2015). https://scalar.usc.edu/works/the-voyages-of-the-clarence/overview-of-mortality-on-ocean-voyages-in-the-1800s

Saint Vincent and the Grenadines. (n.d.). New World Encyclopedia. https://www.newworldencyclopedia.org/entry/Saint_Vincent_and_the_Grenadines

Saletan, W. (2002, April 10). What's wrong with marrying your cousin? Slate Magazine. https://slate.com/news-and-politics/2002/04/what-s-wrong-with-marrying-your-cousin.html

Samaroo, B. (2019). Global Capitalism and Cheap Labor: The Case of Indenture. Springer eBooks, 1795–1811. https://doi.org/10.1007/978-981-13-2898-5_102

Sanadhya, T. (2003). My Twenty-One Years in the Fiji Islands & The Story of the Haunted Line (J. D. Kelly & U. K. Singh, Trans.). Quality Print Limited. (Original work published 1914)

Saval, N. (2019, February 4). How Bauhaus Redefined What Design Could Do for Society. The New York Times. https://www.nytimes.com/2019/02/04/t-magazine/bauhaus-school-architecture-history.html

Schomburgk, R., & Roth, W. E. (1922). Reisen in British-Guiana in den Jahren, 1840–1884. HathiTrust Digital Library. https://doi.org/10.5962/bhl.title.105205 (Original work published 1847)

Semuels, A. (2016, August 19). The Racist History of Portland, the Whitest City in America. The Atlantic. https://www.theatlantic.com/business/archive/2016/07/racist-history-portland/492035/

Sen, A. (2021, June 29). Illusions of empire: Amartya Sen on what British rule really did for India. The Guardian. https://www.theguardian.com/world/2021/jun/29/british-empire-india-amartya-sen

Serino, K., & Stabley, J. (2022, September 16). What to know about calls for reparations for Britain's legacy of slavery in the Caribbean. PBS NewsHour. https://www.pbs.org/newshour/world/what-to-know-about-calls-for-reparations-for-britains-legacy-of-slavery-in-the-caribbean

Shanmugaraj, N. (2022). Disidentifying from the "model minority": How Indian American women rearticulate dominant racial rhetorics. Quarterly Journal of Speech, 109(2), 109-131. https://doi.org/10.1080/00335630.2022.2147581

Sharma, H. (2020, December 23). Why Indian women became the

faces of these Victorian-era postcards. CNN. https://www.cnn.com/style/article/indo-caribbean-women-colonial-postcards/index.html

Sharpe, J. (2022). Life, Labor, and a Coolie Picturesque in Jamaica. Small Axe: A Caribbean Journal of Criticism, 26(2), 24-45. https://doi.org/10.1215/07990537-9901583

Shaw, A. & Raz, A. (2015). Cousin Marriages: Between Tradition, Genetic Risk and Cultural Change. Berghahn Books. https://doi.org/10.1515/9781782384939

Shokoohi, K. (2021, June 27). Straight, white women can be good allies, but they shouldn't be the face of diversity. The Globe and Mail. https://www.theglobeandmail.com/business/careers/article-straight-white-women-can-be-good-allies-but-they-shouldnt-be-the-face/

Siegel, B. R. (2018). Hungry nation: Food, famine, and the making of modern India. Cambridge University Press.

Sinykin, D., & So, R. J. (2024, June 19). Has the DEI Backlash Come for Publishing? The Atlantic. https://www.theatlantic.com/books/archive/2024/06/diversity-publishing-backlash-study/678734/

Smith, M. R. (2023). Andil Gosine's Cane Portraiture and the aesthetics of indenture. Journal of Indentureship and Its Legacies, 3(1), 133–145. https://www.jstor.org/stable/48739009

Snack kills 27 children at School. (2005, March 10). The Guardian. https://www.theguardian.com/world/2005/mar/10/schoolsworldwide.philippines

Sorkin, A. R., Giang, V., Gandel, S., Warner, B., de la Merced, M. J., Hirsch, L., & Livni, E. (2022, September 9). Dissecting the Royal Family's Wealth. The New York Times. https://www.nytimes.com/2022/09/09/business/dealbook/britain-royal-family-wealth.html

Soundararajan, T. (2022). The Trauma of Caste: A Dalit Feminist Meditation on Survivorship, Healing, and Abolition. North Atlantic Books.

Srivastava, R. (2020, March 4). No, you won't get the coronavirus from Chinese food. And don't drink bleach. The Guardian. https://www.theguardian.com/commentisfree/2020/mar/05/no-you-wont-get-the-coronavirus-from-chinese-food-and-dont-drink-bleach

Stanley, S. M. (2020, February 27). The Nuclear Family Was No Mistake: A Response to David Brooks. Psychology Today. https://www.psychologytoday.com/ca/blog/sliding-vs-deciding/202002/the-nuclear-family-was-no-mistake-response-david-brooks

Stanziani, A. (2013). Beyond colonialism: servants, wage earners and indentured migrants in rural France and on Reunion Island (c. 1750–1900). Labor History, 54(1), 64-87. https://doi.org/10.1080/0023656x.2012.759809

Steele, Joelle. (2016). Postcard Publishers: Antique & Vintage Postcard Publishers. https://postcardpeddler.com/article-708.html

Stern, P. J. (2023). Empire, Incorporated: The Corporations That Built British Colonialism. Harvard University Press.

Strabo. (2014). The Geography of Strabo (Vol. 1). [eBook edition]. The Project Gutenberg. https://www.gutenberg.org/cache/epub/44884/pg44884-images.html (Original work published about 17 CE)

"Success Story of One Minority Group in the U.S." (1966, December 26). U.S. News and World Report.

Sullivan, D., & Hickel, J. (2022, December 2). How British colonialism killed 100 million Indians in 40 years. Al Jazeera. https://www.aljazeera.com/opinions/2022/12/2/how-british-colonial-policy-killed-100-million-indians

Suranyi, A. (2021). Indentured servitude: Unfree Labour and Citizenship in the British Colonies. McGill-Queen's University Press.

Tadmouri, G. O., Nair, P., Obeid, T., Al Ali, M. T., Al Khaja, N., & Hamamy, H. A. (2009). Consanguinity and reproductive health among Arabs. Reproductive Health, 6(1). https://doi.org/10.1186/1742-4755-6-17

Tan, A. (2018). Where the Past Begins: Memory and Imagination. Ecco.

Temple, C. (2017, September 6). 10 reasons growing up with cousins is so valuable for your kids. Motherly. https://www.mother.ly/relationships/community-friendship/10-reasons-growing-up-with-cousins-is-the-best/

Teulié, G. (2019). Orientalism and the British Picture Postcard Industry: Popularizing the Empire in Victorian and Edwardian Homes. Cahiers Victoriens et Édouardiens, 89 Spring. https://doi.org/10.4000/cve.5178

Tharoor, S. (2017). Inglorious Empire: What the British Did to India. Penguin.

Thelen, K. (2019). The American Precariat: U.S. Capitalism in Comparative Perspective. Perspectives on Politics, 17(1), 5-27. https://doi.org/10.1017/s1537592718003419

Thompson, K. A. (2006). An Eye for the Tropics: Tourism, Photography, and Framing the Caribbean Picturesque. Duke University Press.

Thompson, S. (2020, July 3). Blackbirding and indentured labour in 19th century Queensland. Asia & the Pacific Policy Society. https://www.policyforum.net/blackbirding-and-indentured-labour-in-19th-century-queensland/

Tinker, H. (1974). A New System of Slavery: The Export of Indian Labour Overseas, 1830–1920. Oxford University Press.

Torabully, K. (2021). Cargo Hold Of Stars: Coolitude. (N. Naomi Carlson, Trans.). Seagull Books. (Original work published 1992)

TuckDB Postcards: A collection of antique postcards published by Raphael Tuck & Sons. (n.d.). TuckDB Postcards. https://www.tuckdbpostcards.org/

Tunstall, E. (2023). Decolonizing Design: A Cultural Justice Guidebook. MIT Press.

Twelve Crewmembers Aboard Chinese Bulker Die of Food Poisoning. (2022, September 30). The Maritime Executive. https://maritime-executive.com/article/twelve-crewmembers-aboard-chinese-bulker-die-of-food-poisoning

Urban, T. (2015, December 17). Everyone on Earth is actually your cousin. Quartz. https://qz.com/557639/everyone-on-earth-is-actually-your-cousin

Vahed, G. (2017). Networks, Caste, and Transnational Identities. In R. S. Hegde & A. K. Sahoo (Eds.), Routledge Handbook of the Indian Diaspora (pp. 330-340). Tayor and Francis.

Vahed, G. (2019). 'An evil thing': Gandhi and Indian Indentured Labour in South Africa, 1893–1914. South Asia: Journal of South Asian Studies, 42(4), 654-674. https://doi.org/10.1080/00856401.2019.1608002

Venkateswaran, P. (2022). Performing Dalit Feminist Youth Activism in South India: Rap, Gaana, and Street Theater. Journal of International Women's Studies, 24(2). https://vc.bridgew.edu/jiws/vol24/iss2/12

Waterton, C. (1885). Wanderings in South America, the North-West of the United States and the Antilles in the Years 1812, 1816, 1820 & 1824: With Original Instructions for the Perfect Preservation of Birds, Etc. for Cabinets of Natural History. Macmillan. https://hdl.handle.net/2027/aeu.ark:/13960/t3223nm9b

Webb, A. (2020, June 15). Boise State faculty, alumnus honor Chinese railway laborers who lost their lives in Idaho. Boise State News.

https://www.boisestate.edu/news/2020/06/15/boise-state-faculty-alumnus-honor-chinese-railway-laborers-who-lost-their-lives-in-idaho/

Wilkerson, I. (2020). Caste: The Origins of Our Discontents. Random House.

Williams, C. (2023, November 8). New monument honoring Chinese railroad workers to be added to Utah Capitol. Deseret News. https://www.deseret.com/utah/2023/11/8/23952001/new-monument-honoring-chinese-railroad-workers-to-be-added-to-utah-capitol/

Winnick, L. (1990). America's "Model Minority". Commentary Magazine. https://www.commentary.org/articles/louis-winnick/americas/

Wonder trees and plants on the world's poorest soils. (n.d.). World Wildlife Fund. https://wwf.panda.org/discover/knowledge_hub/where_we_work/amazon/about_the_amazon/ecosystems_amazon/rainforests/

Wong, G. (2022, April 21). The Rise and Fall of World's Fairs. Smithsonian Magazine. https://www.smithsonianmag.com/history/the-rise-and-fall-of-worlds-fairs-180979946/

Wong, J. S., & Penner, A. M. (2018). Better Together? Interracial Relationships and Depressive Symptoms. Socius, 4. https://doi.org/10.1177/2378023118814610

Woodcock, J., & Graham, M. (2020). The Gig Economy: A Critical Introduction. Polity Press.

World Directory of Minorities and Indigenous Peoples—Guyana. (2018, January). Minority Rights Group International. https://www.refworld.org/docid/4954ce3723.html

Wu, E. D. (2015). The Color of Success: Asian Americans and the Origins of the Model Minority. Princeton University Press.

Yao, D. (2022). Model Minority. In The Canadian Encyclopedia. https://www.thecanadianencyclopedia.ca/en/article/model-minority

Yin, S. (2018, March 1). When Did Americans Stop Marrying Their Cousins? Ask the World's Largest Family Tree. The New York Times. https://www.nytimes.com/2018/03/01/science/cousins-marriage-family-tree.html

Yiu, M. (2022). COVID-19 is a "Yellow Peril" Redux: Immigration and Health Policy and the Construction of the Chinese as Disease. Asian American Research Journal, 2. https://doi.org/10.5070/rj42057359

Yorath, C., & Yorath, C. J. (2000). A Measure of Value: The Story of the D'Arcy Island Leper Colony. TouchWood Editions.

Young, D. (2017, November 22). Do White People Have Cousins? The Root. https://www.theroot.com/do-white-people-have-cousins-1820685828

The Young Lady's Equestrian Manual. (2009). [eBook edition]. The Project Gutenberg. https://gutenberg.org/cache/epub/29248/pg29248-images.html (Original work published 1838)

Young, S. (2023, April 16). Unpapering the cracks: sugar, slavery and the Sydney Morning Herald. University of Melbourne. https://findanexpert.unimelb.edu.au/news/63249-unpapering-the-cracks--sugar--slavery-and-the-sydney-morning-herald

Zakaria, R. (2021). Against White Feminism: Notes on Disruption. W. W. Norton & Company.